Rick Steves'
SWITZERLAND
2005

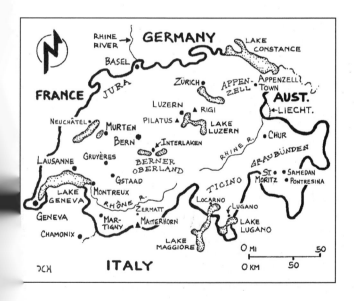

AVALON
TRAVEL

CONTENTS

RESORT TOWNS

Top Destinations in Switzerland

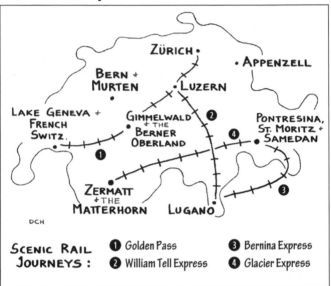

INTRODUCTION

Little, mountainous, efficient Switzerland is one of Europe's most appealing destinations. Wedged neatly between Germany, Austria, France, and Italy, Switzerland melds the best of all worlds—and adds a healthy dose of chocolate, cowbells, and cable cars. Fiercely independent and decidedly high-tech, the Swiss stubbornly hold on to their quaint traditions, too. Join the cheesemakers high atop an alp, try to call the shepherds on an alphorn, and hike to some of the world's most stunning mountain panoramas.

This book breaks Switzerland into its top big-city, small-town, and rural destinations. It then gives you all the information and opinions necessary to wring the maximum value out of your limited time and money in each of these destinations. If you plan three weeks or less in Switzerland, this lean and mean little book is all you need...unless you're a skier. Note that this is a fair-weather book—with a focus on the highlights of summertime fun.

Experiencing Switzerland's culture, people, and natural wonders economically and hassle-free has been my goal for more than two decades of traveling, tour-guiding, and guidebook writing. With this book, I pass on to you the lessons I've learned, updated (in mid-2004) for 2005.

Rick Steves' Switzerland is a tour guide in your pocket. The book includes a balance of cities and villages, mountaintop hikes and lake cruises, thought-provoking museums and sky-high gondola rides. It covers the predictable biggies while mixing in a healthy dose of "Back Door" intimacy.

Along with Luzern, the Matterhorn, and the Glacier Express, you'll experience windswept Roman ruins and ramble through traffic-free alpine towns. I've been selective, including only the most exciting sights. For example, the Swiss countryside is littered with dozens of cute villages. I take you only to the quaintest.

The best is, of course, only my opinion. But after spending half my life researching Europe, I've developed a sixth sense for what travelers enjoy. Just thinking about the places featured in this book makes me want to yodel.

This Information is Accurate and Up-to-Date

This book is updated every year. Most publishers of guidebooks that cover a country from top to bottom can afford an update only every two or three years (and, even then, it's often by letter or e-mail). Since this book is selective, covering only the top destinations in Switzerland, my researchers and I can update it in person each summer. The prices, hours, telephone numbers, and other information in this book are accurate as of mid-2004. Even with annual updates, things change. But if you're traveling with the current edition of this book, I guarantee you're using the most up-to-date information in print (for the latest, see www.ricksteves.com /update). Also at my Web site, check my Graffiti Wall (select "Rick Steves' Guidebooks," then "Switzerland") for a huge, valuable list of reports and experiences—good and bad—from fellow travelers.

This guidebook is designed to help you have a smooth, affordable vacation. Your trip costs at least $10 per waking hour. Your time is valuable. This guidebook will save you lots of time.

About This Book

This book is organized by destination. Each destination is covered as a mini-vacation on its own, filled with exciting sights and homey, affordable places to stay. In each chapter, you'll find:

Planning Your Time, a suggested schedule with thoughts on how best to use your limited time.

Orientation, including tourist information, city transportation, and an easy-to-read map designed to make the text clear and your arrival smooth.

Sights with ratings: ▲▲▲—Worth getting up early and skipping breakfast for; ▲▲—Worth getting up early for; ▲—Worth seeing if it's convenient; No rating—Worth knowing about.

Sleeping and Eating, with addresses and phone numbers of my favorite budget hotels and restaurants.

Transportation Connections, including train information and route tips for drivers, with recommended roadside attractions along the way.

The **appendix** is a traveler's tool kit, with telephone tips, a festival list, a climate chart, and survival phrases in German, French, and Italian.

Browse through this book, choose your favorite destinations, and link them together. Then have a great trip! You won't waste time on mediocre sights because, unlike other guidebook authors, I cover only the best. Since lousy, expensive hotels are a major financial pitfall, I've worked hard to assemble the best accommodations values for each stop. You'll travel like a temporary local, getting the absolute most out of every mile, minute, and dollar. As you travel the route I know and love, I'm happy you'll be meeting some of my favorite Swiss people.

PLANNING

Trip Costs

Five components make up your trip cost: airfare, surface transportation, room and board, sightseeing/entertainment, and shopping/miscellany.

Airfare: Don't try to sort through the mess. Get and use a good travel agent. A basic round-trip flight from the United States to Zürich should cost $600–1,000 (even cheaper in winter), depending on where you fly from and when. Always consider saving time and money in Europe by flying "open jaw" (flying into one city and out of another).

Surface Transportation: For a two-week whirlwind trip of all my recommended destinations, allow $315 per person for public transportation (second-class, 15-consecutive-day Swiss Pass, plus reservation fees for scenic trains) or $600 per person (based on 2 people sharing the car) for a two-week car rental, parking, gas, and insurance. Car rental is cheapest when reserved from the United States. Train passes are normally available only outside of Europe. On a short trip (of a week or less) in Switzerland, you may save money by simply buying tickets as you go. For longer trips, a railpass is usually a good value (see "Transportation," page 16).

Room and Board: You can thrive in this region on $100 a day per person for room and board. A $100-a-day budget per person allows $15 for lunch, $20 for dinner, $5 for snacks, and $60 for lodging (based on 2 people splitting the cost of a $120 double room that includes breakfast). That's doable. Students and tightwads do it on $40 a day ($20 per bed, $20 for meals and snacks). But budget sleeping and eating require the skills and information covered in this chapter (and in much more depth in my book *Rick Steves' Europe Through the Back Door*).

Sightseeing and Entertainment: In big cities, figure $5–10 per major sight, $3 for minor ones, and around $50 for each major alpine lift. Hiking is free, though lifts to some of the best high-altitude trails aren't. An overall average of $25 a day works for most. Don't skimp here. After all, this category directly powers most of the experiences all the other expenses are designed to make possible.

Shopping and Miscellany: Figure $2–3 per postcard, coffee, beer, and ice-cream cone. Shopping can vary in cost from nearly

Budget Tips

Switzerland is pricey, but there are ways to stretch your dollars. For example, many expensive alpine lifts offer discounted "early bird" tickets for the first trip of the day. Train trips get cheaper when you choose the right railpass (see all the deals on page 6). Cut down on restaurant costs by having scenic picnics and seeking out self-service cafeterias (often attached to department or grocery stores), which offer delicious food at a fraction of the cost of dining out. To minimize sightseeing expenses, get the Swiss Museum Passport; it'll save you money if you'll be visiting at least three or four museums while in Switzerland (see page 15).

nothing to a small fortune. Good budget travelers find that this category has little to do with assembling a trip full of lifelong and wonderful memories.

When to Go

The "tourist season" runs roughly from May through September. Summer (July–Aug) has its advantages: the best weather, snow-free alpine trails, very long days (light until after 21:00), and the busiest schedule of tourist fun. In late May, June, September, and early October, travelers enjoy fewer crowds, milder weather, and the ability to grab a room almost whenever and wherever they like.

During the *Zwischenzeit* ("between time," that is, between summer and ski seasons, roughly April, early May, late October, and November), the cities are pleasantly uncrowded—but the weather can be iffy, and resort towns like Zermatt and Mürren are completely dead (with most hotels and restaurants closed).

During ski season (December through March), mountain resorts are crowded and expensive, while cities are quieter (some accommodations and sights are either closed or run on a limited schedule). The weather can be cold and dreary, and nighttime will draw the shades on your sightseeing before dinnertime. You may find the climate chart in the appendix helpful. Pack warm clothing for the Alps, no matter when you go.

Sightseeing Priorities

Depending on the length of your trip, here are my recommended priorities. Assuming you'll be traveling by train, I've taken geographic proximity and likely transportation connections into account.

3 days:	Berner Oberland
5 days, add:	Luzern
7 days, add:	Lausanne and Bern, connecting with Golden Pass scenic rail journey

10 days, add:	Zermatt and Appenzell, linking with Glacier Express train
14 days, add:	Lugano and Pontresina area, connecting with Bernina Express and William Tell Express train rides
16 days, add:	Zürich and Murten
21 days, add:	More day trips (Central Switzerland, French Swiss countryside), more hikes, and time to slow down

The map on page 7 and the two-week itinerary on page 6 include everything in the top 14 days, plus modifications for a longer or shorter trip.

Itinerary Specifics

Design an itinerary that enables you to hit the festivals and museums on the right days. As you read through this book, note special days (festivals, colorful market days, and days when sights are closed). Saturday morning feels like any bustling weekday morning, but at lunchtime, many shops close down through Sunday. Sundays have pros and cons, as they do for travelers in the United States (special events, limited hours, shops and banks closed, limited public transportation, no rush hours). Popular places are even more popular on weekends. Many sights are closed on Monday (head for the hills).

Plan ahead for banking, laundry, postal chores, and picnics. To maximize rootedness, minimize one-night stands. Mix intense and relaxed periods, villages and cities, mountains and museums. Every trip (and every traveler) needs at least a few slack days. Pace yourself. Assume you will return.

Perhaps more than anywhere else in Europe, weather plays a huge factor in your sightseeing in Switzerland. The mountains are stunning—if it's not raining. But bad weather needn't ruin a trip. Switzerland is so small and has such a slick train network that you can easily double back later in your trip to visit the mountaintop hideaway that was clouded over your first time through.

Be flexible. For maximum spontaneity, consider not even reserving your hotels ahead (realizing that this comes with some risk). For example, you might plan on three days split between the city of Bern and the mountainous Berner Oberland region. If it's raining as you approach the area, head for Bern. If it's sunny, make a beeline for the mountains, then hit Bern on your way out of the area. To help you decide, tune into TV stations and Web sites that show the weather in various parts of the country. Many high-altitude observation decks come with 24-hour cameras that pan slowly back and forth, showing you exactly what you'll see when you get up top (for example, www.swisspanorama.com for the Berner Oberland, www.zermatt.ch for Zermatt).

Note that because Switzerland is right in the middle of Western

Switzerland's Best Two-Week Trip (By Train)

Day	Plan	Sleep in
1	Arrive Zürich, head to Appenzell	Appenzell or Ebenalp
2	All day for Appenzell and Ebenalp	Appenzell or Ebenalp
3	Leave early for Luzern	Luzern
4	Luzern	Luzern
5	William Tell Express to Lugano	Lugano
6	Bernina Express to Pontresina area	Pontresina
7	Pontresina area (St. Moritz, Samedan, lifts and hikes)	Pontresina
8	Take Glacier Express; if good weather, head for Zermatt; if bad weather, consider going straight to Lausanne (see below)	Zermatt
9	Zermatt, Matterhorn-view lifts and hikes	Zermatt
10	If good weather, spend more time in Zermatt, go late to Lausanne; if bad weather, leave early for Lausanne	Lausanne
11	Take the Golden Pass to the Berner Oberland. If good weather, go early; if bad weather, linger in Lausanne/Lake Geneva area and leave late	Berner Oberland (Gimmelwald or Mürren)
12	All day for lifts and hikes in the Berner Oberland	Gimmelwald or Mürren
13	More time in the Berner Oberland	Gimmelwald or Mürren
14	Early to Bern, then on to Zürich	Zürich
15	More time in Zürich, or fly home	

Note that Zermatt isn't worth the trip in bad weather. If your reservations are flexible, consider skipping that leg and going straight to Lausanne (take the Glacier Express only to Visp, then change for Lausanne). Visit Zermatt later, when the clouds part.

If you have extra time in Switzerland, I'd suggest spending it in (listed in order of priority)…

1. Murten and Bern
2. Zürich
3. Lausanne and Lake Geneva area
4. Lugano (relaxing) or Luzern area (day trips)

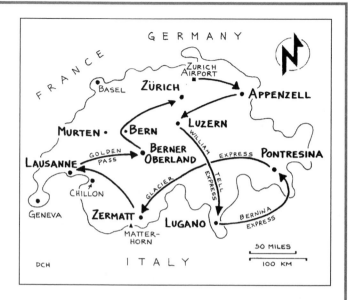

For a short trip of a week or so, consider dropping Appenzell, Pontresina, and the scenic train rides in east Switzerland. Instead, go straight from the Zürich Airport to Luzern, then cut down to Zermatt.

Railpass: The best railpass for this itinerary is a 15-consecutive-day Swiss Pass ($290 second class, $440 first class, 15 percent less for 2 or more traveling together; figure an additional $70 total in reservation fees for all the scenic rail journeys). While this pass doesn't cover mountain lifts, it does earn you a 25 percent discount on most of them.

By Car: While this itinerary is designed to be done by public transportation, it can be done by car with a few modifications. Obviously, you won't take the scenic rail trips. Instead, drive from Appenzell straight to the Pontresina area, then continue through Tirano and on to Lugano (via Lake Como in Italy). From Lugano, drive to Zermatt (crossing again through Italy) and resume the above itinerary, visiting Luzern at the very end before returning to Zürich. Note that the French Swiss countryside and the area around Murten merit more time if you have a car.

Europe, it splices neatly into a multi-country trip. For example, the Appenzell region is a likely gateway to Germany's Bavaria or Austria's Tirol (Innsbruck). Italy's Lake Como is a stone's throw from Lugano or Ticino (in fact, the Bernina Express bus drives right alongside it)—and Milan is not much farther. If you're in Lausanne, you're literally looking at France (across Lake Geneva)—a handy train ride whisks you to Lyon or Chamonix. And big Swiss cities are efficiently connected via night trains and fast day trains to destinations in all of these countries and beyond.

RESOURCES

Swiss Tourist Office in the United States

The Swiss national tourist office is a wealth of information. Before your trip, get the comprehensive "Welcome to the Best of Switzerland" brochure and request any specifics you want (such as regional and city maps, festival schedules, and hiking information).

For questions and brochures, call 877/794-8037 (608 Fifth Ave., New York, NY 10020, fax 212/262-6116, www.myswitzerland .com, info.usa@switzerland.com).

Rick Steves' Books and Public Television Shows

Rick Steves' Europe Through the Back Door 2005 gives you budget travel tips on minimizing jet lag, packing light, planning your itinerary, traveling by car or train, finding budget beds, avoiding rip-offs, using mobile phones, hurdling the language barrier, staying healthy, using your bidet, and lots more. The book also includes chapters on 38 of my favorite "Back Doors," including Gimmelwald and other alpine escapes in Switzerland.

Rick Steves' Country Guides, an annually updated series that covers Europe, offers you the latest on the top sights and destinations, with tips on how to make your trip efficient and fun.

My **City and Regional Guides**, freshly updated every year, focus on Europe's most compelling destinations. Along with specifics on sights, restaurants, hotels, and nightlife, you'll get self-guided, illustrated tours of the outstanding museums and most characteristic neighborhoods.

Rick Steves' Easy Access Europe, written for travelers with limited mobility, focuses on London, Paris, Bruges, Amsterdam, and the Rhine.

Rick Steves' Europe 101: History and Art for the Traveler (with Gene Openshaw) gives you the story of Europe's people, history, and art.

Rick Steves' Best European City Walks & Museums (with Gene Openshaw) provides fun, easy-to-follow, self-guided tours in London, Amsterdam, Paris, Rome, Venice, Florence, and Madrid.

Rick Steves' German Phrase Book has the survival phrases necessary

Rick Steves' Guidebooks

Rick Steves' Europe Through the Back Door
Rick Steves' Best European City Walks & Museums
Rick Steves' Easy Access Europe

Country Guides
Rick Steves' Best of Europe
Rick Steves' Best of Eastern Europe
Rick Steves' France
Rick Steves' Germany & Austria
Rick Steves' Great Britain
Rick Steves' Greece*
Rick Steves' Ireland
Rick Steves' Italy
Rick Steves' Portugal
Rick Steves' Scandinavia
Rick Steves' Spain
Rick Steves' Switzerland

City and Regional Guides
Rick Steves' Amsterdam, Bruges & Brussels
Rick Steves' Florence & Tuscany
Rick Steves' London
Rick Steves' Paris
Rick Steves' Prague & the Czech Republic*
Rick Steves' Provence & the French Riviera
Rick Steves' Rome
Rick Steves' Venice

*Coming in 2005

(Avalon Travel Publishing)

to communicate your way through a smooth and inexpensive trip. You'll be able to make hotel reservations over the phone, joke with your cabbie, and bargain at a street market.

My public television series, *Rick Steves' Europe*, keeps churning out shows. Of 95 episodes (from the new series and from *Travels in Europe with Rick Steves*), four half-hour shows are on Switzerland.

Rick Steves' Postcards from Europe, my autobiographical book, packs 25 years of travel anecdotes and insights into the ultimate 2,000-mile European adventure.

Other Guidebooks
You may want some supplemental information if you'll be traveling beyond my recommended destinations. When you consider the improvements they'll make in your $3,000 vacation, $25 or $35 for extra maps and books is money well spent. Especially for several

Begin Your Trip at www.ricksteves.com

At ricksteves.com, you'll find a wealth of **free information** on destinations covered in this book, including fresh European travel and tour news every month and helpful "Graffiti Wall" tips from thousands of fellow travelers.

While you're there, Rick Steves' **online Travel Store** is a great place to save money on travel bags and accessories specially designed by Rick Steves to help you travel smarter and lighter. These include Rick's popular carry-on bags (wheeled and ruck-sack versions), money belts, day bags, totes, toiletries kits, packing cubes, clotheslines, locks, clocks, sleep sacks, adapters, and a wide selection of guidebooks, planning maps, and *Rick Steves' Europe* DVDs.

Traveling through Europe by rail is a breeze, but choosing the right railpass for your trip (amidst hundreds of options) can drive you nutty. At ricksteves.com, you'll find **Rick Steves' Annual Guide to European Railpasses**—your best way to convert chaos into pure travel energy. Buy your railpass from Rick, and you'll get a bunch of free extras to boot.

Travel agents will tell you about mainstream tours of Europe, but they won't tell you about **Rick Steves' tours**. Rick Steves' Europe Through the Back Door travel company offers more than two dozen itineraries and 250+ departures reaching the best destinations in this book...and beyond. You'll enjoy the services of a great guide, a fun bunch of travel partners (with group sizes in the mid-20s), and plenty of room to spread out in a big, comfy bus. You'll find tours to fit every vacation size, from week-long city getaways (Barcelona, Paris, London, Venice, Florence, Rome), to 12–18-day country and regional tours, to three-week "Best of Europe" adventures. For details, visit www.ricksteves.com or call 425/771-8303, ext 217.

people traveling by car, the added weight and expense of a small trip library are negligible.

Lonely Planet's guide to Switzerland is thorough, well-researched, and packed with good maps and hotel recommendations for low- to moderate-budget travelers (but it's not updated annually—check to see when it was published). The similar *Rough Guide to Switzerland* is written by insightful British researchers (also not updated annually).

Students and vagabonds like the highly opinionated *Let's Go: Austria and Switzerland* (updated annually by Harvard students, has thorough hostel listings). *Let's Go* is best for backpackers who have railpasses and are interested in the youth and night scene.

The popular, skinny *Michelin Green Guide: Switzerland* is excellent, especially if you're driving. Michelin Guides are known for their city and sightseeing maps, dry but concise and helpful information on all major sights, and good cultural and historical background. English editions are sold locally at gas stations and tourist shops.

More Recommended Reading and Movies

To get in the mood for your trip, consider these books and films, which take place partly or entirely in Switzerland.

Non-Fiction: *La Place de la Concorde Suisse* (by John McPhee, in English); *Living Among the Swiss* (memoir by Michael Wells Glueck); *Why Switzerland?* (socioeconomic commentary by Jonathan Steinberg); *The White Spider* (by Heinrich Harrer, on the first Eiger ascent in the 1930s); *The Climb Up to Hell* (by Jack Olsen, on 1957 Eiger climb); and *A Tramp Abroad* (by Mark Twain).

Fiction: *The Magic Mountain* (by Thomas Mann); *Hotel du Lac* (by Anita Brookner); *A Farewell to Arms* (by Ernest Hemingway); *Daisy Miller* (by Henry James); *The Prisoner of Chillon* (epic poem by Lord Byron); *Terminal* (by Colin Forbes); *The Night Manager* (by John le Carré); *I'm Not Stiller* (by Swiss author Max Frisch, available in English); and *Heidi* (children's book by Johanna Spyri).

Movies: *Heidi*, *The Eiger Sanction*, *Five Days One Summer*, *Third Man on the Mountain*, and *Three Colors: Red*. In addition, the following 007 films feature scenes of James Bond skiing in Switzerland: *On Her Majesty's Secret Service* (with scenes of the Schilthorn, in the Berner Oberland), *Goldeneye*, *Goldfinger*, *The Spy Who Loved Me*, and *A View to a Kill*.

Maps

The black-and-white maps in this book are drawn by Dave Hoerlein, one of my veteran tour guides, who is well-traveled in Switzerland. His concise, simple maps are designed to help you locate recommended places quickly and painlessly. In Switzerland, tourist offices offer free (or cheap) maps of the city and region. Better maps are sold at newsstands—take a look before you buy to be sure the map has the level of detail you want.

European bookstores, especially in touristy areas, have good selections of maps. For drivers, I recommend a 1:400,000-scale map of the whole country, or even larger-scale maps of particular regions. Train travelers usually manage fine with the freebies they get with their railpass or from the local tourist offices.

PRACTICALITIES

Red Tape: Currently, Americans need only a passport, but no visa or shots, to travel in Europe. Switzerland isn't a member of the European Union, so you'll generally still have to show your passport when you cross borders. And remember, when you change countries, you must also change telephone cards, postage stamps, and *Unterhosen*.

Time: In Europe—and throughout this book—you'll be using the 24-hour clock. After 12:00 noon, keep going—13:00, 14:00, and so on. For anything over 12, subtract 12 and add p.m. (14:00 is 2:00 p.m.).

Business Hours: Swiss shops are generally open Monday through Friday 9:00–18:30, Saturday 8:00–16:00, and closed Sunday. They are often open later on Thursdays.

Discounts: While discounts for sightseeing and transportation are not listed in this book, youths (under 18) and students (only with International Student Identity Card) often get discounts—but only by asking.

Metric: Get used to metric. A liter is about a quart, four to a gallon. A kilometer is six-tenths of a mile. I figure kilometers to miles by cutting them in half and adding back 10 percent of the original (120 km: 60 + 12 = 72 miles, 300 km: 150 + 30 = 180 miles).

Watt's up? If you're bringing electrical gear, you'll need a two-prong adapter plug (sold cheap at travel stores in the United States) and a converter. Travel appliances often have convenient, built-in converters; look for a voltage switch marked 120V (U.S.) and 240V (Europe).

MONEY

Exchange Rates

I've priced things throughout this book in the local currency. Switzerland, which isn't a member of the European Union, has retained its traditional currency, the Swiss franc.

---

1 Swiss franc (SF) = about 75 cents, and 1.30 SF = about $1.

One Swiss franc is broken down into 100 rappen (or centimes, in French Switzerland). To roughly convert prices from Swiss francs into dollars, subtract one-quarter (for example, 50 SF = about $37—actually, $37.50). There are coins for one, two, and five francs, plus several coins for very small denominations of rappen. The small coin with real value is the 50-rappen (marked with $\frac{1}{2}$ rather than 50—worth about 37 cents). In a handful of change, it's easy to identify as the only one with ridges.

Banking

ATMs are the way to go. Bring an ATM or debit card (with a PIN code) to withdraw funds from cash machines as you travel, and carry a couple hundred dollars in American cash in your money belt as a backup. Switzerland has readily available, easy-to-use, 24-hour

Why No Swiss Euros?

You can't help but wonder why the efficient Swiss are stubbornly hanging on to their old franc while surrounded by countries basking in the ease and convenience of the euro. The answer is simple: It's too expensive for the Swiss to change. The Swiss enjoy lower mortgage interest rates and a more stable currency than the rest of Europe. But even more importantly, a huge part of the Swiss economy is based on providing a safe and secret place for wealthy people from around the world to stash their money. When bank fees are figured in, people who "save" in Swiss banks actually earn negative interest—they *pay* the Swiss to keep their money. Compliance with European Union regulations in order to join the euro zone would mean the end of Switzerland's secret banking industry. The Swiss are not inclined to deal such a devastating blow to their economy.

But even though Switzerland hasn't officially adopted the euro, the majority of Swiss hotels, restaurants, and shops (especially in touristy areas) accept smaller euro bills. Most businesses will not take euro coins or larger bills, and you'll usually get bad rates (and your change in Swiss francs). Many coin-operated phone booths even accept euros (marked with a big yellow €). If you're just passing through the country, never fear: Your euros will work. But if you're staying a while, get some Swiss francs...they're prettier, anyway.

ATMs with English instructions. They'll save you time and money (on commission fees). I traveled painlessly throughout Switzerland in 2004 with my Visa debit card. Before you go, verify with your bank that your card will work, inquire about fees, and alert them that you'll be making withdrawals in Europe; otherwise, the bank may not approve transactions if it perceives unusual spending patterns. Bring an extra copy of your card (or another of your cards) just in case one gets demagnetized or gobbled up by a machine. The German word for "cash machine" is *Bankomat*.

I've cashed my last travelers check, but if you haven't, note that regular banks have the best rates for cashing checks. Many Swiss banks charge a fee per check—so rather than cashing five $100 checks, cash one $500 check. For a large exchange, it pays to compare rates and fees. Bank hours are typically Monday through Friday from 8:00 to 17:00. Post offices (business hours) and train stations (long hours) usually change money if you can't get to a bank.

Just like at home, credit (or debit) cards work easily at larger hotels, restaurants, and shops, but smaller businesses prefer payment in local currency.

Damage Control for Lost or Stolen Cards

You can stop thieves from using your ATM, debit, or credit card by reporting the loss immediately to the proper company. Call these 24-hour U.S. numbers collect: Visa (tel. 410/581-9994), MasterCard (tel. 636/722-7111), and American Express (tel. 336/393-1111).

Providing the following information will help expedite the process: the name of the financial institution that issued you the card, full card number, the cardholder's name as printed on the card, billing address, home phone number, circumstances of the loss or theft, and identification verification: Social Security Number or birth date and your mother's maiden name. (Packing along a photocopy of the front and back of your cards helps you answer the harder questions.) If you are the secondary cardholder, you'll also need to provide the primary cardholder's identification verification details. You can generally receive a temporary card within two or three business days in Europe.

If you promptly report your card lost or stolen, you typically won't be responsible for any unauthorized transactions on your account, although many banks charge a liability fee of $50.

VAT Refunds and Customs Regulations

VAT Refunds: Wrapped into the purchase price of your Swiss souvenir is a Value Added Tax (VAT) of 7.6 percent. If you make a purchase of more than 530 SF at a store that participates in the VAT refund scheme, you're entitled to get most of that tax back. Personally, I've never felt that VAT refunds are worth the hassle, but if you do, here's the scoop.

If you're lucky, the merchant will subtract the tax when you make your purchase (this is more likely to occur if the store ships the goods to your home). Otherwise, you'll need to do all this:

Get the paperwork. Have the merchant completely fill out the necessary refund document, called a "cheque." You'll have to present your passport at the store.

Have your cheque(s) stamped at the border at your last stop in Switzerland by the customs agent who deals with VAT refunds. It's best to keep your purchases in your carry-on for viewing, but if they're too large or dangerous (such as knives) to carry on, then track down the proper customs agent to inspect them before you check your bag. You're not supposed to use your purchased goods before you leave. If you show up at customs wearing your new lederhosen or drindl, officials might look the other way—or deny you a refund.

To collect your refund, you'll need to return your stamped documents to the retailer or its representative. Many merchants work with services such as Global Refund or Premier Tax Free that have offices at major airports, ports, or border crossings. These services, which extract a 4 percent fee, can refund your money immediately in your currency of choice or credit your card (within 2 billing cycles). If you have to deal directly with the retailer, mail the store your stamped documents and then wait. It could take months.

Customs Regulations: You can take $800 in souvenirs per person duty-free back into the United States. The next $1,000 is taxed at a flat 3 percent. After that, you pay the individual item's duty rate. You can also bring in a liter of alcohol (slightly more than a standard-size bottle of wine), a carton of cigarettes, and up to 100 cigars duty-free. To check customs rules and duty rates, visit www .customs.gov.

TRAVEL SMART

Your trip is like a complex play—easier to follow and really appreciate on a second viewing. While no one does the same trip twice to gain that advantage, reading this book in its entirety before your trip accomplishes much the same thing.

Reread entire chapters as you travel, and visit local tourist information offices. Upon arrival in a new town, lay the groundwork for a smooth departure. Buy a phone card and use it for reservations and confirmations.

Enjoy the hospitality of the Swiss people. Ask questions. Most locals are eager to point you in their idea of the right direction. Wear your money belt, pack along a pocket-size notebook to organize your thoughts, and practice the virtue of simplicity. Those who expect to travel smart, do.

Tourist Information
Your best first stop in any new city is the tourist information office (abbreviated in this book as **TI**). Try to arrive, or at least telephone, before it closes. Throughout Switzerland, you'll find TIs are usually well-organized and have English-speaking staff.

As national budgets tighten, many TIs have been privatized. This means they become sales agents for big tours and hotels, and their "information" becomes unavoidably colored. While TIs are eager to book you a room, you should use their room-finding service only as a last resort. TIs can as easily book you a bad room as a good one—they are not allowed to promote one place over another. Go direct, using the listings in this book.

Swiss Museum Passport (Schweizer Museumspass)
This pass, an excellent deal for avid sightseers, covers the entry to more than 300 museums, including many museums listed in this

book (30 SF, valid 1 month). You can buy it at TIs, post offices, major museums, or online at www.museumspass.ch.

If you're only in Switzerland to hike, skip it. But if you'll be sightseeing in the cities, this pass is a no-brainer that pays for itself in three or four visits.

The following sights (covered in this book) are free with the pass:

Zürich—Swiss National Museum and Museum Rietberg.

Luzern—Rosengart Collection, Picasso Museum, Depot History Museum, Bourbaki Panorama, Glacier Garden, Alpineum, Swiss Transport Museum, Richard Wagner Museum, Museum of Art Luzern, and the Museum of Natural History, plus Fortress Fürigen Museum nearby.

Bern—Museum of Fine Arts.

Near Murten—Roman Museum in Avenches.

Near Interlaken—Swiss Open-Air Folk Museum at Ballenberg.

Appenzell Region—Folk Museums in Appenzell Town, Stein, and Urnäsch.

Lausanne—Collection de l'Art Brut, Olympic Museum, and City History Museum.

TRANSPORTATION

By Car or Train?

The train is best for single travelers, those who'll be spending more time in big cities, and those who don't want to drive in Europe. While a car gives you the ultimate in mobility and freedom, enables you to search for hotels more easily, and carries your bags for you, the train zips you effortlessly from town to town, usually dropping you in the center and near the tourist office. Cars are great in the Swiss countryside, but an expensive headache in cities such as bustling Zürich.

Because Switzerland's train network is excellent, I recommend using public transportation here. Only a few areas—like the Appenzell region and the French Swiss countryside—are better by car.

Trains

Trains are generally slick, speedy, and punctual, with synchronized connections. They cover cities well, but some frustrating schedules make a few out-of-the-way recommendations (such as Taveyanne in the French Swiss countryside) not worth the time and trouble for the less determined.

Information: Switzerland has a train info number you can dial from anywhere in

Prices listed are for 2004. For up-to-date prices and details (and easy online ordering), see my comprehensive Guide to European Railpasses at www.ricksteves.com.

SWISS PASS AND SWISS FLEXIPASS

	1st class Individual	1st class Saver	1st class Youth	2nd class Individual	2nd class Saver	2nd class Youth
4 consec. days	$260	$221	$195	$170	$145	$128
8 consec. days	360	306	270	240	204	180
15 consec. days	440	374	330	290	247	218
22 consec. days	500	425	375	335	285	252
1 month	560	476	420	375	319	282
Any 3 days in 1 mo. flexi	250	213	N/A	166	141	N/A
Any 4 days in 1 mo. flexi	294	250	N/A	196	167	N/A
Any 5 days in 1 mo. flexi	338	287	N/A	226	192	N/A
Any 6 days in 1 mo. flexi	386	328	N/A	256	218	N/A
Any 8 days in 1 mo. flexi	450	383	N/A	300	255	N/A

Saverpass prices are per person for 2 or more traveling together. Covers all trains, boats, and buses with 25% off high mountain rides. Kids under 16 free with parent.

SWISS 'N AUSTRIA COMBO PASS

	1st class Individual	1st class Saver	2nd class Youth
Any 4 days in 2 months	$300	$256	$210
Extra rail days (max 6)	36	30	27

Saverpass prices are per person for two or more people traveling together. Youthpasses are for travelers under age 26 only. Children 4-11: half adult fare or Saver price, under 4: free.

FRANCE & SWITZERLAND COMBO PASS

	1st class Individual	1st class Saver	2nd class Youth
Any 4 days in 2 months	$299	$259	$209
Extra rail days (max 6)	36	30	27

Youthpasses are for travelers under age 26 only. Saverpass prices are per person for two or more people traveling together. Children 4-11: half adult fare or Saver price, under 4: free.

SWITZERLAND BY TRAIN

This schematic map indicates the cost in dollars for a one-way, second-class train trip between the cities shown. First class costs 50 percent more. Add up the approximate ticket costs for your trip to see if a railpass will save you money.

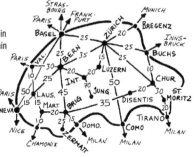

Public Transportation

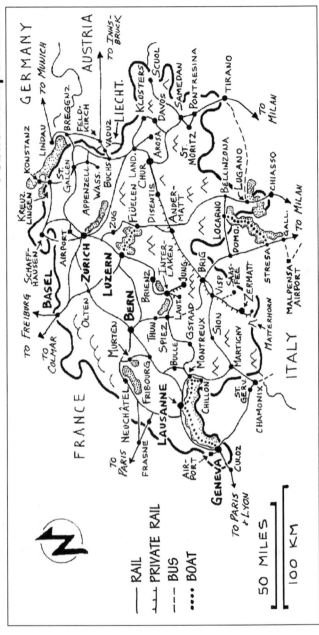

Lift Lingo

The Swiss have come up with a variety of ways to conquer peaks and reach the best viewpoints and trailheads with minimum sweat. Known generically as "lifts," each of these contraptions has its own name and definition—use the right terms, and impress your new Swiss friends.

Cogwheel Train: A train that climbs a steep incline using a gear system, which engages "teeth" in the middle of the tracks to provide traction. Also known as "rack-and-pinion train" or "rack railway."

Funicular: A car that is pulled by a cable along tracks up a particularly steep incline, often counterbalanced by a similar car going in the opposite direction. Funiculars, like cogwheel trains, are in contact with the ground at all times.

Cable Car: A large passenger car, suspended in the air by a cable, which travels between stations without touching the ground. A cable car holds a large number of people (sometimes dozens at a time), who generally ride standing up. When a cable car reaches a station, it comes to a full stop to allow passengers to get on and off.

Gondola: Also suspended in the air by a cable, but smaller than a cable car—generally holding fewer than 10 people, who are usually seated. Gondolas move continuously, meaning that passengers have to hop into and out of the moving cars at stations. Also, while cable-car lines usually have two big cars—one going in each direction—gondolas generally have many smaller cars strung along the same cable.

Confusingly, the "car" compartment of a cable car is sometimes referred to as a "gondola."

the country: toll tel. 0900-300-3004. For Swiss timetables, visit www.rail.ch or http://bahn.hafas.de/bin/query.exe/en. At most train stations, attendants will print out a step-by-step itinerary for you, free of charge. Major stations also have handy travel offices offering general help. Swiss trains and stations are marked "SBB CFF FFS." All those letters mean the same thing ("Swiss Federal Railways"), in three different languages: German, French, and Italian.

Swiss Railpasses

Because of high ticket prices, railpasses are a good deal in Switzerland (assuming you're here for a week or more). But for such a little country, Switzerland has a dizzying array of train passes and deals. Here are the most popular ones:

The **Swiss Pass** is the basic version, covering all trains, boats, and buses, plus a 25 percent discount on lifts. It comes in both consecutive and flexi-day versions. A Swiss Pass Saverpass gives a 15 percent discount to two or more companions traveling together. Second class (available to any age) is 33 percent cheaper than first class. For specific passes and prices, see page 17.

The **Half-Fare Travel Card** gives you 50 percent off all national and private trains, postal buses, lifts, and steamers (99 SF for 1 month, sold only in Switzerland). This can save you money if your Swiss travel adds up to more than $150 in point-to-point tickets. The **Swiss Card** is a variation on this, sold only in America. It includes the same discounts and adds a round-trip train ride from any point of entry (such as the German border or Zürich's airport) to any other point in Switzerland ($166 first class, $124 second class).

Regional passes cover all travel—including trains, buses, boats, and lifts—in a particular area, such as the Berner Oberland (Berner Oberland Pass, see page 112), Zermatt area (see page 172), or Central Switzerland, around Luzern (Tell-Pass, see page 222). Buy these (in Switzerland, not the U.S.) only if you're very focused on a single region, but note that there's usually no need to have both a regional pass and an all-Swizerland pass (or Eurailpass).

Other deals include the **Swiss Family Card**, allowing children under 16 to travel free with their parents (20 SF per child at Swiss stations, or free with Swiss train passes when requested with purchase in the United States).

For more details on all of these passes, see www.ricksteves.com/rail.

Eurailpasses

If you're also traveling to other counties, consider a Eurail Selectpass, which gives you up to 10 travel days (within a 2-month period) in three, four, or five adjacent countries—choose from among Switzerland, Germany, Austria, France, Italy, and other Western European countries. Another possibility is a 17-country Eurailpass (cost-effective only if you're doing a whirlwind trip of Europe). Like the Swiss Pass, these come in Saverpass versions (15 percent cheaper for 2 or more traveling together); unlike the Swiss Pass, if you're over 26, you have to buy a first-class pass.

Railpass Discounts

If you buy a railpass, know what extras are included—for example, boat cruises on the big Swiss lakes. In addition, railpasses can get you discounts on many mountain lifts. Always ask. Note that while Eurailpasses include some deals in Switzerland beyond simple trains (such as on some mountain lifts), the discounts and coverage of these passes generally isn't as extensive as the Switzerland-only passes (for example, lifts in Zermatt are discounted and postal buses nationwide are free with a Swiss Pass, but both are full price with a Eurailpass).

If your railpass is a "flexipass" (that is, a certain number of days in a given span, rather than consecutive days), note that discounted trips (such as on mountain lifts) don't use up a flexi-day, but free trips (like lake boats) do. The "used" flexi-day can also cover your train travel on that day. But if you're not planning to travel more that day, it makes sense to pay for, say, a short boat ride rather than use up a day of your pass for it.

Train Notes

Scenic Rail Journeys: In addition to being convenient for transportation, many of Switzerland's trains are also breathtakingly scenic. Several trips are particularly beautiful, and billed as special "theme" routes for tourists. For many visitors, these are a Swiss highlight, and I've devoted an entire chapter to them (see page 221).

Private Lines: Switzerland has some privately owned train lines. For instance, a large segment of the Glacier Express scenic journey is private. Private lines are usually covered by Swiss railpasses, but not covered by Eurailpasses (though these passes can get you discounts on certain trips). If your railpass doesn't cover an entire journey, pay for the "uncovered" portion at the station before you board the train.

Check Your Bags: If you're town- or mountain-hopping through Switzerland by train, you can lighten your load by sending your baggage ahead (drop it off at the station, pay 10 SF with ticket or railpass, 40 SF without, maximum 55 pounds). Your bag will show up within 24 hours of your arrival (usually faster), and will be held free for five days (after that, you're charged 3 SF/day).

Bike 'n' Rail: Hundreds of local train stations rent bikes for about $5 a day, and sometimes have easy "pick up here and drop off there" plans. For mixing train and bike travel, ask at stations for information booklets.

Car Rental

It's cheaper to arrange your car rental in advance in the United States than in Europe. You'll want a weekly rate with unlimited mileage. For three weeks or longer, leasing is cheaper because it saves you money on taxes and insurance. Comparison-shop through your agent. DER, a German company, often has good rates (U.S. tel. 800/782-2424, www.dertravel.com). It's cheaper to pick your car up in Zürich than at the airport.

Expect to pay about $600 per person (based on 2 people sharing the car) for a small economy car for two weeks with unlimited mileage, including gas, parking, and insurance. I normally rent a small, inexpensive model like a Ford Fiesta. For a bigger, roomier, more powerful but still inexpensive car, move up to a Ford Escort or VW Polo. If you drop your car off early or keep it longer, you'll be credited or charged at a fair, prorated price.

For peace of mind, I splurge for the CDW insurance (about 25 percent extra, or about $15 per day), which covers virtually the full value of the car (minus a small deductible) in case of an accident. A few "gold" credit cards include CDW if you rent the car using that card; quiz your credit-card company on the worst-case scenario. Travel Guard sells CDW insurance for $7 a day (tel. 800/826-4919, www.travelguard.com). With the luxury of CDW, you'll enjoy the autobahn knowing you can bring back the car in a shambles and just say, "S-s-s-sorry."

For driving in Switzerland, your U.S. driver's license is all you need. If you're also planning to drive in Austria and Germany, you're strongly advised to get an international driver's license (at your local AAA office—$10 plus 2 passport-type photos).

Driving

You can get anywhere quickly on Switzerland's fine road system, the world's most expensive per mile to build. Drivers pay a one-time, 40-SF fee for a permit to use Swiss autobahns—check to see if your rental car already has one (if not, buy it at the border, gas station, or car rental agency). Anyone caught driving on a Swiss autobahn without this tax sticker is likely to be stopped and fined. Seat belts are required, and two beers under those belts are enough to land you in jail.

Driving: Distance and Time

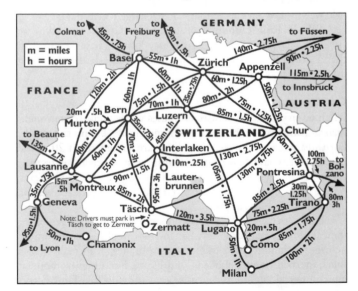

AND LEARN THESE ROAD SIGNS

Speed Limit (km/hr)

Yield

No Passing

End of No Passing Zone

One Way

Intersection

Main Road

Freeway

Danger

No Entry

No Entry for Cars

All Vehicles Prohibited

Parking

No Parking

Customs

Peace

Use good local maps and study them before each drive. Learn which exits you need to look out for, which major cities you'll travel toward, where the ruined castles lurk, and so on.

Know the universal road signs (shown in this chapter and explained in charts in most road atlases and at service stations). *Dreieck* (literally, "three corners") means a "Y" in the road; *Autobahnkreuz* is an intersection. Exits are spaced about 20 miles apart and often have a gas station (*bleifrei* means unleaded), a restaurant, a mini-market, and sometimes a tourist information desk. Exits and intersections refer to the next major or the nearest small town. Look at your map and anticipate which town names to watch out for. Know what you're looking for—miss it, and you're long autobahn-gone. When navigating, you'll see *nord, süd, ost, west,* or *mitte.*

To get to the center of a city, follow signs for *Zentrum* or *Stadtmitte.* Ring roads go around a city. For parking, you can pick up the "cardboard clock" (*Parkscheibe,* available free at gas stations, police stations, and *Tabak* shops) and display your arrival time on the dashboard, so parking attendants can see you've been there less than the posted maximum stay.

COMMUNICATING

Language Barrier

Switzerland has four official languages: German, French, Italian, and Romansh (an obscure Romantic tongue). Most of the destinations in this book are in the German-speaking territory. No matter where you are, most people in larger towns and the tourist trade speak at least some English. Still, you'll get more smiles by using the local pleasantries. See the German, French, and Italian "Survival Phrases" in the appendix.

In German-speaking Switzerland, locals speak sing-songy *Schwyzertütsch* (Swiss German) around the house, but in schools and at work, they speak and write in the same standard German used in Germany and Austria (called "High" German, or *Hochdeutsch*— though many Swiss prefer to call it *Schriftdeutsch,* or "Written German"). The standard greeting is a hearty *Grüezi* (GREWT-see). "Thank you" is derived from French, but pronounced a little differently: *Merci* (MUR-see). They also sometimes use the more German-like *Dunkcha* (DOONK-chah).

German—like English, Dutch, Swedish, and Norwegian—is a Germanic language, making it easier on most American ears than Romance languages (such as Italian and French). German is pronounced just as it's spelled. There are a few potentially confusing vowel combinations: *ie* is pronounced "ee" (as in *Bier,* the German word for "beer"); *ei* is pronounced "aye" (as in *nein,* German for "no"), and *eu* is pronounced "oy" (as in *Deutsch,* German for "German"). Written German always capitalizes all nouns.

Give it your best shot. The locals will appreciate your efforts.

Telephones

Smart travelers learn the phone system and use it daily to reserve or reconfirm rooms, get tourist information, or phone home. Some Swisscom phone booths take only cards, some only coins, some take both, and some (marked with a yellow €) even accept euro coins.

Phone Cards: International phone calls are just about the only thing that's actually cheaper in Switzerland than in other countries. You'll see Swisscom phone booths everywhere. Dialing direct from those booths to the United States costs just eight cents a minute, plus a 35-cent connection charge. Rather than juggle coins at these booths, buy an insertable **Swisscom phone card** *(Telefonkarte),* which is the cheapest bet for both domestic and international calls. These cards are sold at post offices and many newsstand kiosks.

Simply slide it into the slot on the phone, wait for a dial tone and digital readout to show how much value remains on your card, and dial your domestic or international call. The cost of the call is automatically deducted from your card.

In neighboring countries, the official insertable phone cards are more expensive for international calls. In those places, it's smart to buy a special **international phone card** with a scratch-to-reveal personal identification number (PIN). With these cards, the cost for international calls plummets to 10 cents per minute. Since you don't have to insert them in the phone, they can also be used from hotel rooms.

Either type of phone card works only in the country where it's purchased. If you use coins to make your calls, have a bunch handy. Or look for a metered phone ("talk now, pay later") in the bigger post offices. Avoid using hotel-room phones for anything other than local calls.

Dialing Direct: All phone numbers in Switzerland are 10 digits (without area codes) that can be dialed direct throughout the country. For instance, to call a recommended Swiss hotel in Gimmelwald, you'd dial the same number (tel. 033-855-1658) whether you're calling from the Gimmelwald gondola station or from Zürich. If calling the Swiss hotel from outside the country, dial the international access code (011 if you're phoning from the U.S. or Canada; 00 from elsewhere in Europe), Switzerland's country code (41), and then the local number *without* its initial 0 (33-855-1658). Note that when you call internationally to Switzerland, you must drop the initial 0 of the telephone number.

To dial international calls direct, you'll need the international access codes and country codes (see the appendix). To call my office in Edmonds, Washington, from Europe, I dial 00 (Europe's international access code), 1 (U.S. country code), 425 (Edmonds' area code), and 771-8303. European time is six/nine hours ahead of the East/West Coast of the United States.

U.S.A. Direct Services: Since direct-dialing rates have dropped, calling cards (offered by AT&T, MCI, and Sprint) are no longer the good value they used to be. It's much cheaper to purchase a phone card in Switzerland and dial direct.

Mobile Phones: Many travelers now buy inexpensive mobile phones in Europe to make both local and international calls. (Typical American mobile phones don't work in Europe, and those that do have horrendous per-minute costs.) For about $75, you can get a phone with $20 worth of calls that will work in the country where you purchased it. You can buy more time at newsstands or mobile phone shops. For about $100, you can get an "unlocked" phone that will work in most countries if you pick up the necessary chip per country (about $25 each). If you're interested, stop by any European shop that sells mobile phones; you'll see prominent store window displays. Find an English-speaking clerk to help you. Confirm with the clerk whether the phone works only in Switzerland or throughout Europe. You'll need to pick out a policy; different policies offer, say, better rates for making calls to fixed phones rather than mobile phones. Receiving calls is generally free. If you're on a tight budget, skip mobile phones and buy phone cards instead.

E-Mail and Mail

E-mail: More and more hoteliers have e-mail addresses and Web sites (listed in this book). Note that mom-and-pop pensions, which can get deluged by e-mail, are not always able to respond immediately to a message you've sent.

Internet cafés are available at just about every destination in this book, giving you reasonably inexpensive and easy Internet access. Your hotelier can direct you to the nearest place.

Mail: To arrange for mail delivery, reserve a few hotels along your route in advance and give their addresses to friends. If you have an American Express card, most AmEx offices will hold your mail for free. Allow 10 days for a letter to arrive. Phoning and e-mailing are so easy that I've dispensed with mail stops altogether.

If you need to mail items home (be warned, it's expensive), you can buy boxes and tape at most post offices.

SLEEPING

In the interest of smart use of your time, I favor hotels and restaurants handy to your sightseeing activities. Hotels are expensive in Switzerland, so I've scoured the options and presented you with the best values, from $10 bunks to plush $200 doubles.

Accommodations in Switzerland are normally very comfortable and come with breakfast. Plan on spending $80–130 per hotel double, and $60–80 for a double with the bathroom down the hall in a cheap hostel-type place or a private home. A triple is much cheaper than a double and a single. While hotel singles are most expensive, private accommodations *(Zimmer)* have a flat per-person rate. Hostels and dorms always charge per person. Especially in private homes, where the boss changes the sheets, people staying several nights are most desirable. One-night stays are sometimes charged extra.

In recommending hotels, I favor small, family-run places that are central, inexpensive, quiet, clean, safe, friendly, English-speaking, and not listed in other guidebooks. I also like local character and simple facilities that don't cater to American "needs." Obviously, a place meeting every criterion is rare, and all of my recommendations fall short of perfection—sometimes miserably. But I've listed the best values for each price category, given the above criteria.

Sleep Code

To give maximum information in a minimum of space, I use these codes to describe accommodations listed in this book. Prices listed are per room, not per person. When a range of prices is listed for a room, the price fluctuates with room size or season.

  S = Single room (or price for 1 person in a double).
  D = Double or Twin. Double beds are usually big enough for non-romantic couples.
  T = Triple (often a double bed with a single bed moved in).
  Q = Quad (an extra child's bed is usually cheaper).
  b = Private bathroom with toilet and shower or tub.
  s = Private shower or tub only (the toilet is down the hall).
 no CC = Does not accept credit cards; pay in local cash.
  SE = Speaks English.
 NSE = Does not speak English. Used only when it's unlikely you'll encounter English-speaking staff.

According to this code, a couple staying at a "Db-150 SF" hotel would pay a total of 150 Swiss francs (about $115) for a double room with a private bathroom. The hotel accepts credit cards or cash in payment; you can assume a hotel takes credit cards unless you see "no CC" in the listing.

I've divided the rooms into three categories, based on the price for a standard double room with bath:

$$\$\$\$ \textbf{Higher Priced}$$
$$\$\$ \textbf{Moderately Priced}$$
$$\$ \textbf{Lower Priced}$$

Any room without a bathroom has access to a bathroom in the corridor (free unless otherwise noted). All rooms have a sink. For environmental reasons, towels are often replaced in hotels only when you leave them on the floor. In cheaper places, they aren't replaced at all, so hang them up to dry and reuse.

Unless I note otherwise, the cost of a room includes a breakfast (sometimes continental, but usually buffet). The price is usually posted in the room. Before accepting, confirm your understanding of the complete price. I appreciate feedback on your hotel experiences.

Making Reservations

It's possible to travel at any time of year without reservations, but given the high stakes, erratic accommodations values, and quality of the gems I've found for this book, I'd recommend calling for rooms at least several days in advance as you travel (and book well in advance during festivals, such as Luzern's Karneval). If there's any reason to travel without reservations, it's to remain flexible, so you can modify your itinerary as you go to adapt to the weather (spending rainy days in cities and sunny days in the mountains). If tourist crowds are minimal, you might make a habit of calling between 9:00 and 10:00 on the day you plan to arrive, when the hotel knows who'll be checking out and just which rooms will be available. I've taken great pains to list telephone numbers with long-distance instructions (see "Dialing Direct," above). Use the telephone and the convenient telephone cards. Most hotels listed are accustomed to English-only speakers. A hotel receptionist will trust you and hold a room until 16:00 without a deposit, though some will ask for a credit-card number. Honor (or cancel by phone) your reservations. Trusting people to show up is a hugely stressful issue and a financial risk for B&B owners. Don't let these people down—I promised you'd call and cancel if for some reason you can't show up. Don't needlessly confirm rooms through the tourist offices; they'll take a commission.

If you know exactly which dates you need and really want a particular place, reserve a room long before you leave home. To reserve from home, e-mail, call, or fax the hotel. E-mail is free, phone and fax costs are reasonable, and simple English is fine. To fax, use the form in the appendix (e-mailers can find it online at www.ricksteves.com/reservation). A two-night stay in August would be "2 nights, 16/8/05 to 18/8/05" (Europeans write the date day/month/year, and European hotel jargon uses your day of departure). Hotels often require one night's deposit to hold a room. Usually a credit-card number and expiration date will be accepted as the deposit. If that's the case, you can pay with your card or cash when you arrive; if you don't show up, you'll be billed for one night. Reconfirm your reservations a day or two in advance for safety. Ask about the hotel's cancellation policy when you reserve—sometimes you have to cancel as far as two weeks ahead to avoid being charged.

Camping and Hosteling

Campers can manage with *Let's Go* listings and help from the local TI (ask for a regional camping list). Your hometown travel bookstore also has guidebooks on camping in Europe. You'll find campgrounds just about everywhere you need them. Look for *Campingplatz* signs. You'll meet lots of Europeans— camping is a popular middle-class-family way to go. Campgrounds are cheap (about $10 per person), friendly, safe, more central and convenient than rustic, and rarely full.

Hostelers can take advantage of the wonderful network of hostels. Follow signs marked *Jugendherberge*

(with triangles) or with the logo showing a tree next to a house. Generally, travelers without a membership card ($28 per year, sold at hostels in most U.S. cities or online at www.hihostels.com, U.S. tel. 202/783-6161) are admitted for an extra $5.

Swiss hostels are open to members of all ages. They usually cost $10–20 per night (cheaper for those under 27) and serve good, cheap meals and/or provide kitchen facilities. If you plan to stay in hostels, bring your own sheet (or pay extra at each place to rent one). While many hostels have a few doubles or family rooms available upon request for a little extra money, plan on gender-segregated dorms with 4–20 beds per room. Hostels can be idyllic and peaceful, but school groups can raise the rafters. School groups are most common on summer weekends and on school-year weekdays. I like small hostels best. While many hostels may say over the telephone that they're full, most hold a few beds for people who drop in, or they can direct you to budget accommodations nearby.

EATING

The Swiss eat when we do and enjoy a straightforward, no-nonsense cuisine. Specialties include delicious fondue, rich chocolates, a melted cheese dish called raclette, *Rösti* (hash browns), fresh dairy products (try muesli with yogurt), 100 varieties of cheese, and Fendant—a good, crisp, local white wine.

Eateries

There are many kinds of restaurants. Hotels often serve fine food. A *Gaststätte* is a simple, less expensive restaurant. A *Weinstübli* (wine bar) or *Bierstübli* (tavern) usually serves food. Mountain huts—called *Hütte*—generally have hot chocolate and hearty meals.

If you're not too hungry, order from the *kleine Hunger* (small hunger) section of the menu. Many restaurants offer half portions, which is a great relief on your budget (although two people save even more by sharing one full portion).

Most restaurants tack a menu onto their door for browsers and have an English menu inside. Only a rude waiter will rush you. Good service is relaxed (slow to an American). To wish others "Happy eating!," offer a cheery *"Guten Appetit!"* When you want the bill, ask for *"Die Rechnung, bitte."*

Swiss restaurants are expensive, but there are several excellent budget alternatives. The Co-op and Migros grocery stores are the hungry hiker's best budget bet; groceries—while about 50 percent more than U.S. prices—are a huge savings over any restaurant. These supermarkets also often come with cheap self-service cafeterias, with good food at much lower prices than restaurants with table service. In most big cities, you'll find Manor department stores,

Tips on Tipping

Tipping in Europe isn't as automatic and generous as it is in the United States—but for special service, tips are appreciated, if not expected. As in the United States, the proper amount depends on your resources, tipping philosophy, and the circumstance, but some general guidelines apply.

Restaurants: At restaurants with table service, tipping is optional, though appreciated (up to 10 percent). If you order your food at a counter, don't tip.

Taxis: To tip the cabbie, round up. For a typical ride, round up to the next franc or two on the fare (to pay a 13-SF fare, give 15 SF); for a long ride, to the nearest 10 (for a 75-SF fare, give 80 SF). If the cabbie hauls your bags and zips you to the airport to help you catch your flight, you might want to toss in a little more. But if you feel like you're being driven in circles or otherwise ripped off, skip the tip.

Special services: Tour guides at public sites sometimes hold out their hands for tips after they give their spiel; if I've already paid for the tour, I don't tip extra, though some tourists do give a franc or two, particularly for a job well done. I don't tip at hotels, but if you do, give the porter a franc or two for carrying bags and leave a few francs in your room at the end of your stay for the maid if the room was kept clean. In general, if someone in the service industry does a super job for you, a tip of a couple of francs is appropriate...but not required.

When in doubt, ask: If you're not sure whether (or how much) to tip for a service, ask your hotelier or the TI; they'll fill you in on how it's done on their turf.

which usually feature wonderful self-service eateries called "Manora"—with lush salad bars, tasty entrées, and fresh-squeezed juices (I've listed several specific Manora locations in this book). Bakeries are another great place for a snack or affordable light meal.

Swiss Cuisine

Here at a crossroads of Europe, the food has a wonderful diversity: heavy *Wurst*-and-kraut Germanic fare; delicate, subtle French cuisine; and pasta dishes *all' Italiana*.

Aside from clocks and banks, Switzerland is known for its cheese. Gruyère cheese is hard, with a strong flavor; Emmentaler is also hard, but milder. Appenzeller is the incredibly pungent cheese from the northeast of Switzerland, with a smell that verges on nauseating...until you taste it. Two of Switzerland's best-known specialties are cheese-based. *Käse fondue* is Emmentaler and Gruyère cheese melted with white wine, garlic, nutmeg, and other seasonings. You eat it with a long fork, dipping cubes of bread into it. Raclette is cheese slowly melted by a special appliance; as it softens, scrape a mound off and eat it with potatoes, pickled onions, and gherkins. (In restaurants, raclette often comes as little slices of cheese already melted.)

Another must-try dish, most typical in the mountains of the German-speaking areas, is *Rösti:* traditional hash browns with alpine cheese, often served with an egg cracked over it...yum.

Of course, each region has its own specialties. In French-speaking Switzerland, white wine and heavy cream are used in many dishes, and horsemeat (formerly imported from Eastern Europe, now imported from the U.S.) is common. The cuisine in eastern Switzerland (Pontresina, St. Moritz) uses chestnuts in many forms, wild mushrooms, and air-dried beef. Southwestern Switzerland (Zermatt area) specializes in all kind of cheese, and their favorite white wine is Fendant.

Despite all the cheese and potatoes, the Swiss tend to be health-conscious. Menus often feature a *Fitnessteller* ("fitness plate")—usually a large mixed salad that comes with a steak, chicken, or fish. *Bio* means organically grown, and a *Bioläderli* is a store that sells organic products.

Swiss wine (about two-thirds white) is good, but expensive. Try the dry, white Fendant, great with cheese dishes. If you're in Murten, sample the local Vully wine. Fruity St. Saphorin grows on the slopes above Lake Geneva. Menus list drink size by the tenth of a liter, or deciliter (dl). Order wine by the *Viertel* (quarter liter, or 8 oz.) or *Achtel* (eighth liter, or 4 oz.). Order it *süss* (sweet), *halbe trocken* (medium), or *trocken* (dry). You can say, "*Ein Viertel Weisswein* (white wine), *bitte* (please)." *Rotwein* is red wine; a *Pfiff* is two deciliters (around 8 oz.) of red wine. *Bocalino* is a small, decorated eight-ounce ceramic jug with a light Swiss red wine called Dole.

As for beer: *Dunkles* is dark, *helles* is light, *Flaschenbier* is bottled, and *vom Fass* is on tap. *Pils* is barley-based (a *Stange* is a *Pils* in a tall, fluted glass). *Weizenbier* is wheat-based, poured slowly to build its frothy head thick and high, and served in a large rounded-top glass with a wedge of lemon. *Radler* (literally "biker"—for athletes who want to get refreshed, not drunk) is half beer and half lemon-lime soda. When you order beer, ask for *ein Halbe* for a half liter (not always available), or *eine Mass* for a whole liter (about a quart).

Instead of Coke, try a local favorite: Rivella, a carbonated, vita-min-rich soft drink made with 35 percent milk serum. Its unusual (but not unpleasant) taste doesn't resemble milk at all; it's more like chewable vitamins. It comes in three colors: red is regular, blue is low-calorie, and green is mixed with green tea. Tap water—which many waiters aren't eager to bring you—is *Leitungswasser* or *Wasser vom Fass*. They would rather you buy *Mineralwasser* (*mit/ohne Gas*, with/without carbonation).

As an alternative to hot chocolate, try Ovomaltine. The Swiss have a fondness for this hot drink—a malt-derived vitamin supplement, flavored with chocolate so kids will drink it. (In the U.S., our "Ovaltine" is an Asian variation on this drink—considered by the Swiss to be a cheap copy.)

And, of course, there's chocolate. The Swiss changed the world in 1875 with their invention of milk chocolate. Nestlé, Suchard, and Lindt are the major producers. Stroll the chocolate aisle of a grocery store and take your pick.

TRAVELING AS A TEMPORARY LOCAL

We travel all the way to Europe to enjoy differences—to become temporary locals. You'll experience frustrations. Certain truths that we find "God-given" or "self-evident," such as cold beer, ice in drinks, and bottomless cups of coffee, are suddenly not so true. One of the benefits of travel is the eye-opening realization that there are logical, civil, and even better alternatives. A willingness to go local ensures that you'll enjoy a full dose of Swiss hospitality.

While Europeans look bemusedly at some of our Yankee excesses—and worriedly at others—they nearly always afford us individual travelers all the warmth we deserve.

While updating this book, I heard over and over again that my readers are considerate and fun to have as guests. Thank you for traveling as temporary locals who are sensitive to the culture. It's fun to follow you in my travels.

Send Me a Postcard, Drop Me a Line

If you enjoy a successful trip with the help of this book and would like to share your discoveries, please fill out the survey at www.ricksteves.com/feedback or e-mail me at rick@ricksteves.com. I personally read and value all feedback. Thanks in advance—it helps a lot.

Judging from the happy postcards I receive from travelers, it's safe to assume you'll enjoy a great, affordable vacation—with the finesse of an independent, experienced traveler.

Thanks, and happy travels—*gute Reise!*

BACK DOOR TRAVEL PHILOSOPHY
From *Rick Steves' Europe Through the Back Door*

Travel is intensified living—maximum thrills per minute, and one of the last great sources of legal adventure. Travel is freedom. It's recess, and we need it.

Experiencing the real Europe requires catching it by surprise, going casual..."Through the Back Door."

Affording travel is a matter of priorities. (Make do with the old car.) You can travel—simply, safely, and comfortably—anywhere in Europe for $100 a day plus transportation costs. In many ways, spending more money only builds a thicker wall between you and what you came to see. Europe is a cultural carnival, and, time after time, you'll find that its best acts are free and the best seats are the cheap ones.

A tight budget forces you to travel close to the ground, meeting and communicating with the people, not relying on service with a purchased smile. Never sacrifice sleep, nutrition, safety, or cleanliness in the name of budget. Simply enjoy the local-style alternatives to expensive hotels and restaurants.

Extroverts have more fun. If your trip is low on magic moments, kick yourself and make things happen. If you don't enjoy a place, maybe you don't know enough about it. Seek the truth. Recognize tourist traps. Give a culture the benefit of your open mind. See things as different, but not better or worse. Any culture has much to share.

Of course, travel, like the world, is a series of hills and valleys. Be fanatically positive and militantly optimistic. If something's not to your liking, change your liking. Travel is addictive. It can make you a happier American, as well as a citizen of the world. Our Earth is home to six billion equally important people. It's humbling to travel and find that people don't envy Americans. They like us, but with all due respect, they wouldn't trade passports.

Globe-trotting destroys ethnocentricity. It helps you understand and appreciate different cultures. Travel changes people. It broadens perspectives and teaches new ways to measure quality of life. Many travelers toss aside their hometown blinders. Their prized souvenirs are the strands of different cultures they decide to knit into their own character. The world is a cultural yarn shop. And Back Door travelers are weaving the ultimate tapestry.

Come on, join in!

SWITZERLAND
(Schweiz, Suisse, Svizzera)

Switzerland is one of Europe's richest, best organized, and most expensive countries. Like the Boy Scouts, the Swiss count cleanliness, neatness, punctuality, tolerance, independence, thrift, and hard work as virtues...and they love pocketknives. Their high income, a great social security system, and the spectacular Alps give the Swiss plenty to be thankful for.

Nearly half of Switzerland, Europe's most mountainous country, consists of uninhabitable rocks, lakes, and rugged Alps. Despite the country's small size, it is unusually diverse. Its wild geography has kept people apart historically, helping its many regions maintain their distinct cultural differences. Switzerland is at a linguistic crossroads of Europe: Two-thirds of the people speak German, 20 percent French, 8 percent Italian, and a small group in the southeast speak Romansh, a descendant of ancient Latin.

Historically, Switzerland is one of Europe's oldest democracies, yet women didn't get the vote until 1971. Born when three states (cantons) united in 1291, the Confederation Helvetica grew to the 26 cantons of today. (The "CH" decal on cars doesn't stand for chocolate.) The country is named for the Celtic Helvetia tribe that lived here back in Roman times. The Confederation Helvetica government is decentralized, and cantonal loyalty is very strong.

Stubbornly independent (or maybe just smart), Switzerland loves its neutrality and stayed out of both World Wars. But it's far from lax when it comes to national defense. Every fit man serves in the army and stays in the reserve. Each house has a gun and a fully stocked bomb shelter. (Swiss vacuum-packed emergency army bread, which lasts two years, is also said to function as a weapon.) Switzerland bristles with 600,000 rifles in homes and 12,000 heavy guns in place. Airstrips hide inside mountains behind camouflaged doors. With the push of a button, all road, rail, and bridge entries to the country can be destroyed, sealing off the country from the outside world. Sentiments are changing, though, and Switzerland has

How Big, How Many, How Much

- Switzerland is 16,000 square miles (half the size of Ireland, or twice the size of Massachusetts)
- About 7.5 million people (470 people per square mile)
- 1 Swiss franc (SF) = about 75 cents, and 1.30 SF = about $1

come close to voting away its entire military. Today you can visit once-hidden military installations—now open to the public as museums (for an example, see page 80).

In 2002, Switzerland legalized marijuana use. When polls showed that over 30 percent of the country had used marijuana, the Parliament decided to decriminalize the drug, rather than criminalize a third of its population. The new law is still hazy—the Swiss can possess and use pot, but they can't sell it. While not wanting to clog its prisons with petty pot smokers, the country doesn't want to be known as another Holland, either. Each spring, there's a push for stricter control. Word gets out that Switzerland is no haven for pot, and then things ease up.

Prices are high. More and more locals call sitting on the pavement around a bottle of wine "going out." Hotels with double rooms under $80 are rare. Even dormitory beds cost $15. If your budget is tight, be sure to chase down hostels (many have family rooms) and keep your eyes peeled for *Matratzenlagers* (literally, "mattress dorms"). Hiking is free, though major alpine lifts run around $50.

While Switzerland's booming big cities are cosmopolitan, traditional culture survives in the alpine villages. Spend most of your time getting high in the Alps. On Sunday, you're most likely to enjoy traditional music, clothing, and culture. August 1 is the festive Swiss national holiday.

A Swiss Timeline

Switzerland has a unique and impressive story—forging unity from diversity and somehow remaining above the fray when Europe goes ballistic. Despite four languages, diverse geography, ill-defined borders, and many religious sects—and despite being surrounded by Continental Europe's four big powers (France, Germany, Austria, and Italy)—the Swiss cantons banded together to form an independent federal system that still works today.

500,000,000 B.C.: The ocean floor is rocked by earthquakes that fold the earth upward, creating the Alps.

53 B.C: Julius Caesar defeats the Helvetia, a Celtic tribe. The Romans' language, Latin, would eventually evolve into the French, Italian, and Romansh languages spoken in Switzerland today.

c. A.D. 300: Germanic tribes invade and settle.

c. 600: An Irish missionary named Columbanus arrives and converts the pagan Swiss to Christianity.

800: Swiss lands are part of Charlemagne's empire, later called the Holy Roman Empire, under German kings.

1256–1273: During a period in which no emperor rules, the Swiss develop a measure of independence. When Austrian Hapsburgs are brought in to reign, the Swiss resent foreign control.

1291: On August 1, Swiss citizens swear the oath, "We will be a single nation of brothers..." and rise up against Hapsburg rule. The three cantons of Uri, Schwyz, and Unterwalden unite, proclaiming independence and democratic institutions.

In a legend of the time, the Swiss William Tell refuses to bow to the Hapsburg hat, a symbol of their power. As punishment, he's forced to shoot an apple off his own son's head. He does so, then leads a rebellion.

In fact, the Swiss often outbattled the more powerful Hapsburgs, but they had to fight for two full centuries to drive the Hapsburgs out, earning a reputation as Europe's fiercest warriors. Swiss mercenaries (like the Swiss Guards that protect the Vatican today) became a major export.

1332: Luzern joins the Swiss Federation, soon followed by more cantons.

1499: A treaty makes Switzerland independent in fact, if not in name.

1500s: During the Reformation, Switzerland is bitterly divided, but offers a haven for free thinkers. Ulrich Zwingli establishes Protestantism in Zürich, John Calvin (a Frenchman) brings followers to Geneva, and Erasmus (from Holland) teaches at Basel.

1648: The Treaty of Westphalia officially makes Switzerland independent.

1798: French revolutionary forces occupy Switzerland and try to establish a strong central government. It doesn't stick, so Napoleon restores canton power (1803).

1815: The Congress of Vienna proclaims Switzerland with today's borders.

1848: Amid a Europe-wide wave of liberal reforms, Switzerland's tradition of democracy is established in a constitution. The new Confederation features a modern, bicameral parliament modeled after America's but with less power given to the executive branch.

1864: The International Red Cross is founded by a Genevan, adopting the Swiss flag with colors reversed as its symbol.

1872–1882: The Gotthard railway is built over

the Alps. A wave of breathtaking mountain engineering follows, taming much of the Alps and bringing vacationers safely and effortlessly to previously unheard-of heights.

1914–1918: In World War I, Switzerland declares neutrality, and Geneva serves as the postwar seat of the League of Nations (a forerunner to the United Nations).

1939–1945: When World War II breaks out, 850,000 Swiss men grab their rifles and mobilize to protect the borders while they declare neutrality. Critics charge that, though neutral, Switzerland's open trade policies helped supply Nazi Germany.

c. 1945: After the war, their policy of neutrality leads the Swiss to refuse membership in the UN, NATO, and the EU.

1989: The final canton (Appenzell) grants women the right to vote.

2002: Switzerland joins the United Nations, but decides to hold off on EU membership.

2003: Land-locked Switzerland wins the world's most prestigious sailboat race, the America's Cup.

2005: Today, Switzerland's 26 cantons are autonomous, part of a loose federalist democracy. Four political parties rule in an ever-changing array of coalitions, as they have since World War II. The economy thrives on tourism, banking, engineering, chemicals, watches, textiles, water power...and chocolate.

ZÜRICH

Zürich is one of those cities that tourists tend to skip right through. Since it's a transportation hub, people fly in or change trains here, but don't give stopping a serious thought. The local graffiti jokes: *Zürich = zu reich, zu ruhig* ("too rich, too quiet"). But even though you won't find a hint of Swiss Miss in Switzerland's leading city—and with limited time, I'd certainly spend it up in the mountains—Zürich is surprisingly comfortable and enjoyable for a quick visit. There's much more to Switzerland than yodeling and Alpine-meadow-munching cows.

Zürich was founded by Romans in 58 B.C. as a customs post. Roman Turicum eventually became Zürich. It gained city status in the 10th century, and by the 19th century it was a leading European financial and economic center. Today, it's home to the world's largest gold marketplace and fourth largest stock exchange (after New York, London, and Tokyo). Assuming you've got the money to enjoy it, Zürich is by many measures the world's most livable city. Its 350,000 people (1 million in greater Zürich) are known for their wealth and hard work. Zürich is the only place in Switzerland where you'll see men in ties running in the streets.

Planning Your Time

While Luzern and Bern provide more charming urban experiences, Zürich is worth a quick visit. With two weeks in Switzerland, I'd spend a day here. Begin by visiting the impressive Swiss National Museum, then wander along the river, using my self-guided walk (see page 40), and take a river/lake cruise. With less time, do only the self-guided walk. With more time, take your pick of the many art museums.

ORIENTATION

Zürich sprawls around the northern tip of the long, skinny Lake Zürich (Zürichsee). The grand Bahnhofstrasse cuts through Zürich's

 glitzy shopping center, connecting the train station and the country's top historical museum (Swiss National Museum) with the lake-front in a 15-minute walk. Running parallel to that, across the Limmat River, is the Niederdorf neighborhood—a vibrant, cobbled, Old World zone of colorful little shops, cafés, and restaurants.

Tourist Information

A helpful TI is located in the great hall of the train station (under the fat blue angel, May–Oct Mon–Sat 8:00–20:30, Sun 8:30–18:30, shorter hours off-season, tel. 044-215-4000, www.zuerich.com). Pick up their city guide and map, browse the racks of brochures, and ask about their daily walking tours. This TI sells a one-day Swiss Pass not available elsewhere in the country (95 SF for unlimited travel on trains, buses, and boats throughout Switzerland).

For a whirlwind visit, consider the **ZürichCARD,** which covers transportation by train, tram, bus, and boat; admission to 43 museums; a 50 percent discount on the city walking tour; and "welcome drinks" in many restaurants (15 SF/24 hrs, 30 SF/72 hrs, sold at TI). The one-day card will pay for itself if you do the walking tour and at least one museum or boat cruise in a day. If you like museums and Zürich is your first stop on a long trip through Switzerland, this is a good opportunity to buy a Swiss Museum Passport at the TI (see page 15 for details).

Tours: You can tour Zürich with a **guided walk** (2 hrs, 20 SF, 10 SF with ZürichCARD, leaves from TI daily at 15:00 and also weekends at 11:00, mid-April–Oct) or by **bus** (2 hrs, 32 SF, 16 SF with ZürichCARD, May–Oct daily at 10:30 and 13:00). The TI has details on both tours.

Arrival in Zürich

By Train: The slick train station (with a TI and mall, see "Introductory Zürich Walk," next page) is on the north end of town; to reach most of the recommended hotels, cross Walchebrücke bridge in front of the station.

By Plane: From Zürich Airport, catch the train to the train station downtown (5.40 SF, 15 min, leaves every 10 min 5:00–24:00) rather than take a 50-SF taxi ride. For more on the airport, see page 54.

Getting Around Zürich

A ticket good on the trams and buses costs 2.10 SF (2 hrs for 3.60 SF, 24-hr transit pass for 7.20 SF). All transportation is covered by the ZürichCARD, mentioned above.

Helpful Hints

Bikes: A city program called "*Züri rollt*" allows you to borrow a bike for free (May–Oct, leave passport and 20-SF deposit, daily 7:30–21:30, various locations, including 200 yards down track 18 at train station—look for *Velogate* or *Züri rollt* signs). For more information, ask the TI.

Laundry: Try Speed Wash (Mon–Sat 7:00–22:00, Sun 10:30–22:00, Weinbergstrasse 37, tel. 044-242-9914).

Phone System Change: Until recently, all Zürich phone numbers began with 01; now they begin with 044. However, the 01 numbers will continue to work through March 2007, and you may still see numbers printed this way in older sources.

Introductory Zürich Walk

This handy walking tour is the perfect orientation for travelers blitzing Zürich from the train station. It crisscrosses the river, connecting the city center's main sights en route to the boat dock for a lazy lake-cruise finale (or a quick tram back to the station). Allow about an hour for the walk.

Train Station: Zürich's central station has great energy. This major European transportation hub handles 2,000 trains a day, including InterCity expresses to many major capitals. Built in 1870, its vast main hall was once lined with tracks. Today, it's a farmers market (Wed 11:00–20:00) and community hall—busy with concerts, exhibitions, and even beach volleyball. The station sits over a vast underground modern shopping mall (open late—until 20:00—and on Sundays).

Above you, find the fat blue angel, Zürich's "Guardian Angel" protecting all travelers. The angel, who's been here since 1997 to celebrate the 150th anniversary of the Swiss rail system, looks toward the **Swiss National Museum**, just across the street. It's the best museum in town, offering an essential introduction to Swiss history. To maximize your education, tour this museum before starting the walk (see "Sights and Activities," page 48).

Bahnhofstrasse: The station fronts Zürich's main shopping boulevard. Bahnhofstrasse, stretching from here to the lake, is lined with all the big-name shops. Head on down. The big boulders on the sidewalk mark the most exciting places that thieves in cars would choose for a "crash and dash," usually the finer jewelry stores.

On the right, the only **park** on this pedestrian- and tram-only boulevard is dedicated to Zürich's most important teacher, Johann

Introductory Zürich Walk

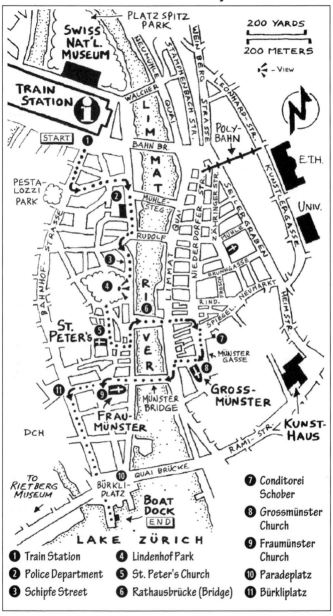

❶ Train Station
❷ Police Department
❸ Schipfe Street
❹ Lindenhof Park
❺ St. Peter's Church
❻ Rathausbrücke (Bridge)
❼ Conditorei Schober
❽ Grossmünster Church
❾ Fraumünster Church
❿ Paradeplatz
⓫ Bürkliplatz

Heinrich Pestalozzi (1746–1827). He promoted the notion, still prevalent in today's Switzerland, that a good education should be available for everyone (not only for sons of rich families). Parks like this are rare in central Zürich because of sky-high property values—among the most expensive in the world.

Turn left at Werdmühleplatz, continue toward the Limmat River (following signs to *Stadtpolizei*), and make a short stop at the **Police Department,** facing the river. Don't be shy—show your ID and enter for a free peek at an amazing wall painting by Swiss artist Augusto Giacometti. His famous "Hall of the Flowers" (*Blüemlihalle*, 1926), awash in bright colors, reflects the relief and joy the artist felt when World War I ended.

Along the Limmat River: From here, walk along the river upstream toward the church spires (without crossing the river). Back when the city's trade depended on river traffic, this small riverside street, called Schipfe, used to be the harbor of Zürich. Pass a fun riverside restaurant (at Schipfe 16, see "Eating," page 54) and an arcade. Twenty yards before the ugliest bridge in Switzerland, head uphill two blocks, and then right up Pfalzgasse, to enjoy a great view from another park...

Lindenhof: Important forts and strategic buildings stood on this hilltop square from Roman times through Carolingian times. But when Zürich became a free city in the 13th century, the townspeople destroyed the fort and established a law forbidding any new construction. The citizens realized that whoever lived on this hill would rule over the city—and they didn't want any more rulers. Today, this is a people's square, where locals relax under linden trees (for which the square is named) and enjoy the commanding city view.

Survey Zürich beyond its river. The **university** (behind the green spire) is the largest in Switzerland, with 25,000 students. Left of that is Zürich's renowned technical college—the ETH (Eidgenössische Technische Hochschule, or Federal Institute of Technology), with 15,000 students. The ETH has graduated 25 Nobel Prize winners, including Albert Einstein and Wilhelm Röntgen (who discovered X-rays). The boats moored under the street are traditional farmer delivery vehicles, sculled with one oar like Venetian gondolas. Lining the far side of the river, Niederdorf is

today's lively restaurant, café, and bar district (see "Eating," page 51). On a clear day, you can see the Alps (behind the twin domes).

Take the stairs just left of the chess players down to Strehlgasse, and follow Glockengasse, passing to the left of the Golden Bell. Continue down tiny Robert-Walser-Gasse—passing a characteristic eatery, Reblaube Gaststube, made famous by visits from Goethe in 1779—to St. Peterhofstatt, a square with Zürich's oldest church.

St. Peter's Church: Founded in the 7th century, this church has one of Europe's largest clock faces (28 feet in diameter). The town watchman used to live above the clock. If he spotted a fire, he would ring the alarm and hang a flag out of the window facing the blaze. This system seems to have worked—Zürich never suffered a major fire. In the 18th century, this church had such a well-loved preacher, Johann Kaspar Lavater (1741–1801), that people reserved their seats for Sunday Mass. The minister, a friend of Goethe, had long discussions over glasses of wine with the "German Shakespeare" in the nearby Reblaube Gaststube, mentioned above.

Continue past the church on Schlüsselgasse and take the first left, down the narrow Thermengasse (literally "Bath Street"). Under your feet are excavations of a **Roman bath,** discovered by accident in 1984. A sketch on the wall shows the bath. Studs elevated the floor, which was heated from below.

The lane empties out on **Weinplatz,** a wine market of centuries past (notice the grape-picker on the fine little fountain). Zürich's fountain water, which is regularly checked for quality, is as good as bottled mineral water. A wall mural inside the Barchetta bar shows the medieval river action. (Note the dock here for river and lake cruises—see "Sights and Activities," page 48.)

Rathausbrücke: The city's oldest bridge goes back to Roman times. Cross the bridge, passing the 17th-century, Renaissance-style City Hall, and walk a block uphill to Marktgasse—the gateway to the bustling **Niederdorf** neighborhood. To the left, down Niederdorfstrasse, is the best place for colorful streets, fun shopping, restaurants, and nightlife. You can explore this area now...or, better yet, tonight.

To continue our walk, go the opposite direction (right), heading down **Münstergasse.** At #19, pop into Schwarzenbach, which still advertises "merchandise from the colonies" out front and sells things the old-fashioned way inside (in loose bags, by the weight). Inhale. Pick up 100 grams of dried bananas from Togo or some Thai sticks...coconut, of course. Across the street, Zürich's popular Conditorei Schober, a riot of silk flowers, serves famously good (and expensive) hot chocolate and champagne truffles. Try not to look at the kinky knights on the plaque opposite #17.

Ahead is the "big cathedral" (literally)...

Grossmünster: It was here that Huldrych Zwingli sparked the Reformation in German-speaking Switzerland (see "Switzerland's

Switzerland's Zwingli Reformation

Today's Evangelical Reformed Church of Switzerland was founded by Huldrych Zwingli (1484–1531), who preached in Zürich from 1519 through 1531. A follower of the humanist philosopher Erasmus of Rotterdam, Zwingli believed that the true foundation of the church was based on preaching the Holy Scriptures freely. In 1522, most of German-speaking Switzerland embraced Zwingli's ideas—and that required leaving the Roman Catholic Church.

Zwingli was 33 in 1517, when German church reformer Martin Luther posted his revolutionary 95 Theses (which questioned the practice of selling forgiveness, salvation, church offices, and so on). Within two years, sellers of indulgences were refused entry to Zürich. As the Reformation swept Switzerland, things heated up. In 1523, rioters were storming churches, and authorities called for an orderly removal of all images in Zürich houses of worship (except stained glass windows).

The new, reformed Swiss church let priests marry. (Zwingli—like Luther—promptly took advantage of this freedom.) Fancy Masses were replaced by simple services. At Zürich's main church, the Grossmünster, preachers studied Latin, Greek, and Hebrew in order to translate the Bible into the people's German. In 1531, the Zwingli Bible (the first complete Bible translated into German) was published. It's still used today (like the King James Bible is in English).

Zwingli gave the Swiss church an unusual austerity: no altar, no pictures, and for a while, not even any music. Church services focused on preaching. Holy communion was celebrated only on holidays. This puritanical simplicity permeated Swiss society in general.

Zwingli Reformation" sidebar, above). The domes of its towers (early examples of neo-Gothic) are symbols of Zürich. They were rebuilt following a 1781 fire, and after much civic discussion, were left a plain stone color. Step inside and sit down...let the strength and purity of the 12th-century Romanesque architecture have its way with you. The simple round arches feel strong, and the wide triumphal arch separating the nave from the altar makes you feel like a winner. The impact of the architecture is made stronger since it's uncluttered—Zwingli's reforms led to a clean sweep of Catholic decor in 1519.

In the front are three choir windows by Augusto Giacometti (c. 1933, perhaps Switzerland's most famous modern artist, known for his gnarled and stretched-super-thin metal statues). Mary and the baby Jesus

Zwingli (no fan of the "separation of church and state") established an ironclad city law: The government's duty was to oversee public worship, and only preaching true to the Bible was to be tolerated.

But Zwingli's reforms were by no means universally supported. Oh, it was a mess: Switzerland's Protestant movement split over baptism. Luther and Zwingli split over the Eucharist (is Christ's body really *in* the bread, or there only in a spiritual sense?). And, as old-school Catholics predicted, putting the Bible into the hands of regular people brought chaos—enabling every Tom, Dick, and Hanz to "carve his own path to Hell." Switzerland was embroiled in a religious civil war, as Protestant cantons fought Catholic ones. In 1531, while fighting as a "citizen soldier," Zwingli was killed in battle. His friend and partner Heinrich Bullinger succeeded him as the leader of German-speaking Swiss Protestantism.

Bullinger collaborated with John Calvin as Swiss Protestantism matured. The Protestant focus on preaching promoted the translation and interpretation of the Bible. Everyone was reading the Bible directly, which promoted literacy. The Reformation provided a basis of the autonomous community spirit, strong work ethic, and high literacy of a prosperous Switzerland for the future. The Swiss church became a place where equals would meet and worship God. Zwingli's heritage included transferring the notion of social charity from being a church phenomenon to being the social welfare responsibility of any self-respecting modern state. The foundations of Swiss democracy and its present social policies are rooted in Zwingli's teaching. And these Swiss reformers planted the seeds of what became the Presbyterian Church in the United States.

meet the three kings bearing their gifts, while angels hover above with offerings of flowers. In the crypt (stairs below altar), you'll see an original 15th-century statue of Charlemagne (a copy now fills its niche on the river side of the church exterior). The church is open daily 9:00–17:00 (pick up English bio of Zwingli). For 2 SF and 200 steps, you can enjoy a fine city view from atop the tower.

Leaving the church, go right and into the corner, where a door leads to a fine Romanesque cloister ringed with fanciful 12th-century carvings (free, Mon–Fri 9:00–18:00, closed Sat–Sun). Upon entering, take eight steps to the left and meet the sculptor (self-portrait on the highest arch).

Cross the river to another tall-steepled church.

Fraumünster: This was founded as an abbey church for a convent outside the town walls in 853. The current building, which sits on the same footprint as its Carolingian predecessor, dates from 1250. With the Reformation of Zwingli, the church was taken by the Zürich town council in 1524 and—you know the drill—gutted

Fraumünster's Chagall Windows

The church's claim to fame is its 30-foot-tall stained glass windows by Marc Chagall (1887–1985), the Russian-born French artist. Chagall gave an exhibit in Zürich in 1967. It was such a hit that the city offered the world-famous artist a commission. To their surprise, the 80-year-old Chagall accepted. Having stood in the church's spacious chancel (50 feet by 40 feet by 60 feet), he intuitively felt it was a place where his unique mix of religious themes could flourish.

For the next three years, he threw his heart and soul into the project, making the sketches at his home on the French Riviera, then working in close collaboration with a glass-making factory in Rheims. After the colored panes were made, Chagall personally painted the figures on with black outlines, which were then baked into the glass. Chagall spent weeks in Zürich overseeing the installation and completion.

His inimitable painting style—deep colors, simple figures, and shard-like Cubism—is perfectly suited to the stained glass medium. Blending Jewish and Christian traditions, Chagall created a work that can make people of many faiths comfortable.

The five windows (left to right) depict Bible scenes, culminating in the central image of the crucified Christ:

1. The Prophets (red): The prophet Elisha (bottom) looks up to watch a horse-drawn chariot carry off his mentor Elijah to heaven. Further up, Jeremiah (blue in color and mood) puts his hand to his head and ponders the destruction of wicked Jerusalem. Up in heaven (top), a multicolored, multifaceted God spins out his creation, sending fiery beams down to inspire his Prophets on earth. This window is artificially lit, as it's built into an interior wall.

2. Jacob (blue—Chagall's favorite color): Jacob (bottom, in deep purple amid deep blue) dreams of a ladder that snakes up to heaven, with red-tinged angels ascending and descending, symbolizing the connection between God above and Jacob's descendants (the Children of Israel) below.

to fit Zwingli's taste. Today, it's famous for its windows by Chagall, described in the "Fraumünster's Chagall Windows" sidebar, above (free, daily May–Oct 9:00–18:00, Nov–April 10:00–16:00).

From the Fraumünster to Lake Zürich: From the church, Poststrasse (continuing away from the river) takes you back to Bahnhofstrasse and the busy **Paradeplatz**. Survey the scene: The train station is a 10-minute walk to your right, and the lake is a few minutes to your left. You're facing Sprungli, Zürich's top

3. Christ (green): The central, biggest window depicts the central figure in God's plan of salvation—Jesus Christ, who as the Messiah fulfills the promises of the Old Testament prophets. Mother Mary suckles baby Jesus (bottom) amid the leafy family tree of Jesus' Old Testament roots. The central area is an indistinct jumble of events from Christ's life, leading up to his crucifixion. The life-size Christ is crucified in a traditional medieval pose, but he's surrounded by a circle that seems to be bearing him, resurrected, to heaven. Chagall signed and dated the work (1970).

4. Zion (yellow): King David (bottom right) strums his harp and sings a psalm, while behind him stands his mistress Bathsheba, who gave birth to Solomon, the builder of Jerusalem's temple. At the end of history, an angel (top) blows a ram's horn, announcing the establishment of a glorious New Jerusalem, which descends down (center), featuring red, yellow, and green walls, domes, and towers.

5. The Law (blue): Moses, with horns of light and the Ten Commandments (top), looks sternly down on lawbreaking warriors on horseback wreaking havoc. At the bottom, an angel (in red) embraces the prophet Isaiah (very bottom) and inspires him to foretell the coming of the Messiah (in red, above the angel). Bible scholars note that Isaiah (who predicted the Messiah) points from this window across to King David (in window 4), whose descendant was Jesus (born on the same level in window 3), who fulfills the promise.

Everyone comes away with a different interpretation of this complex work, which combines images from throughout the Bible. The tall, skinny windows seem to emphasize the vertical connection between heaven above and earth below, both bathed in the same colored light. Some think Chagall used colors symbolically: blue and green represent the earth, while red and yellow are heavenly radiance. But all recognize that the jumble of images—as complex as God's universe—reaches its Point Omega in the central act of Christ's crucifixion.

café for the past century. Its "Luxemburgerli" macaroons—little cream-filled, one-inch macaroon-meringue hamburgers—are a local favorite (you can buy just a couple; if you buy 100 grams, you'll get a selection of 12). The café upstairs offers elegant finger-sandwich lunches. To the right is Credit Suisse (with a ground floor full of fancy shops). A bit farther (at #31) is the fine little Beyer watch museum (the watchmaker's personal collection, in the basement of his watch shop; 5 SF, Mon–Fri 14:00–18:00, closed Sat–Sun).

Finish this walk at the lake. Turning left, follow Bahnhofstrasse to Bürkliplatz and the boats. **Lake Zürich** is 17 miles long, 2.5 miles wide, and—because it's relatively shallow—warm enough for swimming. From here, you can enjoy the lakeside promenade (a fine strolling path 3 miles in either direction, left is sunnier) or a short cruise (see below). Tram #11 zips you back to the station, as does the riverboat.

SIGHTS AND ACTIVITIES

Limmat River and Lake Zürich Cruises—There are two basic boat-ride options: 1) small, low-floating buses that take local commuters and joy-riding visitors up and down the river and to points nearby on the lake; and 2) big, romantic lake ships taking tourists on longer rides around Lake Zürich. All boats leave from Bürkliplatz (lake end of Bahnhofstrasse) and are covered by railpasses (but it costs a flexi-day—handy if you're already using that day for a train trip to or from Zürich). None of the boats comes with commentary.

The riverboat-buses (very low, to squeeze under the bridges) make a 60-minute loop around the Zürich end of the lake and down the river to the train station and Swiss National Museum (2/hr, daily 10:00–22:00, schedule posted at pier 6, buy ticket on boat; 3.60 SF for any ride, short or long; free with 24-hr transit pass or ZürichCARD). These can be handy for connecting the lake and the Swiss National Museum.

The big, touristy, lake-only boats leave daily from spring through fall (5.40 SF for basic 90-min version, 2/hr, 11:00–19:00). They also offer longer trips, jazz and dinner cruises, and so on. The ticket kiosk is near pier 1; boats depart from piers 1 through 6.

▲Swiss National Museum (Schweizerisches Landesmuseum)—This massive museum, in a neo-Gothic castle next to the train station, presents a wide range of artifacts from Swiss history. In the late 19th century, it was clear that the world was changing, and the Swiss wanted to protect their unique heritage. A national competition was held, and Zürich (promising to provide a piece of land, pay for construction, and donate an impressive collection) won the privilege of hosting the country's National Museum. The quirky building is a mish-mash of architectural themes from around the country. The museum, while huge and entertaining, is decidedly old-school—but a slick new wing is planned to open in 2008 (5 SF, covered by ZürichCARD and Swiss Museum Passport—see page 15, Tue–Sun 10:00–17:00, closed Mon, Museumstrasse 2, tel. 044-218-6511; good café in courtyard that leads into Platzspitz Park).

Here are a few highlights, by floor: The **basement** features exhibits on medieval bookmaking and winemaking; an intricate diorama of the pivotal Battle of Murten (see page 102); and a room of huge church bells with an inviting rubber mallet (unique in Europe...bang away). The **ground floor** has pre-Reformation church art—all the fancy stuff the Protestants gutted from the churches so they could "concentrate." There's also a Zwingli room about the Reformation in Switzerland and medieval living rooms. On the **first** and **second floors** are living rooms from the Renaissance and the 18th and 19th centuries. The **third floor** is home to a small toy exhibit, plus traditional folk costumes from around the country.

Platzspitz Park—What used to be a riverside hangout for drug addicts has been cleaned up and—apart from a rusty needle here and there—is now a safe, family-friendly place, ideal for picnics (free, daily 6:00–21:00, behind train station and Swiss National Museum, clean WC). From here, you can take a boat down up the lake (included in 24-hr transit pass or ZürichCARD, departures at :05 and :35, see above).

Kunsthaus Zürich—Switzerland's top collection of modern art includes Swiss artists (Alberto Giacometti, Johann Heinrich Füssli, and Ferdinand Hodler) as well as international greats such as Munch, Picasso, Kokoschka, Beckmann, Corinth, Monet, and Chagall. The younger generation is also represented, with works by Rothko, Merz, Twombly, Beuys, Bacon, and Baselitz (10 SF, covered by ZürichCARD, Tue–Thu 10:00–21:00, Fri–Sun 10:00–17:00, closed Mon, Heimplatz 1, tram #3, #5, #8, or #9 or bus #31 to Kunsthaus stop, tel. 044-253-8497, www.kunsthaus.ch).

Museum Rietberg—Filling historic villas set in a beautiful park, this museum houses art from Asia, Africa, America, and the South Pacific (6 SF, covered by ZürichCARD and Swiss Museum Passport—see page 15, Tue–Sun 10:00–17:00, Wed until 20:00, closed Mon, tram #7 to Museum Rietberg stop, Villa Wesendonck, Gablerstrasse 15, tel. 044-206-3131).

E.G. Bührle Collection—This collection is a must for lovers of the French Impressionists, their forerunners, and their followers. Here you'll find exceptional paintings by Manet, Degas, Cézanne, Monet, Renoir, Gauguin, van Gogh, Picasso, and Braque. You'll also see a smattering of Dutch Baroque and 18th-century Venetian works, plus religious sculptures from medieval times to the Renaissance (9 SF, Tue, Fri, and Sun 14:00–17:00, Wed 17:00–20:00, closed Mon, Thu, and Sat, tram #2 or #4 to Wildbachstrasse stop, or bus #77 to Altenhofstrasse stop, Zollikerstrasse 172, tel. 044-422-0086, www.buehrle.ch).

SLEEPING

High season is May, June, September, and October. There are about 10 days a year when festivals and conventions send prices higher. My listings are near the train station, ideal for those passing through or leaving on an early-morning train or plane (train to airport: 5.40 SF, 15 min, leaves every 10 min).

Sleep Code

(1.30 SF = about $1, country code: 41)
S = Single, **D** = Double/Twin, **T** = Triple, **Q** = Quad,
b = bathroom, **s** = shower only, **no CC** = Credit Cards not
accepted, **SE** = Speaks English, **NSE** = No English. Unless otherwise noted, credit cards are accepted, English is spoken, and
breakfast is included.

To help you sort easily through these listings, I've divided
the rooms into two categories, based on the price for a standard
double room with bath:

$$$ **Higher Priced**—Most rooms 200 SF or more.
 $$ **Moderately Priced**—Most rooms between
         150–200 SF.
  $ **Lower Priced**—Most rooms 150 SF or less.

Across the River from the Train Station

With this efficient, handy neighborhood as your home base, you're a
quick stroll away from the train station, Swiss National Museum,
riverboat dock, a huge underground mall of services and shops
(under the station), and the Niederdorf restaurant and nightlife zone
(down Stampfenbachstrasse). To reach these hotels, exit the train
station from the huge hall with the "Guardian Angel" sculpture and
the TI (see "Introductory Zürich Walk," page 40). Cross the river
on the Walchebrücke bridge and continue straight through the passageway to Stampfenbachstrasse, where you'll see Hotel Arlette and
the Bristol; the Leoneck is two blocks further away. The Martahaus
is a little further south (towards the lake).

$$$ Hotel Arlette is a bit worn, but comfortable. Since it's a
business hotel, its 30 rooms are cheaper on weekends (Sb-110–165
SF, Db-150–210 SF, generally 20 percent cheaper Fri–Sun, includes
small breakfast, Stampfenbachstrasse 26, tel. 044-252-0032, fax
044-252-0923, hotel.arlette@bluewin.ch, family Schlotter).

$$ Hotel Bristol, run by Martin Hämmerli and his friendly
staff, offers 54 modern and cozy rooms an eight-minute walk from
the station. This is a business-quality place with family-run warmth
(Sb-110–150 SF, Db-150–195 SF, Tb-190–220 SF, Qb-200–240
SF, 5 percent discount if booked direct with this book in 2005,
includes breakfast, Internet access, laundry, Stampfenbachstrasse 34,
tel. 044-258-4444, fax 044-258-4400, www.hotelbristol.ch, info
@hotelbristol.ch). Helpful Maggie at the reception desk answers
travel questions.

$$ Hotel Leoneck offers 78 modern yet kitschy, bovine-themed rooms at a good price. The hotel—and the fine attached
Crazy Cow restaurant (daily 6:30–24:00)—somehow manage to

make Swiss cows seem cool; enjoy the "moo-velous" mural in your room (Sb-100–120 SF, Db-150–160 SF, Tb-185–210 SF, Qb-240–260 SF, includes small breakfast, half are non-smoking rooms, elevator, Internet access, some street noise—ask for quieter back room, Leonhardstrasse 1, tel. 044-254-2222, fax 044-254-2200, www.leoneck.ch, info@leoneck.ch, Herr Gold and his friendly staff SE). From the station, walk 12 minutes uphill (see above), or use the Bahnhofstrasse exit and find tram #10 (direction Bahnhof Oerlikon, 2 stops to Haldenegg, look for Crazy Cow restaurant).

$$ **Martahaus Hotel,** run by a YWCA-type organization, is open to all and has a special mission to help women and disabled travelers. Despite its youthful-prison ambience, its 100 bomb-hardened rooms feel cozy and perfectly safe (bunk in 6-bed boys' dorm or girls' dorm-38 SF, includes breakfast, D-100–115 SF, Db-150–160 SF, T-135 SF, Qb-200 SF, side facing old town is quiet, side facing street is 15 percent cheaper and a little noisy, elevator, Zähringerstrasse 36, tel. 044-251-4550, fax 044-251-4540, www.martahaus.ch, info@martahaus.ch). They also run a cheap, not-so-central, women-only guesthouse.

Elsewhere in Zürich

$$$ **Walhalla Hotel,** just behind the train station, has 48 modern, spacious rooms (Sb-100–150 SF, Db-160–220 SF, breakfast-15 SF, Limmatstrasse 5, tel. 044-446-5400, fax 044-446-5454, www .walhalla-hotel.ch, walhalla-hotel@bluewin.ch).

$ **City Backpacker Hotel Biber,** buried right in the middle of the Niederdorf action three floors above a restaurant, offers the cheapest backpacker beds in the old center (65 beds in 6-bed dorms for 31 SF each, no breakfast, lockers, kitchen, Internet access, no curfew, reception open daily 7:00–11:00 & 15:00–22:00, Niederdorfstrasse 5, tel. 044-251-9015, www.city-backpacker.ch, sleep @city-backpacker.ch).

EATING

Niederdorf is Zürich's dining district, and the traffic-free Niederdorfstrasse is its restaurant row. While the countless eateries lining this main drag won't offer the best values, the people-watching is hard to beat. Browse the street and survey the eating options (including many colorful ethnic places). All the recommendations below are within a few minutes' walk of this spine of Zürich's people zone. They're listed clockwise, in order from the train station through Niederdorf and back down again along the train-station side of the Limmat River.

Commihalle Restaurant, near the recommended hotels, is a popular Italian chain. The 34-SF "Tavolata" special—ideal for big

Zürich Hotels and Restaurants

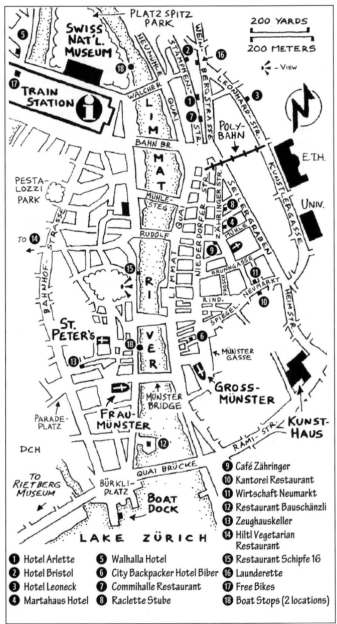

1 Hotel Arlette
2 Hotel Bristol
3 Hotel Leoneck
4 Martahaus Hotel

5 Walhalla Hotel
6 City Backpacker Hotel Biber
7 Commihalle Restaurant
8 Raclette Stube

9 Café Zähringer
10 Kantorei Restaurant
11 Wirtschaft Neumarkt
12 Restaurant Bauschänzli
13 Zeughauskeller
14 Hiltl Vegetarian Restaurant
15 Restaurant Schipfe 16
16 Launderette
17 Free Bikes
18 Boat Stops (2 locations)

eaters—gets you a dressy antipasto buffet, pasta dish, main meat dish, and dessert-buffet finale (open daily, but "Tavolata" available only Tue–Sat 18:15–21:30, plain but dressy interior, fine outside seating, Stampfenbachstrasse 8, tel. 044-250-5960).

Raclette Stube is the place to be if you're looking for cheese—you'll climb into bed smelling like a cheeseball. The menu is classic and simple: just fondue (25 SF) or all-you-can eat raclette (33 SF). The food is heavy: essentially bread, potatoes, and lovingly-chosen cheeses. Since these dishes are traditionally eaten in cold weather, this place can feel a little lonely in summer. But in winter, locals love their fondue and raclette—and prefer to eat them out, in places like this, rather than stink up their homes (Zähringerstrasse 16, tel. 044-251-4130).

Café Zähringer is an artsy, bohemian co-op with a passion for serving reasonably priced healthy food to people who want to take time to keep life in balance (daily until 24:00, 20-SF daily specials, always good veggie plates, organic produce, salad bar by the weight—just point, also meat dishes, wok dishes, famously good coffee; stay-a-while interior or leafy seating on the square a block from where Lenin lived before heading back to Russia, Zähringer Platz 11, tel. 044-252-0500). You may also enjoy the sweet smell of an herb not on the menu.

Kantorei Restaurant serves well-presented modern Swiss cuisine with an Italian touch in a classy but unpretentious atmosphere. Sit inside or out on the quiet square next to a fountain (daily 9:00–24:00, 30-SF plates, good vegetables, half portions available, Neumarkt 2, tel. 044-252-2727).

Wirtschaft Neumarkt, tucked away in the old town, offers "authentic international" dishes. In good weather, the restaurant's long and fun-loving garden is packed with locals eating well under chestnut trees. The upper garden is best, so it's usually filled with diners who made reservations (30-SF plates, 60 SF for 3 courses, lunch specials, extensive wine list and good beer on tap, Neumarkt 5, tel. 044-252-7939).

Restaurant Bauschänzli is a block inland from the boat docks at Bürkliplatz. Filling a small island in the river, it's a fun-loving and popular self-serve restaurant offering Zürich's best beer-garden experience—like a Munich *Biergarten* without the kraut. Help yourself to beer and wine from big casks (grab the glass or carafe of your choice). *Citro* (lemonade) is mixed with lager to make a shandy (or *Radler*). *Süssmost* is apple juice. The garden is open daily in good weather May through mid-September, followed in fall by a raucous Oktoberfest. It comes with live Bulgarian folk music (daily 15:00–17:00 & 19:00–21:30, Stadthausquai 2, tel. 044-212-4919).

Zeughauskeller fills an atmospheric 500-year-old armory with medieval battle gear (William Tell's crossbow?) and happy eaters enjoying typically Swiss cuisine. Their traditional meals include lots of soft meats (but no cheese—which the Swiss don't like to smell unless they're eating it). *Kalbsgeschnetzeltes*—calf's liver with *Rösti*—is a house specialty and a local fave (15- to 30-SF plates, plenty of beer and wine, daily until 23:00, near Paradeplatz at Bahnhofstrasse 28, tel. 044-211-2690).

Hiltl Vegetarian Restaurant is a treat for vegetarians. In 1898, Ambrosius Hiltl was fighting rheumatoid arthritis. His doctor said, "No more meat." So, Ambrosius established the world's first vegetarian restaurant. Today, his great-great-great-grandson, Rolf, carries on the family tradition. While historic photos decorate the walls, the loyal clientele's attention is on the enticing buffet and friendly conversation. At dinner, along with the salad buffet, there's an Indian buffet (endorsed by Indian tourists). Fill your plate, which is sold by the weight—generally 22–28 SF per hearty meal. At lunch, the salad bar is cheaper, but has no Indian options. The à la carte menu comes with delightful salads, curries, and fancy fruit juices. Hiltl's food is legendary for its freshness and lack of preservatives (daily 7:00–23:00, non-smoking, 2 blocks off Bahnhofstrasse where it kinks at Sihlstrasse 28, tel. 044-227-7000).

Restaurant Schipfe 16, gorgeously and peacefully situated on the river, with an old-town view (along the "Introductory Zürich Walk," page 40), is part of a city-run organization providing work for hard-to-employ people. Don't expect polished service...but you're contributing to a worthy cause and enjoying healthy and decent food at a very good price (lunch only, 18-SF daily specials, Mon–Fri 10:00–16:00, closed Sat–Sun, Schipfe 16, tel. 044-211-2122).

TRANSPORTATION CONNECTIONS

From Zürich by train to: Luzern (2/hr, 1 hr), **Interlaken** (hrly, 2.25 hrs), **Bern** (2/hr, 1.25 hrs), **Murten** (2/hr, 2–2.5 hrs, transfer in Bern, Fribourg, or Kerzers), **Appenzell** (2/hr, 1.75 hrs with transfer in Gossau or 2.25 hrs with transfer in St. Gallen), **Lausanne** (2/hr, 2.5 hrs), **Chur** (hrly, 1.5 hrs), **Lugano** (hrly, 2.75–3.25 hrs), **Munich** (every 2 hrs, some direct in 4.5 hrs, some 5.25 hrs with transfer in Stuttgart), **Frankfurt** (at least hrly, 4–4.5 hrs, some direct but most with transfer in Basel or Stuttgart).

Zürich Airport
Smooth, compact, and user-friendly, the Zürich Airport is a major transportation hub and an eye-opening introduction to Swiss efficiency. There are three levels: 1) train station on the bottom floor, with train info and ticket desk; 2) main level, with a top-end food court, Migros supermarket, fancy souvenir shops, Swiss Post Office (easy to mail things home—pack light), banks, ATMs, and lockers;

and 3) departures, upstairs. Eateries and ATMs are plentiful before and after the immigration checkpoint. For flight information, call the automated toll number: 0900-300-313 (press 2 for English).

The train station underneath the airport can whisk you about anywhere you'd want to go in Europe, including downtown Zürich (5.40 SF, 15 min, leaves every 10 min 5:00–24:00, much cheaper than the 50-SF taxi ride). Your train ticket into Zürich is good for the following two hours on all city public transportation.

If catching an early-morning flight, don't spend a fortune to stay near the airport (Hilton, Db-from 250 SF, tel. 044-828-5050). Sleep near the train station downtown (see above), then zip to the airport in the morning on the frequent and fast train.

From Zürich Airport by train to: Luzern (2/hr, 1.25 hrs), **Interlaken** (hrly, 2.5 hrs), **Bern** (2/hr, 1.5 hrs), **Murten** (hrly, 2.75 hrs, change in Fribourg, Switzerland), **Appenzell** (2/hr, 1.5 hrs with transfer in Gossau, or 2 hrs with transfer in St. Gallen), **Lausanne** (2/hr, 2.75 hrs), **Chur** (hrly, 2 hrs, change at Zürich main station), **Lugano** (hrly, 3–3.5 hrs), **Munich** (4/day, 4.25 hrs).

LUZERN
and CENTRAL SWITZERLAND

Luzern has long been Switzerland's tourism capital. Situated on the edge of a lake, with a striking Alpine panorama as a backdrop, Luzern has drawn visitors like Goethe and Queen Victoria for centuries. Since the Romantic era, Luzern has been a no-brainer on the "Grand Tour" route of Europe. And with a charming old town, a pair of picture-perfect wooden bridges, a gaggle of world-class museums, and a famous weeping lion, there's still enough in Luzern to earn it a place on any Swiss itinerary.

Luzern also makes a fine home base for exploring the surrounding region, known as Central Switzerland (Zentralschweiz). A wide variety of boat trips, mountain lifts, and other excursions make fun day trips.

Planning Your Time

Luzern is worth at least a full day and two nights. To get the most out of your day, begin with the TI's two-hour walking tour (see "Tours," below), or follow the self-guided walk in this chapter (see "Reuss River Stroll," page 58). Then hit the museums that interest you most: art buffs will visit the Rosengart and Picasso museums; gearheads will have a ball at the Swiss Transport Museum; and geologists dig the Glacier Garden. In the late afternoon, take a peaceful boat trip on Lake Luzern, then wander the town's scenic bridges at sunset.

With more time, there's plenty to fill two or even three days. Tour more museums, or consider one of the many easy and thrilling day trips.

Luzern

Luzern ("Lucerne" in English) is a charming mid-size city with about 60,000 residents (and a metro area sprawling to nearly 200,000). It sits where the Reuss River meets Lake Luzern (Vierwaldstättersee). South of the river is the train station and bustling new town (Neustadt), and north of the river is the quaint, traffic-free old town (Altstadt). The river is spanned by a series of pedestrian bridges, including two classic wooden ones: the Chapel Bridge, with its famous stone water tower, and the Mill Bridge. Museums, restaurants, and hotels are scattered on both sides of the Reuss.

ORIENTATION

Tourist Information

Luzern's helpful, modern **TI** is right in the train station (mid-June–mid-Sept daily 8:30–19:30, May–mid-June and mid-Sept–Oct Mon–Fri 8:30–18:30, Sat–Sun 9:00–18:30, Nov–April Mon–Fri 8:30–17:30, Sat–Sun 9:00–13:00, Bahnhofstrasse 3, tel. 041-227-1717, phone not answered on weekends, www.luzern.org). Pick up some of the well-produced brochures, such as the *City Guide* (loaded with handy information and museum discounts; see "Helpful Hints," next page), *Cultural Guide,* and many more. The TI also provides a free room-booking service (with some great last-minute deals) and sells tickets to various activities around town (such as boat trips). If you have kids (or are one), ask about the pedal boats.

All the museums mentioned in this chapter are covered by the Swiss Museum Passport (described on page 15, sold at the TI).

Arrival in Luzern

By Train: Luzern's train station is refreshingly user-friendly. The TI is near the front of track 3. Most other important amenities are down the escalators at the front of the tracks, in an underground shopping mall called RailCity. There you'll find the ticket desks, WCs, ATMs, lockers, a convenient self-service cafeteria, a grocery store with long hours, and lots of other shops and restaurants. If all of the other stores in town are closed (for example, on Sunday), your best bet is RailCity.

For the quickest route into the old town, go into the underground RailCity and follow signs to Altstadt (to avoid crossing the busy streets above).

In front of the train station is the main drag, Bahnhofplatz, where buses fan out in every direction (and where my self-guided walk begins—see next page).

Getting Around Luzern

Virtually everything of interest in Luzern is accessible by foot. The one destination you may want to reach by bus or boat is the Swiss Transport Museum, which is a long 25-minute walk around Lake Luzern (the lake is across from the train station). To get there, use bus #6 or #8, or take a boat to "Verkehrshaus" from the dock at the train station. Buses to sights all over the city leave from in front of the station.

Public transportation prices in Luzern depend on which zones you travel in; a single ticket within the primary zone (Zone 10)—including to the Swiss Transport Museum—costs 1.80 SF. A 3-day pass costs 12 SF, and an 8-day pass is 30 SF (though it's unlikely you'd need either). The TI's City Guide includes a map of bus routes.

Helpful Hints

Sightseeing Discounts with Free "Visitor's Card": When you check into your Luzern hotel, have them stamp your *City Guide* tourist brochure. This stamped brochure becomes a "Visitor's Card" (Gästekarte) that gives you minor discounts at all of Luzern's museums (noted below). Remember to ask for this discount when buying entrance tickets.

Internet Access: An Internet point is inside the TI (20 min/4 SF). You'll see other Internet signs scattered around town.

Post Office: The main post office (Hauptpost) is kitty-corner from the train station (Mon–Fri 7:30–18:30, Sat 8:00–16:00, closed Sun).

TOURS

With many beautiful and interesting landmarks, Luzern lends itself to exploring with a tour. Try the two-hour **walking tour** in English, offered every morning in summer (18 SF, 9:45, daily May–Oct, 2/week Nov–April, departs from TI). There's also a tacky **tourist train** that does a 40-minute circuit with headphone commentary (8 SF, 24-SF combo-ticket also includes walking tour and saves 2 SF, daily April–Oct every hour from 11:00, less frequently off-season, tel. 041-220-1100).

Reuss River Stroll

This self-guided orientation stroll will give you a brief overview of the town—going up along the Reuss River, then across one of Luzern's famous wooden bridges, then back through the old town. Begin at Bahnhofplatz, the busy zone between the lake and the train station. Stand in front of the big stone arch.

Bahnhofplatz: This is the transportation hub of Luzern—and all of Central Switzerland. From the area in front of the station,

Reuss River Stroll

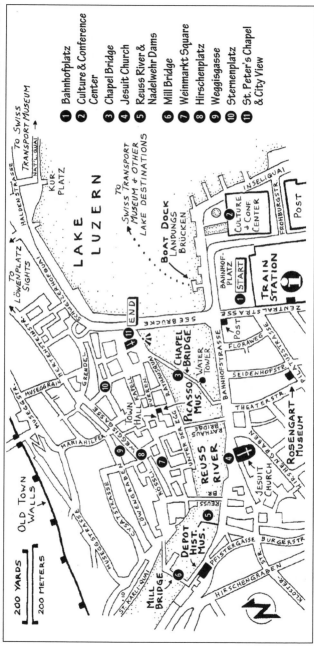

1. Bahnhofplatz
2. Culture & Conference Center
3. Chapel Bridge
4. Jesuit Church
5. Reuss River & Nadelwehr Dams
6. Mill Bridge
7. Weinmarkt Square
8. Hirschenplatz
9. Weggisgasse
10. Sternenplatz
11. St. Peter's Chapel & City View

buses zip you anywhere in town. Along the lakefront, you can catch a boat for a lazy cruise around Lake Luzern. And underneath you is an extensive shopping mall, honeycombed with pedestrian passageways leading to different parts of town. The big stone **arch** was the entrance of the venerable old train station, which was built in the late 19th century when Switzerland became a top tourist spot, with Luzern as its main attraction. But it burned down in 1971 and was replaced with the modern station.

The huge, new building with the big overhanging roof (on your right, with your back to the station) is the...

Culture and Conference Center (Kultur- und Kongresszentrum): This building, finished in 1998 by Parisian architect Jean Nouvel, features a concert hall that hosts the Luzern Festival, one of Switzerland's biggest music events (mid-Aug–mid-Sept, www.lucernefestival.ch). Lake water is pumped up, into, through, and out of the building; if you wander around its far side, you'll see open channels that go right through the middle of the structure (now blocked by benches, so distracted tourists don't fall in), as well as a big pond. The architect claims this design recalls earlier times, when Luzern was swamplands...but it more likely recalls his own original plans for the building. Nouvel wanted to put it out in the middle of the lake. When he was voted down by the people of Luzern, he decided to surround it with water anyway (www.kkl-luzern.ch).

Now walk in the opposite direction from the conference center, across the busy street (or, better, use the handy network of underpasses). Stroll Bahnhofstrasse along the river until you have a good view of Luzern's most famous landmark, the wooden...

Chapel Bridge (Kapellbrücke): Luzern began as a fishing village. By the 13th century, traffic streaming between northern and southern Europe went through the nearby Gotthard Pass—and

Luzern became a bustling trading center. In the 14th century, this bridge was built—at an angle, to connect the site of today's white Jesuit Church (just downstream) with the pointy Gothic towers of the Benedictine Monastery, on the far side of the lake. Between these points was the octagonal stone **Water Tower** (Wasserturm), which predates the bridge by a century. The bridge also served a defensive purpose—notice that the "window" openings facing the lake are smaller than the inland side.

Wander out onto the bridge itself. At first, look for the colorful 17th-century paintings overhead—depicting scenes from Luzern and Swiss history. The coats of arms on the paintings tell you which aristocratic families sponsored them. But then the paintings stop. In 1993, a leisure boat moored under the bridge caught fire, and before long, Luzern's wooden landmark was in flames. (Notice the wood is lighter—that is, newer—in the middle of the bridge than at the ends.) Chapel Bridge was painstakingly rebuilt, but the paintings were irreplaceable (the few you see here are reproductions). Boats are no longer allowed under the bridge, it's now strictly non-smoking, and you'll notice tiny security cameras everywhere.

Now head back to the train-station end of the bridge, and continue up the river. Enter the big, white...

Jesuit Church (Jesuitenkirche): This was the first major Baroque church in Switzerland (built 1666–1677). Even though Luzern was a relatively small town back then, the pope wanted to

establish a strong presence in Central Switzerland, empowering the local Catholics during the tense times of the Protestant Reformation. The interior of the church used to drip with Baroque stucco—but those decorations proved too heavy, and the walls came a-tumblin' down. (It's been retouched in lighter Rococo style.) Notice the decorations on the ceiling, celebrating the Jesuit missionary (and church patron) Francis Xavier. Right in the center, look for this church and Luzern's landmark Chapel Bridge. Notice that Xavier's cart is pulled by an elephant, a leopard, and a camel—to commemorate his mission trips to the exotic Far East (church open daily 6:00–18:30, www.jesuitenkirche-luzern.ch).

Now head back out and continue strolling downriver (left). As you walk along the banks towards Luzern's *other* wooden bridge, consider this information about the...

Reuss River: This big river actually flows *out* of the lake—opposite of what you might expect. Lake Luzern is filled with snowmelt, which trickles into the south end. The water leaves the lake here, and heads for the Rhine. Luzern is responsible for controlling this flow of water and preventing floods. In the mid-19th century, the city built an ingenious system of segmented dams (*Nadelwehr,* literally, "water spikes"). When the water is highest (in the spring), they insert more dam seg-

ments; as the summer wears on and the water level drops, they gradually remove the segments. In the winter, they close the dam entirely to keep the lake level high enough for boats.

As you continue along the river, you'll pass the fun Depot History Museum on your left (see "Museums," below), before coming to the wooden...

Mill Bridge (Spreuerbrücke): Unlike the rebuilt Chapel Bridge, this one's original—with locals hoping to keep it that way (try to find the low-profile security cameras). Cross the bridge, noticing the 17th-century *Dance of Death* paintings overhead—also original. Look closely: In each painting, there's a skeleton. This reminds viewers that nobody, in any walk of life, can escape death (an especially poignant message in times of war and plague, when these were painted).

This bridge sits where Luzern's mills were once located (*Spreu* means "chaff"—the sheath surrounding wheat, which was separated at the mill). The tradition of harnessing nature's power continues today. As you reach the old town across the bridge, look for the stream of water spurting into the air at an angle. It's coming from an underwater hydroelectric plant, which creates enough power for 1,000 households (the strength of the squirt shows how much electricity is being produced).

As you cross the bridge, you'll find yourself in Mühlenplatz, the square at the entrance to the old town. The riverfront Hug bakery on your right is a good place for lunch or a snack (see "Eating," page 73). At the top of the square, head right on Kramgasse, then take the first left onto Weinmarktgasse, which leads to...

Weinmarkt Square: In medieval Luzern, this square served as a marketplace for wine (as the name implies). Notice the big mural on the green building at the top of the square. The Last Supper, right? Take a closer look: It's actually the wedding feast at Cana, where Jesus turned water into wine. In front of the mural are stairs leading up to a "stage" where the Passion Play was performed (this tradition ended when the Jesuits left in the 19th century). On the right (as you face the mural), notice the old yellow pharmacy that knows its limitations. Above the bay window is the wise saying, *Amor medicabilis nvllis herbis* (roughly, "No medicine can cure a broken heart"). Across the square from the pharmacy is a modern building. Many locals don't appreciate its less traditional design, but there's a secret message hiding in those strange zigzags. Start at the top left and read: W-E-I-N-M-A-R-K-T.

Leave the square on the left side of the big mural. You'll walk one block to...

Hirschenplatz: This square hasn't always been a square—notice the footprints of two former buildings in the middle. It's named for the Hirschen ("Deer") Restaurant, with the elaborate golden sign. Across from that, try to guess who used to have a shop in the big green building. Yep—the jeweler (see all the rings?). To the right of that building, look for the painting of a famous German writer with the legend, *"Goethe logierte hier 1779."* Goethe—the "German Shakespeare"—visited Luzern, and stayed in a hotel on this corner. Unfortunately, he didn't like the town very much...a fact that the people of Luzern still take personally.

Continue out of the square on the busy **Weggisgasse**. As you stroll, realize that every building in the old town—whether new or rebuilt—is required to offer residential apartments to prevent this historic zone from becoming only office space and touristy shops. After a few blocks, you'll come to the Manor department store, with a tasty and convenient top-floor cafeteria (see "Eating," page 73). Turn right after the Manor store and walk one block to...

Sternenplatz: This square is dominated by the very colorful facade of the Restaurant Fritschi. The paintings feature symbols from Luzern's annual Mardi Gras celebration—the city's biggest

event, called Karneval here. Karneval is celebrated by Mr. and Mrs. Fritschi, pictured near the top of this building, wearing masks and throwing oranges. Flanking them are their trusty servants, a nanny and a jester—who, in this case, bear a striking resemblance to the restaurant's owners. Below them is the story of Karneval: The cock calls at 5:00 in the morning the Thursday before Ash Wednesday (on the left), and the people get up to frighten winter away. Mr. and Mrs. Fritschi arrive on their wagon to kick off the festivities (on the right). Flying around the scene are oranges—traditionally tossed from the Fritschis to their adoring fans. This special seasonal fruit, which can't grow in winter, marks the beginning of spring.

Continue down the street at the bottom of the square (Hans-Holbein-Gasse), and you'll stumble on a colorful fountain with masks of Herr and Frau Fritschi and their servants. Continue around to the riverfront, walking around **St. Peter's Chapel,** the namesake of Chapel Bridge—which you've arrived at once again. This is *the* classic Luzern view: the Chapel Bridge and Water Tower, with Mount Pilatus hovering in the background. Snap a couple of pictures and continue your sightseeing.

SIGHTS

Museums
Luzern is charming enough that simply strolling the streets and bridges and cruising the lake would be enough for a happy day of sightseeing. But the city also offers a bevy of world-class museums, with a little something for everyone: art, history, geology, transportation, music, and natural history, as well as fun, modern, interactive spots. Modern art lovers should buy the 18-SF combo-ticket to enjoy both the Rosengart and the Picasso museums.

▲**Rosengart Collection (Sammlung Rosengart Luzern)**—
Rosengart is the first and last name in Luzern art. In the 1930s and
1940s, wealthy resident Siegfried Rosengart palled around with all-
star modern artists, financing and collecting their works. This
museum displays the fruits of his labor, with three floors of all the
big names from the late 19th and early 20th centuries (15 SF, 13 SF
with Visitor's Card, 18-SF combo-ticket also includes Picasso
Museum, covered by Swiss Museum Passport, good English booklet-
2.50 SF, otherwise no English info, daily April–Oct 10:00–18:00,
Nov–March 11:00–17:00, a few blocks from the train station in the
new town at Pilatusstrasse 10, tel. 041-220-1660, www.rosengart.ch).

The ground floor features an extensive Picasso collection (mostly
lesser works from the 1950s and 1960s). Several other Rosengart
Picassos were donated to the city, becoming the core of the Picasso
Museum across the river (see below). Upstairs are a few early Picassos,
as well as middle- and lower-tier works by Braque, Monet, Renoir,
Miró, Chagall, Cézanne, Matisse, Modigliani, and Pissarro. In the
basement are 125 small works by Paul Klee, displayed in chronologi-
cal order. Watch as the artist discovers colors, and blossoms from a
doodler and sometime watercolor artist into a true painter.

▲▲**Picasso Museum Luzern**—In 1978, the Rosengart family
donated eight Picassos to the city of Luzern. Over the years, the collection has grown to fill three floors of a creaky old building next
door to the Town Hall. The "Picassos" here are nothing special, but
Picasso himself is: Over 200 black-and-white candid photographs
of the artist, by American David Douglas Duncan, make this
museum a ▲▲▲ experience for Picasso fans. I've seen a passel of
Picassos, but never have I gotten a feel for the artist's personality as I
did here (8 SF, 5 SF with Visitor's Card, 18-SF combo-ticket
includes Rosengart Collection, covered by Swiss Museum Passport,
5-SF English brochure, borrow insightful descriptions of photographs at entry, daily April–Oct 10:00–18:00, Nov–March
11:00–17:00, in the Am-Rhyn-Haus at Furrengasse 21, tel. 041-
410-1773).

You'll see various Picasso works—a few paintings, as well as lots
of ink sketches, and even a ceramic pigeon. A fun room traces the
artistic evolution of the playful *Self-Portrait as an Owl*. Look for the
portraits of Angela Rosengart—Siegfried's daughter and a friend of
Picasso's.

David Douglas Duncan's intimate photos of Picasso and his
family, scattered around the museum (mostly on the top floor), do a
remarkable job of capturing the very human personality of this
larger-than-life artistic giant. The photos—taken in Picasso's later
years, and many featuring his wife, Jacqueline—provide insight into
his artistic process, as well as his lifestyle, showing him at work and
at play. As a fly on the wall of his chaotic studio, you'll see Picasso in

the bathtub, getting a haircut, playing dress-up, moving to a new house, horsing around with his kids, entertaining his guest Gary Cooper, and getting a ballet lesson from Jacqueline. You'll meet his pet goat, Esmerelda, and his dachshund, Lump. The excellent English descriptions—which you'll borrow when you buy your ticket—are essential for getting the stories behind the photos.

▲▲**Depot History Museum (Depot Historisches Museum Luzern)**—This high-tech museum—a "depot" for the accumulated bric-a-brac of Luzern's past—presents the history of the city in two parts: a dull exhibit and a fun tour (10 SF, 8 SF without tour or with Visitor's Card, covered by Swiss Museum Passport, Tue–Sun 10:00–17:00, closed Mon, Pfistergasse 24, tel. 041-228-5424, www.hmluzern.ch).

The museum is in one of Luzern's oldest surviving buildings, which used to house military weapons and uniforms. Their collection is just too big to display effectively, so they've come up with an innovative concept: Throw all of their archived stuff together and display it on three crowded floors. You'll wander through shelves of old weapons, stained-glass windows, sculptures, and old-fashioned tourism posters. The items are displayed without much rhyme or reason, and each is labeled with a barcode. You'll use a scanner (included with entry) to scan the items you're interested in, and get the history (in English). The scanner can also be rigged to link several items together into a cohesive tour.

All these bits and pieces, presented without much context, are difficult to appreciate (even with the scanner). But one of Luzern's most enjoyable experiences is the educational and fun-loving "backstage" tour of the museum by a dynamic guide—well worth the cost of entry alone. Your guide will sneak you into the actual warehouse of the museum, showing you items in deep storage, and becoming different characters to bring all those dusty old odds and ends—and the history of Luzern and Switzerland—to life. It's a great combination of entertainment and education, presented by lively actors instead of stodgy old historians. There are various tour themes (like weapons, archaeology, and costumes), but only some are available in English. It's essential to call ahead to see when the English tour is scheduled on the day of your visit (usually 1/day, sometimes more, generally 45 min, tel. 041-228-5424).

Other Museums—There's much more. Music fans may want to venture out to the **Richard Wagner Museum,** housed in a building where the composer lived (6 SF, 5 SF with Visitor's Card, mid-March–Nov Tue–Sun 10:00–12:00 & 14:00–17:00, closed Mon, along the lakefront south of train station at Wagnerweg 27, tel. 041-360-2370). If you didn't get your fill at Luzern's two modern art museums, stop by the **Museum of Art Luzern** (Kunstmuseum Luzern; 10 SF, 8 SF with Visitor's Card, more for special exhibits,

Tue–Sun 10:00–17:00, Wed until 20:00, closed Mon, Europaplatz 1, tel. 041-226-7800, www.kunstmuseumluzern.ch). The **Museum of Natural History** (Natur-Museum), with an emphasis on interactive exhibits, is great for kids (6 SF, 5 SF with Visitor's Card, Tue–Sun 10:00–17:00, closed Mon, Kasernenplatz 6, tel. 041-228-5411, www.naturmuseum.ch).

Near Löwenplatz

The following sights are clustered around Löwenplatz, a square that's a 10-minute walk from the old town (under the big, yellow, red-roofed building, behind the tour buses). This is the heart of touristy Luzern, with a must-see monument and a trio of tacky but fun attractions. If you're doing the two bigger attractions here (Glacier Garden and Bourbaki Panorama), you might as well buy the **Lionpass**, which saves you money and also includes the Alpineum (17 SF, a 6-SF savings over individual admissions). Note that even the goofy museums are covered by the Swiss Museum Passport (see page 15).

I've listed the museums below in descending order of respectability (or ascending order on the international "tacky tourist trap" scale).

▲▲Lion Monument (Löwendenkmal)—This famous monument is a must-see if you're visiting Luzern—if only because when you get back home, everyone will ask you, "Did you see the lion?" The huge sculpture (33 feet long by 20 feet tall) is carved right into a cliff face,

over a reflecting pool in a peaceful park (free, open sunset to dusk). Though it's crowded with tourists, this spot is genuinely affecting: The mighty lion rests his paws on a shield, with his head cocked to one side, tears streaming down his cheeks. In his side is the broken-off end of a spear, which is slowly killing the noble beast. This heartbreaking figure represents the Swiss mercenaries who were killed fighting in the French Revolution. The inscription reads, *Helvetiorum fidei ac virtuti*—"To the loyalty and bravery of the Swiss."

▲Bourbaki Panorama—Here's your chance to get right in the middle of a great painting—literally. This exhibit features an enormous, historical, epic, 360-degree painting (on a 33-foot-tall wraparound canvas with a circumference of 360 feet). The 1-SF booklet explains it all and makes for a nice souvenir. These panoramic paintings were in vogue in the 19th century, when realism was king. Standing completely surrounded by a landmark historical event—such as a key military occasion (as here) or the crucifixion—was the ultimate in "reality painting" (8 SF, 7 SF with Visitor's Card, covered by the Swiss Museum Passport, daily 9:00–18:00, Löwenplatz 11, tel. 041-412-3030, www.panorama-luzern.ch).

The painting depicts the dramatic conclusion of the Franco-Prussian War. On February 1–3, 1871, the 87,000-man French Army—led by the panorama's namesake, General Bourbaki—trudged through the snow across the Swiss border. Once in Switzerland, they gave up their weapons and surrendered to the Swiss—who, the story goes, took excellent care of the French, nursing them back to health before sending them home.

The Bourbaki Panorama was painted by Edouard Castres, who was actually there (as a Red Cross volunteer) on that frigid February morning. The painting was completed in just five months in 1881; it was thoroughly refurbished in 2000, when several life-size figures were added in the foreground. Also new are sound effects that fill the hall as you view the painting. There's a good museum with more background on the Franco-Prussian War and Bourbaki's army, as well as details about this and other panorama paintings. The building is also home to a library, movie theaters, shops, and restaurants.

Glacier Garden (Gletschergarten)—This complex is a strange sort of mini-theme-park with an eclectic hodgepodge of exhibits, most loosely relating to Alpine geology. While it's very touristy, and the various pieces don't quite hang together (such as the fun but out-of-place Hall of Mirrors), it adds up to a pleasant if overpriced activity (10 SF, 8.50 SF with Visitor's Card, covered by Swiss Museum Passport, daily April–Oct 9:00–18:00, Nov–March 10:00–17:00, Denkmalstrasse 4, tel. 041-410-4340, www.glaciergarden.org).

Pick up the English info booklet as you enter, and follow the numbers on the confusing one-way path. First, you'll walk through the actual **geological formations** that give the museum its name. While geologists would get a thrill out of this, it was just a bunch of holes to me. Then you'll enter the **museum**, with exhibits about glacial processes, as well as (downstairs) huge 3-D reliefs of late-18th-century Luzern, and the Alps and lakes of Central Switzerland. Back upstairs, you'll cross directly into the **Amrein's House**, an old chalet with some original furnishings and models of traditional Swiss buildings. As you leave, you have the option of hiking up the steep **Tower Walk**, which leads to another old chalet and an observation tower.

At the end, be sure to visit the **Hall of Mirrors**. This undeniably enjoyable attraction, over 100 years old, is a delightfully low-tech fun house. You'll grope your way through twisting corridors—with mirrors on all sides—decorated like a Disneyfied Alhambra. It's confusing, dizzying, and claustrophobic, but goofy fun. As you run into yourself (literally) again and again, you'll lament the poor sap who has to clean the smudge marks off all those mirrors (walk slowly and—if you don't mind looking foolish—with arms outstretched). As you leave, giggling and nauseated, you'll ask yourself: So, what exactly did that have to do with glaciers?

Alpineum—This disappointing attraction, overshadowed by its substantial gift shop, displays a handful of paintings and reliefs of famous Swiss mountain peaks and panoramas. These are the same views you'll see if you visit the peaks in person—but in a musty, outmoded, tourist-trap environment. The exhibit also includes English explanations and miniature models of traditional houses, trains, boats, people, and cows. Visit this only if you're also doing the Glacier Garden and Bourbaki Panorama, in which case the Lionpass gets you in free (5 SF, 4 SF with Visitor's Card, covered by Swiss Museum Passport, April–Oct daily 9:00–12:30 & 13:30–18:00, closed Nov–March, Denkmalstrasse 11, tel. 041-410-6266, www.alpineum.ch).

Around the Lake

One of Luzern's top museums, the Swiss Transport Museum, is across the lake from the train station. It's a long 25-minute walk, most of it along a beautiful promenade (see "Riverfront Stroll," below). This is a pleasant stroll, even if you're not going to the museum.

To make a beeline to the museum, take bus #6 or #8 from the station, and get off at the Verkehrshaus stop (when you see the big, barrel-shaped, can't-miss-it IMAX theater). For a more scenic approach, take a boat from in front of the train station (to Verkehrshaus; 8 SF round-trip second class, 10 min each way).

Riverfront Stroll—This delightful pathway was built during the tourism boom in the 19th century, when this part of the bay was filled in and fancy resort hotels went up—giving this city the nickname "Monte Carlo of Switzerland." Simply follow the tree-lined waterfront promenade (Nationalquai) that begins near the Hofkirche (the big church with the pointy spires). Believe it or not, Luzern's wooden Chapel Bridge used to stretch all the way to this church.

▲▲Swiss Transport Museum (Verkehrshaus)—This enormous complex is the Smithsonian of Switzerland. The vast museum grounds include hundreds of exhibits in several different buildings, covering virtually all modes of transportation. It's a fun excursion, but it's pricey and a little overwhelming—demanding at least a half day. If you're in town for only one day, I'd skip this and enjoy the museums and ambience in the old town. But if you have a second day, brought your kids, or are obsessed with trains, planes, and automobiles, this is time well spent.

Cost: 24 SF, 22 SF with Visitor's Card, covered by Swiss Museum Passport (see page 15). In addition to the exhibits, there are a wide variety of shows and demonstrations (pick up schedule—and inquire about English—as you enter). These include a planetarium show (included in entry price), an IMAX theater (costs 16 SF extra, www.imax.ch), and a 400-foot-high tethered balloon ride called Hiflyer (costs 16 SF extra, good weather only, www.hiflyer .ch). There are also combo-tickets available (32 SF for museum plus IMAX or Hiflyer, 45 SF for all three).

Hours and Information: Daily April–Oct 10:00–18:00, Nov–March 10:00–17:00, Lidostrasse 5, tel. 0848-852-020, www .verkehrshaus.ch).

Touring the Museum: Starting in the first building, you'll come across a 30-minute show about the Gotthard Tunnel. Then you'll wander through endless halls of train engines and tram cars. As you exit, you'll be face to face with some Swissair jetliners, and

surrounded by pavilions devoted to various vehicles (such as planes, cars, boats, motorcycles, spaceships, and high-mountain lifts). Many of the exhibits are interactive, like the parasailing simulator, where you lie down on a smoothly gliding platform and peer down at the countryside below. Tucked around back, there's even an art museum dedicated to the work of local painter Hans Erni (12 SF extra, worthwhile only for Erni fans and art buffs).

Upstairs in the boat and cable car building, be sure to seek out the **Swissarena**—an enormous (more than 2,000 square feet) aerial photograph of Switzerland (www.swissarena.ch, follow signs that look like a Swiss map in a CBS-style eye). This photo map, spread out on the floor like laminated linoleum, is detailed enough to show virtually every single building within Switzerland's borders. Slide on the Swiss slippers, borrow a map and magnifying glass, and glide across Switzerland, looking for the places you've visited so far.

SLEEPING

Luzern hotels are expensive. Even my higher-priced listings are a little rough around the edges...to get spick-and-span, you'll pay even more than these rates. Budget options are popular—it's smart to book ahead for these places. The cheapest places (the last 4 listed below) are comfortable enough, but feel institutional. I've listed high-season prices (April–Oct); you'll pay marginally less off-season.

$$$ Hotel zum Weissen Kreuz is your super-central splurge option, if you want to pay a premium to sleep in the center of the old town. This historic building has 22 rooms with appropriately old-fashioned furnishings (Sb-100–150 SF, Db-180–195 SF, Tb-230–250 SF, prices depend on size and demand, elevator, Furrengasse 19, tel. 041-418-8220, fax 041-418-8230, www.hotel -wkreuz.ch, info@hotel-wkreuz.ch).

Sleep Code

(1.30 SF = about $1, country code: 41)
S = Single, **D** = Double/Twin, **T** = Triple, **Q** = Quad,
b = bathroom, **s** = shower only, **no CC** = Credit Cards not
accepted, **SE** = Speaks English, **NSE** = No English. Unless otherwise noted, credit cards are accepted, English is spoken, and
breakfast is included.

To help you sort easily through these listings, I've divided
the rooms into three categories, based on the price for a standard
double room with bath:

$$$ **Higher Priced**—Most rooms 160 SF or more.
  $$ **Moderately Priced**—Most rooms between 130–160 SF.
   $ **Lower Priced**—Most rooms 130 SF or less.

$$$ **Jailhotel Löwengraben** is as much an experience as a place to sleep, on a nondescript street a few steps from the heart of the old town. This innovative place is in the renovated former city prison. It has 133 beds in 55 rooms (including 4 over-the-top themed suites). Most rooms are stuffy, with cot-like beds, tiny barred windows, and reinforced doors—so it still *feels* like a prison. In some rooms, they've even kept some of the original fixtures (like sinks). It's overpriced for the lack of conventional comfort, but it's fun enough to bring curious tourists roaming the halls (S-99 SF, Sb-120–130 SF, D-130 SF, twin Db-165 SF, Db with 1 big bed-190 SF, Db suites-250–300 SF, Tb-210 SF, Qb-240 SF, non-smoking, Löwengraben 18, tel. 041-417-1212, fax 041-417-1211, www.loewengraben.ch, hotel@loewengraben.ch).

$$$ **Hotel des Alpes** is your best bet if you want to sleep right on the river in the old town. Its lobby hides above a busy restaurant, but the 45 rooms are modern and fresh, with new bathrooms. Rooms facing the river, which cost a bundle, come with beautiful views (riverview rooms: Sb-150 SF, Db-240 SF; back-side rooms: Sb-125 SF, Db-195 SF, some rooms have balconies for the same price—usually for longer stays, elevator, Furrengasse 3, tel. 041-410-5825, fax 041-410-7451, www.desalpes-luzern.ch, info@desalpes-luzern.ch).

$$$ **Hotel Baslertor**, and its cheaper annex, $ **Hotel Pension Rösli** (across the street), offer well-located rooms for various budgets. The Baslertor's 30 rooms, with old, dark furnishings, are more expensive, come in three sizes (small Db-150 SF, medium Db-175 SF, large Db-200 SF, extra bed-25 SF) and enjoy an elevator and an atmospheric breakfast room. The Rösli pension has six rooms with even older furnishings and no elevator (Db-125 SF). If you need a single, you'll pay the same at either place (125 SF), so you might as well opt for the Balsertor. Both hotels charge 15 SF per person extra

Luzern Hotels and Restaurants

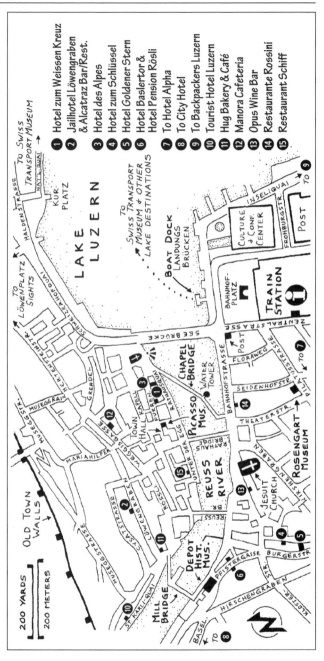

1 Hotel zum Weissen Kreuz
2 Jailhotel Löwengraben & Alcatraz Bar/Rest.
3 Hotel des Alpes
4 Hotel zum Schlüssel
5 Hotel Goldener Stern
6 Hotel Baslertor & Hotel Pension Rösli
7 To Hotel Alpha
8 To City Hotel
9 To Backpackers Luzern
10 Tourist Hotel Luzern
11 Hug Bakery & Café
12 Manora Cafeteria
13 Opus Wine Bar
14 Restaurante Rossini
15 Restaurant Schiff

for breakfast. Contact either place through the Baslertor (Pfistergasse 17, tel. 041-249-2222, fax 041-249-2233, www.baslertor.ch, info @baslertor.ch).

$$ Hotel zum Schlüssel brags it's the oldest hotel in town, hosting guests since 1543. Today, it's a fine, low-key, mid-budget option, with six simple, cozy rooms above a smoky, local-style restaurant on a peaceful square near the river (Sb-95 SF, Db-140 SF, newer Db-160 SF, Tb-210 SF, Qb-280 SF, Franziskanerplatz 12, tel. 041-210-1061, fax 041-210-1021, Wernli family).

$$ Hotel Goldener Stern, a slightly lesser value, offers 16 humble but acceptable rooms with some street noise over two restaurants (Sb-95 SF, D-100 SF, Db-140 SF, Tb-180 SF, Qb-200 SF, prices fluctuate with demand and length of stay, elevator, Burgerstrasse 35, tel. 041-227-5060, fax 041-227-5061, www.goldener -stern.ch, hotel@goldener-stern.ch, Amrein family).

$ Hotel Alpha is a modern, stark place, offering 60 rooms (most with toilet down the hall) in a pleasant residential area a 10-minute walk from the center. While the renovated, blue-floored rooms on the lower floors are nice (if institutional), those on the fourth and fifth floors are old and shabby (S-65 SF, twin D-98 SF, twin Db-120 SF, Db with 1 big bed-130 SF, T-129 SF, Q-164 SF, measly breakfast, elevator, Internet access, comfy TV room, kitchen, popular with students, reception open 7:00–24:00 in summer, 7:00–22:00 in winter, Zähringerstrasse 24, at intersection with Pilatusstrasse, tel. 041-240-4280, fax 041-240-9131, www.hotelalpha.ch, info@hotelalpha.ch).

$ City Hotel has 38 basic rooms in an urban-feeling location surrounded by a maze of busy streets, just beyond the Mill Bridge in the new town. The lobby is a tacky and eclectic mix of a big-screen TV, old furniture, and a newspaper kiosk, with a pizzeria next door—but the rooms are reasonable and well-priced (Sb-80 SF, Db-120 SF, Tb-150 SF, elevator, Baselstrasse 15, tel. 041-240-2323, fax 041-240-2324, www.hotel-cityhotel.ch, info@hotel-cityhotel.ch).

$ Backpackers Luzern is the city's best hostel option. It's calm and well-run, sharing a modern, blocky building with student dorms and some double rooms in a peaceful residential area a 15-minute walk south of the train station. There are 30 rooms with balconies, a pair of kitchens for guests (open 16:00–23:00), a welcoming lounge, no curfew, Internet access, and laundry (9 SF per load for full service). The walk to the center is mostly along the lake, through pretty parks and next to a fine beach (28 SF per person in 4-bed rooms, 34 SF per person in 2-bed rooms, includes sheets, no breakfast but can use water boiler and toaster, reception open 7:30–10:00 & 16:00–23:00, elevator, Alpenquai 42, tel. 041-360-0420, fax 041-360-0442, www.backpackerslucerne.ch).

$ Tourist Hotel Luzern, with 40 rough but acceptable rooms on the river, is a last resort. This basic, crank-'em-out place comes with musty halls, cheap, spongy mattresses, and outmoded leopard-print decor. (Backpackers, above, is a far better hostel option, but it's not central.) I list this divey place only because of its excellent location, right on the river in the old town (dorm beds-35–40 SF per person, S-69–75 SF, Sb-90–120 SF, D-98–112 SF, Db-120–160 SF, T-120–138 SF, Tb-180–200 SF, Q-156–180 SF, Qb-200–240 SF, elevator, Internet access, laundry, St. Karliquai 12, tel. 041-410-2474, fax 041-410-8414, www.touristhotel.ch, info@touristhotel.ch).

EATING

Restaurants in the old town are pricey and popular with tourists—two good reasons to look elsewhere. Here are some places handy to sightseeing, but frequented by both tourists and locals.

Hug is a cuddly-named bakery and café right at the old town end of the Mill Bridge, handy for a lunch break in the middle of the sightseeing action. They have pastries and tasty sandwiches for a take-away picnic (3–6 SF), as well as a selection of basic traditional Swiss dishes (like fondue and *Rösti*, 15–20 SF) to enjoy at outdoor tables overlooking the river or in the glassed-in terrace. Many people come simply to sip a coffee or beer, or to savor an ice-cream sundae with a river view (Mon–Fri 7:00–18:30, Sat 7:00–17:00, Sun 10:00–17:00, in good weather also open for dinner in summer, Mühlenplatz 6).

Manora, a cafeteria on the fifth floor of the Manor department store in the old town, is ideal for a fast, tasty, efficient lunch. Choose between a fresh salad bar (big plate-10.20 SF) or a variety of main dishes (10–15 SF). Wash it down with an energizing glass of fresh-squeezed juice. In good weather, climb the stairs to the outdoor terrace, with views over the rooftops of Luzern. This place is popular with locals and very crowded 12:00–13:00—eat early or late, and send your travel partner up top to claim an outdoor table (Mon–Wed 9:00–18:30, Thu-Fri 9:00–21:00, Sat 8:00–16:00, closed Sun, Weggusgasse 5).

Opus, next to the big Jesuit Church, is a trendy wine bar with tasty food. You have several options: main dishes with international flair (20–40 SF); a lush and varied salad bar (a small plate piled high makes a light and healthy dinner for 15 SF); or your choice of dried meats and cheeses (20–25 SF, choose and cut your own fresh bread to go with it). Sit in the mod, colorful interior or out front, right on the river (open long hours daily, Bahnhofstrasse 16, tel. 041-226-4141, www.restaurant-opus.ch).

Alcatraz is a super-modern, innovative bar and restaurant in one wing of the former prison. The bar is filled with young, hip, chain-smoking locals. The restaurant—all black paint and white leather—serves breakfast (6:30–10:00), lunch (11:00–14:00), and dinner (18:00–23:00)...but after 23:00, the tables disappear and it becomes a happening nightspot until the wee hours. They call the food *"eurasisch"*—a melding of European and Asian flavors. Though the extensive wine list is intimidating—with bottles more expensive than your hotel room—the food is reasonably priced (pastas 20–30 SF, main dishes 30–40 SF, cheaper half portions available, restaurant closed but bar open on Sun, Löwengraben 18, tel. 041-417-1212, www.alcatraz-club.ch).

Restaurante Rossini, packed with happy eaters on the riverfront, offers good handmade pizzas and pastas (20–25 SF, Mon–Sat 7:30–24:30, Sun 10:00–24:30, Bahnhofstrasse 7, tel. 041-210-8050).

If you *must* eat on the riverfront embankment in the old town, locals give **Restaurant Schiff** a slight edge on the competition for its good food and relatively reasonable prices (most main dishes 25–35 SF, open long hours daily, across the river from Jesuit Church, Unter der Egg 8, tel. 041-418-5252).

TRANSPORTATION CONNECTIONS

Luzern is marvelously well-situated in Switzerland, with great connections to anywhere in the country. Note that Luzern is on both the Golden Pass and the William Tell Express (page 222) scenic rail lines (see Scenic Rail Journeys chapter).

From Luzern by train to: Zürich (2/hr, 1 hr), **Zürich Airport** (2/hr, 1.25 hrs), **Bern** (every 2 hrs direct, 1.5 hrs; or 2/hr with transfer in Olten, 1.5–2 hrs), **Interlaken** (hrly, 2 hrs direct to Ost station), **Lausanne** (every 2 hrs direct, 2.75; more with transfer in Olten), **Lugano** (hrly, 3 hrs), **Chur** (hrly, 2.25 hrs, change in Thalwil).

Note that if you're heading to **Zermatt**, the most scenic route is to take the first half of the William Tell Express to Göschenen. There you'll change to a train to Andermatt, where you can catch the Glacier Express (page 241) on the second half of its journey to Zermatt. The whole trip takes about five and a half hours. (You'll save about 30 minutes—but miss much of the scenery—if you go via Olten or Bern instead. But unless you have a Swiss Pass, you'll pay more for the Andermatt-to-Zermatt section than the route via Olten or Bern.)

Central Switzerland:
Day Trips from Luzern

Luzern—perched on the edge of a super-scenic lake and ringed by conquerable mountain peaks—is the perfect springboard for Alpine excursions. The following side-trips—including a boat cruise, two different mountain lifts, and a military fortress—each take less than a day from Luzern.

If you're serious about day-tripping, consider a **Tell-Pass**. This pass includes two days of free passage on lifts, boats, and several area train lines in a seven-day period (with a 50 percent discount on the other 5 days; 135 SF, or 108 SF with a Swiss Pass; buy at TIs, train stations, and boat docks, April–Oct only, www.tellpass.ch). While this can be a good deal for those home-basing themselves in the region for a week, it probably won't pay for itself on a quick visit.

Note that the military fortress is open only on weekends from April through October.

Possible Do-It-All Day Trip: To combine most of these adventures (the fortress, a mini-lake cruise, and the Pilatus mountain lift) into one jam-packed day trip, try this: Take an early train or boat to Stansstad and tour Fortress Fürigen, then have lunch in Stansstad. Catch the 14:00 boat to Alpnachstad (20-min ride). Get off and follow the walkway underneath the road to get to the Pilatus cogwheel train (departing 14:25, arriving at the summit at 14:55). When you're ready to return to Luzern, catch the gondola for the seven-minute ride down to Fräkmüntegg (4/hr, last departure at 17:15, or 18:00 July–Aug), where you have a chance to do the luge ride before changing to a smaller gondola down to Kriens (they run constantly until 17:30, or 18:15 July–Aug, 30-min ride, don't get off at Krienseregg). In Kriens, walk five minutes, following the white signs to "Luzern bus." (You don't want the bus stop in front of the building.) Bus #1 (2.40 SF, not covered by Eurailpass, but free with Swiss Pass) gets you to Luzern's main station in 10 minutes. Whew!

Boats of Note: These boats can help you connect the excursions in this chapter—**Stansstad** (Fortress Fürigen) **to Alpnachstad** (where you catch Pilatus cogwheel train; 6 boats/day, 20–35 min, plus 2 steamboats/day July–Aug, 8 SF), **Stansstad to Luzern** (7 boats/day, 60–75 min, plus 2 steamboats/day July–Aug, 14 SF), **Alpnachstad to Luzern** (7 boats/day, 90 min, 18.60 SF).

Lake Cruises

Lake Luzern (or Lucerne) is the English name for the lake, but locals call it the Vierwaldstättersee—literally, the "Lake of Four Forest Cantons," since it lies where four of Switzerland's political units intersect. More people cruise this lake than any other in Switzerland...and you'll likely be one of them.

There are various routes and destinations (33 stops in all), ranging from a one-hour sampler (basically around Luzern's "harbor") to a full-blown six-hour exploration (to Flüelen, at the far end of the lake, and back again). Some routes are round-trip; on others, you'll get out, explore, and take the next boat back. Romantics will hitch a ride on one of the five old-fashioned paddleboat steamers.

Lake Luzern Area

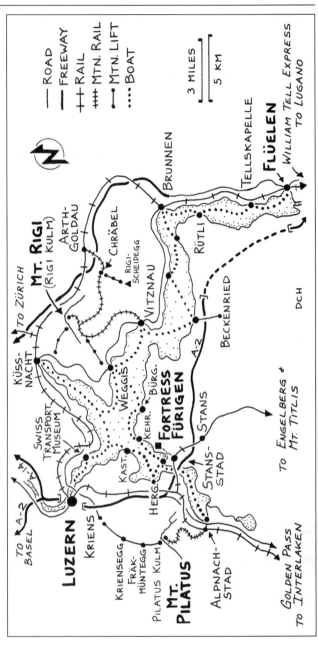

The easiest and most efficient trip is to boat across from the train station to the Swiss Transport Museum (Verkehrshaus, see page 68; 8 SF round-trip, second class, 10 min each way). For an easy two-hour excursion, consider taking the boat from Luzern out to Weggis or Vitznau (under Mount Rigi, across the lake; see "Mountain Lifts," below), then back to Luzern (24 SF round-trip, second class to Weggis, 30 SF to Vitznau). You can buy tickets and get advice on which trip best fits your schedule at the Luzern TI.

Boats leave from right in front of the Luzern train station. They're operated by the Lake Lucerne Navigation Company (tel. 041-367-6767, www.lakelucerne.ch). Note that these boats are free with a Eurailpass or Swiss Pass. But remember that if you're using a flexipass, the boat trip costs a flexi-day. If it's convenient, do the lake cruise the day you arrive or depart—since it's covered on the same flexi-day you're already using for the train trip.

Mountain Lifts

There's no shortage of mountain lifts in Central Switzerland. The two most famous and most accessible from Luzern are listed below.

Mount Pilatus

Pilatus looms behind Luzern, offering the city a dramatic back-drop...and an enjoyable destination. While legend dictates that it's named for Pontius Pilate—whose body is supposedly in one of its lakes, kicking up a fuss if disturbed—it more likely comes from a Latin word meaning "cloudy." It's also said to be infested with drag-ons. With good luck, none of these three factors will interfere with your visit.

You can climb Pilatus (to the overlook platform, at 7,000 feet, called "Pilatus Kulm") two different ways: by cogwheel railway (the world's steepest, at 48 percent grade) or gondola (in 3 stages). The **cogwheel railway** leaves from the lakeside town of Alpnachstad (hourly train from Luzern to Alpnachstad, 20 min, or 90 min by

boat; cogwheel railway runs mid-May–mid-Nov only, goes at least hourly, daily 8:45–17:45, 30 min up, 40 min down; for the best views going up, take a downhill-facing seat on the right side). The **gondola** leaves from the town of Kriens, virtually a suburb of Luzern (from in front of Luzern train station, take city bus #1 for 15 min to Kriens; gondola goes continuously, daily July–Aug 8:30–17:30, April–June and Sept–Oct until 16:45,

Nov–March until 15:45, closes periodically for maintenance Oct-Nov). From Kriens, you'll take a small gondola to Krienseregg (recreation area with trails and playground), then on to Fräkmüntegg (total trip 30 min). At Fräkmüntegg, you'll have a chance to zip down Switzerland's longest luge ride, called "Dragon Speed" (8 SF, 4,400 feet long, good weather only, www.rodelbahn.ch). From Fräkmüntegg, it's another seven minutes in a bigger cable car to the observation platform at Pilatus Kulm.

Up top, **Hotel Bellevue** acts as the visitor center, with a good information office, restaurants, a souvenir shop, and free Internet terminals. **Hotel Pilatus-Kulm** hosts temporary exhibits. Its three restaurants have the original furnishings from 1889; there's also a modern self-service cafeteria. Check out the fancy WC: When you open a door, a red dragon claims the stall for you. The terrace below is full of free and comfortable deck chairs.

Costs: A one-way segment to the top, no matter how you go, costs 29 SF; a round-trip costs 58 SF (with your choice of cogwheel train or gondola for each leg; does not include your transportation between Luzern and the cogwheel railway or gondola stations). Eurailpass and Swiss Pass holders get a 30 percent discount. When you buy your ticket, tell them which way you want to go up and down (it's most interesting to go up one way, down the other). Don't throw your ticket away, as you'll have to scan it several times until you finally exit the last station. Be warned: Buying a one-way ticket and hiking all the way down was a fatal decision for two Americans in 2003.

The handiest way to visit Pilatus from Luzern is with the popular **Golden Round Trip** package. This includes the bus to Kriens, the cable car up to Pilatus, the cogwheel railway down to Alpnachstad, and a lazy 90-minute boat trip back to Luzern (or the same route, reversed; 79 SF second class, 43 SF with Eurailpass or Swiss Pass, 14 SF less to return by train instead of boat, May–Oct only). Figure out the best route with the help of Luzern's TI, or check www.pilatus.ch (tel. 041-329-1111, fax 041-329-1112).

Hikes: These walks lead to great viewpoints. I've listed them roughly in order of difficulty, from easiest to most strenuous. All leave from the summit, Pilatus Kulm.

Two short **Dragonpaths** lead through tunnels to various viewpoints in the rock. These paths come with signs illustrating dragon tales by the famous Swiss artist Hans Erni.

A 10-minute hike takes you up to **Esel** (or "Donkey," commemorating the pre-cable-car days, when Queen Victoria came up to Pilatus on the back of a donkey). Below, Esel hides an impressive part of Switzerland's anti-aircraft defense system. Find the gray, round structures within the imitation rock. Modern missiles behind the camouflage point to the skies. The biggest radar in Switzerland towers above Hotel Pilatus-Kulm in an off-limits military zone.

Hiking to **Tomlishorn** (35 min), you'll spot more camouflaged military installations. Stop at the yellow sign for "Echo" and shout your message out to the world. Somebody out there keeps yelling it back.

A 90-minute hike leads to the 6,700-foot cross-capped summit of **Matthorn** (not Matterhorn). This is moderately strenuous—generally uphill, with lots of ups and downs. A visitors' book invites you to sign and leave your impressions on this breathtaking spot.

Sleeping at the Summit: You can spend the night on the summit of Pilatus. Linger outside to enjoy the views with the marmots and mountain goats...or head inside for the hotels' free nightly entertainment: movies and a disco on alternating nights. $$$ **Hotel Bellevue** is a modern, round building with 27 rooms—clean and bright, with Nordic-style furniture (Sb-111 SF, Db-192 SF). $ **Hotel Kulm** is a historic building from 1900 with basic, sink-only rooms (S-77 SF, D-124 SF). Both hotels come with a big breakfast and share the same contact information (tel. 041-329-1212, fax 041-329-1213, www.pilatus.ch, hotels@pilatus.ch).

Mount Rigi

This long, shelf-like mountain, across the lake from Luzern, provides sweeping views of Central Switzerland (and, on a clear day, Germany and France, too). Even though it's at a lower altitude than Pilatus (5,900 feet), this so-called "Queen of the Mountains" claims to offer the best vistas in the area. The mountain is laced with hiking trails and other attractions to while away an afternoon.

As with Pilatus, there are two ways to approach the topmost viewpoint, Rigi Kulm: via cogwheel railway (from Arth-Goldau or Vitznau), or with a cable car (from Weggis).

To go by **cogwheel railway**, you have two options: from the town of Arth-Goldau (around "behind" Rigi, accessible by train from Luzern), or from Vitznau (right on Lake Luzern, accessible by boat—but not train—from Luzern). The train from Luzern to Arth-Goldau takes 30 minutes; once there, you'll take the cogwheel railway up to Rigi Kulm (35 min, departs hourly, coordinated with arrival of certain trains from Luzern, daily 8:00–17:25). Or take the boat from Luzern to Vitznau (about 1 hr), then a different cogwheel train from there up to Rigi Kulm (30 min, departs hourly, daily 7:10–21:10).

To go by **cable car**, take the boat from Luzern to Weggis (30–45 min), then board the cable car to Rigi Kaltbad (10 min, departs hourly, Mon–Fri 7:20–18:45, Sat–Sun 8:15–18:45); there you'll switch to the cogwheel train that brings you the rest of the way up to Rigi Kulm.

You can combine these various railways and lifts to come and go as you choose; before ascending, figure out your complete route at the Luzern TI. No matter how you go, the price from the base of the mountain to Rigi Kulm is 32 SF one-way, 58 SF round-trip, plus the cost of getting from Luzern to the cogwheel train or cable-car stations. Figure a total of 88 SF per person for the total round-trip from Luzern (plan on 5–6 hrs). Note that cogwheel train and cable-car prices are discounted 25 percent with a Eurailpass and 50 percent with a Swiss Pass; the train trip from Luzern to Arth-Goldau and the boat trips to Vitznau and Weggis are also included in your pass (but you'll have to use one of your flexi-days). The schedules and prices listed here are for peak summer season (May–Oct); they may vary in shoulder and ski seasons (confirm at Luzern TI, or check www.rigi.ch).

Fortress Fürigen Museum of War History (Festung Fürigen Museum zur Wehrgeschichte)

Most visitors come to Luzern to confirm all their stereotypical images of Switzerland, and the city happily responds: picture-perfect mountains around a gorgeous lake, surrounded by tidy villages and lush meadows full of happy cows. The Fortress Museum of Fürigen shows you another face of the country—the reason why Switzerland was able to remain peaceful and neutral: its elaborate and secret system of bunkers and fortresses.

Time your visit for a weekend, because the museum is closed on weekdays (and Nov–March). Enter through an innocent-looking wooden barrack. Put on your Swiss army coast, grab the English brochure that explains each room, and you're on your way. The radio station was placed near the entrance to assure clear reception. The living quarters were gas-proof, complete with specially sealed doors and devices to monitor the air for poison. The bunker is always chilly, but no worries: Visitors are loaned original Swiss Army coats. The museum is a petting zoo of 20th-century weaponry. Visitors can fiddle with and even aim guns, knowing all the ammo is now imaginary. Imagine the photo op—you, in a Swiss military uniform, manning a cannon.

Historical photographs take you back to World War II. Fortress Fürigen was built in 1941 as part of a new military strategy: to protect Switzerland with fortresses hidden in the Alps, called *Réduitfestung* (roughly "shelter fortress"—see sidebar, next page). In case of a Nazi invasion, the Swiss government would retreat to a secret bunker in the Berner Oberland, and Swiss troops would abandon the border regions and gather around this Alpine strong-hold. Fortress Fürigen was meant to protect roads and rail lines that led from Luzern and Zürich along Lake Luzern into the Berner Oberland. This was one of a network of fortresses in the area. After World War II, they were retooled with a new focus: the threat of the Soviet Union and nuclear war.

Swiss Military Readiness

Strolling through a peaceful Swiss village—charming pastoral greenery studded with rustic farmhouses between an Alp and a lake—my friend walked with me to the door of a nondescript

barn. He said, "Stand here," and slid open the door to reveal a solitary mighty gun—pointing right at me. Crossing a field, kicking a stray soccer ball back to a group of happy grade-schoolers, we came to another barn. This time I noticed the "wooden" door was actually metal, with a clever paint job. Inside was a military canteen, now selling snacks to civilians, and a steel ladder leading down into a military-gray world that felt like a vast submarine. A network of passages, just big enough for heavily armed soldiers to race down single file, led to a series of gun barns and subterranean command rooms with charts locating other installations in the area.

Switzerland may be famous for its neutrality, but it's anything but lax defensively. Travelers marvel at how Swiss engineers have conquered their Alps with the world's most-expensive-per-mile road system. But no one designs a Swiss bridge or tunnel without designing its destruction. Each comes with built-in explosives, so, in the event of an invasion, the entire country can be blasted into a mountain fortress.

Even today, you can't get a building permit without an expensive first-class bomb shelter worked into the plan. Old tank barriers (nicknamed "Toblerones" for their shape) stand ready to be dragged across the roads to slow any invasion. Sprawling hospitals are dug into mountains, still ventilated to be kept dry and ready for use. And halfway up Alpine cliffs, Batcave-type doors can slide open, allowing fighter jets to zoom into action from hidden airstrips cut out of solid rock. As you approach each summit, look for the explosive patches ominously checkering the roads.

But the end of the Cold War in 1989 brought changes even to neutral Switzerland. Western armies began cutting back on their military spending, and Switzerland followed suit, with deep cuts in its defense budget. The Swiss Army met its tighter budget in part by closing many of the 15,000 hidden fortresses that protected the country's strategic roads, train lines, and mountain passes. Some of the forts, such as Fortress Fürigen, have been turned into tourist attractions no more formidable than medieval castles.

Big guns in the fortress could shoot over six miles, and machine guns protected the immediate access routes to the bunker. This fortress could house and feed 100 people for three weeks. But in 1990, with the end of the Cold War, the practical Swiss decommissioned the fortress, refit it with vintage WWII and early Cold War gear, and opened it to the curious public.

Cost and Hours: Entry costs 5 SF, covered by Swiss Museum Passport (see page 15). Sadly, the museum is open only on weekends from late spring through early fall (April–Oct Sat–Sun 11:00–17:00, closed Mon–Fri and Nov–March, tel. 041-618-7522).

Getting There: Fortress Fürigen is near the lakefront town of Stansstad (on Kehrsitenstrasse), below the village of Fürigen, not far from Luzern. It's easy by **train** from Luzern (hrly, :14 past each hour, direction Engelberg, 5.60 SF one-way, 15-min ride).

From the train station in Stansstad, you have two options: walking direct (15 min), or detouring up to a fun funicular.

To **walk**, follow brown signs to "Festungsmuseum" or "Kehrsiten" (down Bahnhofstrasse to Stanserstrasse, cross and follow brown signs, right on Achereggstrasse, left passing swimming pool sign and tennis courts, and finally along the lake).

For the **funicular**, catch the yellow postal bus from the station up to the village of Fürigen (direction Bürgenstock, tell driver you want to get off at Fürigen). Cross the road and follow signs to left to "Fürigen." Pass Hotel Fürigen and turn left at the parking lot. The gray wooden pavilion is the station of a funky, short, and steep funicular back down to Stansstad. Ring the bell and sit down in the 1923, box-like cabin (3/hr, April–Oct only, 5-min joyride, 4 SF). Exit and follow to the right; the entrance to the fortress museum is just around the corner. Those taking the more dramatic cogwheel train up to Pilatus won't be impressed by this detour.

You can also get to Stansstad from Luzern by **boat** (7/day, 60–75 min, plus 2 steamboats/day July–Aug, 14 SF). From Stansstad's boat dock, walk 10 minutes up to the main street (Achereggstrasse) and keep left, following the brown signs for "Festungsmuseum."

Drivers arriving in Stansstad can follow white signs to "Kehrsiten" for lakeside parking (1 SF/hr, free WC, 5-min walk along lake to museum entrance).

BERN and MURTEN

Enjoy urban Switzerland in the charming, compact capital of Bern. Ramble the ramparts of Murten, Switzerland's best-preserved medieval town, and resurrect the ruins of an ancient Roman capital in nearby Avenches.

Planning Your Time

On a quick trip, big Bern and little Murten—only a half hour apart by train or car—are each worth a half day. Either makes a fine day trip or overnight stop. If you like cute, small towns (as I do), make Murten your home base. Otherwise, choose busier Bern.

Bern is a handy on-the-way stop between other destinations (such as going from the Berner Oberland to Murten or Zürich). If you're day-tripping, put your bag in a locker at the Bern station, spend a few hours taking my self-guided Introductory Bern Walk (page 86) and visiting some museums, and catch a late-afternoon train to your next stop. You could combine the destinations in this chapter by ending your busy Bern day in Murten—where you can spend the evening wandering the walls and savoring a lakeside dinner. In the morning, linger in Murten or move on to your next destination.

Murten, while easy by train, is even better by car. With a car, I'd sleep in Murten, visit Avenches, and enjoy the view.

Bern

Stately but human, classy but fun, the Swiss capital gives you the most delightful look at urban Switzerland. Window-shopping and people-watching along the arcaded streets and lively market squares are Bern's top attractions, but there's more to this city. Enjoy Bern's fine museums, quaint-for-a-capital ambience, and much-adored mascot bears.

Bern and Murten

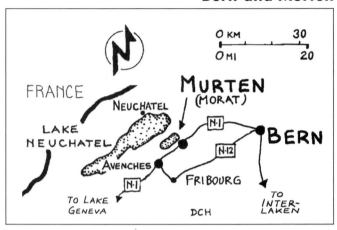

The city, founded in 1191, has managed to avoid war damage and hasn't burned down since a great fire in 1405. After the fire, wooden buildings were no longer allowed, and Bern gained its gray-green sandstone complexion (with stones quarried from nearby). During its 12th- and 13th-century growth spurt, the frisky town grew through two walls. Looking at the map of the city contained within a bend of the Aare River, you can get a sense of how it started with a castle at the tip of the peninsula and expanded with a series of walls—each defending an ever-bigger city from its one accessible-by-land side. The clock tower marks the first wall (1218). A generation later,

another wall was built (in 1256, at today's prison tower). The final wall—where today's train station sits—was built in 1344.

In 1353, Bern became the eighth canton to join the Swiss Federation. Its power ended with the conquest by Napoleon in 1798. But in 1848, Bern rose again to become the Swiss capital.

Today, the German-speaking town has 130,000 people (one-third Protestant and two-thirds Catholic). Its pointy towers, sandstone buildings, and colorful fountains make Bern one of Europe's finest surviving medieval towns.

ORIENTATION

User-friendly Bern is packed into a peninsula bounded by the Aare River. The train station is located where the peninsula connects to the mainland. From there, a handy main drag leads gradually downhill, straight through the middle of town, past most of the major sights, to the tip of the peninsula (and, across a bridge, the bear pits).

Tourist Information

Start your visit at the **TI** inside the train station (June–Sept daily 9:00–20:30, Oct–May Mon–Sat 9:00–18:30, Sun 10:00–17:00, tel. 031-328-1212, www.bernetourism.ch). Pick up a 1-SF map of Bern (and maps for any other Swiss cities you'll be visiting), and browse through their free brochures: general information booklet, museum guide, booklet on bus and walking tours, transit map, monthly *What's On* events guide, and informative leaflets on various sights. Ask about walking tours and the city sightseeing tour by raft on the Aare River (June–Sept). There's a second TI at the bear pits (June–Sept daily 9:00–18:00; March–May and Oct daily 10:00–16:00; Nov–Feb Fri–Sun 11:00–16:00, closed Mon–Thu).

Arrival in Bern

Bern's bustling **train station** is a thriving, multistory mall. The trains almost get lost. On the upper level, you'll find a **Migros** grocery store (daily 8:00–21:00) and a **pharmacy** (daily 6:30–22:00). Near the TI are **lockers** (5 SF) and **WCs** (2 SF). From the station, it's a 30-minute downhill stroll through the heart of town to the bear pits and Rose Garden. The Introductory Bern Walk (page 86) lays out the most interesting route.

Drivers approaching by freeway should follow signs to Bern Zentrum, then Bahnhof, and Bahnhof Parking. There's a huge pay garage behind the train station (Bahnhof). While not the cheapest option, this is your easiest for a quick visit. The old town is essentially car-free (only service vehicles and public transit allowed).

Getting Around Bern

The city is walkable, though the trams can be handy. A standard single ticket costs 2.60 SF, a shorter trip *(Kurzstrecke)* runs 1.70 SF, and a 24-hour ticket is 7 SF. The best plan: Walk from the train station to the far end of town, then catch the made-for-tourists tram #12 back to the station (buy 1.70-SF *Kurzstrecke* from machine at bus stop, tram goes about every 6 min).

Helpful Hints

Closed Day: Most of Bern's museums are closed on Monday.

Bike Rental: Free loaner city bikes are available at Bahnhofplatz (to the right as you exit the station). Look for the *Bern rollt* kiosk. Leave your photo ID and a 20-SF deposit (daily 7:30–21:30, summer only). You can also rent bikes year-round at Velostation, behind the train station baggage office (5 SF/day, Mon–Fri 7:00–19:00, closed Sat–Sun).

Bookstore: Stauffacher is a huge bookstore with an entire floor of English books, a fine travel section, and an inviting café with a terrace and good salads (a block below the train station at Neuengasse 34).

Tours: Town walks leave daily at 14:30 from the TI (90 min, 15 SF, June–Sept). Bus tours leave daily at 11:00, also from the TI (2 hours, 30 SF, May–Nov). Rafting tours are supposedly available by request daily June through September (40 SF, minimum 4 people, reserve through TI).

Introductory Bern Walk

This orientation walk begins at the station and ends at the bear pits, at the far end of town. From the bear pits, you can catch the tram or browse your way back to your starting point.

Train Station: The station is a bright and airy shopping center, with a first-class TI (next to train information center), long-hours exchange desk, and all the shops you could need. On the ground floor are scant remnants of the town's third wall. (Notice the 1353 etching showing Bern as it looked the year it entered the Swiss Federation.) The fortified wall was replaced in the 19th century by the train station. All city buses and trams come and go from here.

From the train station TI, cross Bahnhofplatz, walk 50 yards, and turn left (around the church) onto Spitalgasse. This marks the start of one long street (with four names)—the spine of both the peninsula and this walk—that rambles downhill through the heart of town to the bridge and bear pits.

Notice the first of Bern's 11 historical **fountains,** the Bagpiper. These colorful 16th-century fountains are Bern's trademark. The city commissioned them for many reasons: to brighten up the cityscape of gray stone buildings, to show off the town's wealth, and to remind citizens of great local heroes and events. They also gave local artists something to work on after the Reformation deprived them of their most important patron, the Catholic Church.

Continue down Spitalgasse until you reach...

Bärenplatz: In summer, a daily market is held on this square (busiest on Tue and Sat mornings). The street runs under the **Prison Tower** (Käfigturm)—once a part of the city wall (c. 1256). Renovated 1641–1644, the tower served as a prison until 1897 (*Käfig* means "cage"). Notice how the hand on the clock really is a hand— and how it was built in a slower-paced era, when just an hour hand told time concisely enough. The bears on the tower are from Bern's coat of arms. Live ones await you at the end of this walk.

To the left (100 yards), you'll see the **Dutch Tower.** Swiss soldiers were famous mercenaries who fought all over Europe. Returning from a battle in the Netherlands, the soldiers brought back the habit of smoking. But smoking was forbidden within the

Introductory Bern Walk

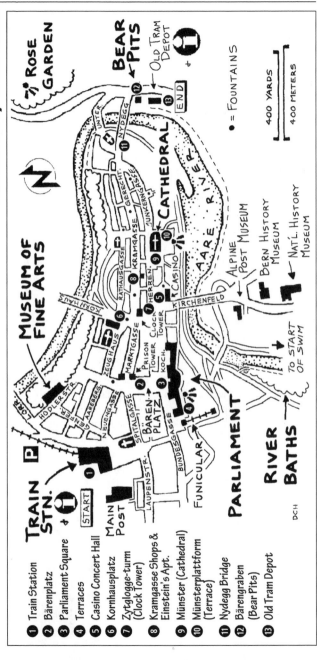

ROSE GARDEN

BEAR PITS

OLD TRAM DEPOT

MUSEUM OF FINE ARTS

CATHEDRAL

AARE RIVER

Alpine Post Museum

Bern History Museum

Nat'l. History Museum

PARLIAMENT

RIVER BATHS

FUNICULAR

TRAIN STN.

START

MAIN POST

BÄREN-PLATZ

To START OF SWIM

• = FOUNTAINS

400 YARDS
400 METERS

N

KICHENFELD
CASINO
HERREN-
KRAMGASSE
RATHAUSGASSE
GERECHT.
JUNKERNGASSE
NYDEGG
UNTER
KORNHAUS
ZEUGHAUS
MARKTGASSE
Clock Tower
Prison Tower
KOCH.
SPITALGASSE
N.EUENGASSE
A.AARBERG
AMTHAUS
HODLER-STR.
ORK.
LAUPENSTR.
BUNDESGASSE

DCH

❶ Train Station
❷ Bärenplatz
❸ Parliament Square
❹ Terraces
❺ Casino Concert Hall
❻ Kornhausplatz
❼ Zytglogge-turm (Clock Tower)
❽ Kramgasse Shops & Einstein's Apt.
❾ Münster (Cathedral)
❿ Münsterplattform (Terrace)
⓫ Nydegg Bridge
⓬ Bärengraben (Bear Pits)
⓭ Old Tram Depot

city walls of Bern—so they hid in this tower to smoke secretly. (European smokers expect that, with current trends, this tower may regain its historic function within just a few years.)

Further left is a modern and controversial **fountain** by the Swiss surrealist Meret Oppenheim. Made in 1983, it symbolizes growth and life, and is supposed to demonstrate communication between an object of art and the beholder. It worked well...too well, in fact, as most citizens immediately communicated their dislike and wanted it destroyed. But Bern's politicians proved braver than expected, and the fountain survived. Time has transformed Oppenheim's gray concrete column into a multicolored pillar decorated with moss, grass, and flowers. Locals like it only in the winter, when it's covered with ice. The grand building beyond the fountain—once the city orphanage—is the police station.

As each of the town's successive walls was torn down, they provided Bern with vast, people-friendly swaths of land which function as elongated "squares"—popular today for markets and outdoor cafés. With your back to the modern fountain, stroll to the end of Bärenplatz, filled with market stalls and lined with fun places to eat (see "Eating," page 95). It leads (on the opposite side) to the...

Parliament (Bundeshaus): You may see some high-powered legislators, but you wouldn't know it—everything looks very casual for a national capital. The fine granite plaza in front of the parliament (built in 2004 to replace a parking lot) is a favorite spot for demonstrations. Facing the square on the left is the Swiss National Bank—this country's Fort Knox, with piles of gold buried under the square.

Standing in front of the Parliament, check out the statuary. The woman on the top of the building represents political independence, the one on the left (under 1291) stands for freedom, and the one on the right (1848) symbolizes peace.

Drop by the welcoming glass pavilion (left side, under the arcade) and pick up the generous literature on the Swiss government. Its bicameral system was inspired by the U.S. constitution, with one big difference: Executive power is shared by a committee of seven, with a rotating ceremonial president and a passion for consensus. This is a mechanism to avoid power grabs by any single individual...a safeguard the Swiss love.

You can visit the Parliament building on a guided **tour** (free 45-min tours up to 6 times daily Mon–Fri, English often at 14:00 as well as other times, tours are canceled if fewer than 5 people show up, must deposit passport before tour; no tours, but you can watch when in session in

March, June, mid-Sept–mid-Oct, and Dec; tel. 031-322-8522, www.parliament.ch). Call the day before to confirm times of English tours.

Continuing past the Parliament info kiosk, walk around behind the Parliament to the terraces, where you have a commanding view over the Aare River and Bern's biggest swimming pool, the **Marzilibad**. On a clear day, you can see the peaks of the Eiger, Mönch, and Jungfrau (see Gimmelwald chapter)—and the far less imposing "mountain" of Bern, the **Gurten**. The Gurten is the city's favorite recreation spot, offering music festivals in summer and very modest skiing opportunities for children in winter.

Follow the tree-lined pedestrian lane left a few hundred yards to Kirchenfeld Bridge (great river views from halfway across, many museums just across). The **Casino** isn't for gamblers—it's the home of Bern's Symphony Orchestra.

With your back to the river, follow the tram tracks down another swath of land created by the removal of a city wall, to...

Kornhausplatz: This square is ornamented by the colorful **Ogre** (*Chindlifresser,* literally, "child-eater") fountain. Two legends try to explain this gruesome sight. It's either a folkloric representation of the Greek god Chronos, or a figure that was intended to scare children off the former city walls. The building behind on the left used to be the granary, and now houses the modern public library and the huge Kornhauskeller.

Wander down the stairs into the **Kornhauskeller**. Once the vast city wine cellar, now an Italian restaurant (see "Eating," page 95), this cellar was built in high Baroque style (1718) and renovated with paintings inspired by the Pre-Raphaelites in 1897. The 12 columns show traditional costumes of Bernese women.

Back on Kornhausplatz, step under the clock tower where Marktgasse becomes Kramgasse to see the fancy clock ornamenting its downhill side.

Zytglogge-turm: Bern's famous clock tower was part of the original wall marking the first gate to the city (c. 1250). The clock performs four minutes before each hour: The happy jester comes to life, Father Time turns his hourglass, the rooster crows (in German,

that's "kee-kee-ree-kee" rather than "cock-a-doodle-doo"), and the golden man on top hammers the bell. Apparently, this non-event was considered entertaining in 1530. To pass the time waiting for the action, read the TI's leaflet explaining what's so interesting about the fancy old clock (the golden hour hand is an hour behind for half the year because of the modern innovation of daylight saving time). You can determine the zodiac, today's date, and the stage of the moon—look at the black-and-gold orb. Enthusiasts can tour the medieval mechanics—early Swiss engineering at its best—and see the billows that enable the old rooster to crow (May–Oct daily at 11:30, also at 16:30 July–Aug, 9 SF, buy ticket from guide, 50-min tour).

Under the clock are the old regional measurements (Swiss foot, the bigger Bernese foot, and the *elle,* or "elbow," which was the distance from the elbow to the fingertip) and the official meter and double meter. It took a strong man like Napoleon to bring consistency to measurements in Europe, and he replaced the many goofy feet and elbows of medieval Europe with the metric system used today (c. 1800).

Continue your stroll down the main drag...

Kramgasse: Bern has wide streets like this one, but not many squares. In the Middle Ages, craftsmen exhibited their goods on the sidewalks under simple roofs. Eventually, these were formalized, buildings expanded out, and arcades evolved.

The lanes of old Bern are lined with over three miles of arcades, providing lots of arcaded shopping opportunities. This is my kind of shopping town: Prices are so high, there's no danger of buying (shops generally open Mon–Fri 9:00–18:30, Thu later, Sat 8:00–16:00, closed Sun).

Most shops are underneath the arcades, but don't miss the ones in the **cellars** that you can access only from the main road. The cellars, marked by old-time hatches, were originally for storing potatoes and coal, and later, wine. People said "merry Bern" was floating on wine, just as Venice was floating on water. The merry times ended in 1798, when the French invaded (and drank all the wine). The cellars were once again used for potatoes, and the city got a new nickname: "sad Bern." Napoleon's soldiers not only liberated Bern from its wine, but also from the tremendous treasury the city was known for. Napoleon used money looted from Bern to finance his Egyptian crusade.

The apartment that **Einstein** called home during several of his happiest and most productive years is 200 yards down Kramgasse from the clock tower (on the right, at Kramgasse 49). The museum that's there now doesn't do much for me, but I guess everything's relative (3 SF, Tue–Fri 10:00–17:00, Sat 10:00–16:00, closed Sun–Mon and Dec–Jan, Kramgasse 49, tel. 031-312-0091).

Just below Einstein's house, at the Samson Fountain, turn right and crawl through the narrow Münstergässchen to the...

Bern Cathedral: Bern's 15th-century Münster, Catholic-turned-Protestant, is capped with a 330-foot-tall tower, the highest in Switzerland (finished only in 1893). The church was dedicated to St. Vincent of Zaragoza. During the Reformation, religious icons were destroyed by Protestants (an act called iconoclasm—see page 189). This church's main portal, with its striking gold-leaf highlights, seems pretty un-Protestant. It probably survived because its theme, the Last Judgment, showed that no matter how rich you are or what rank you have in Church hierarchy, *anyone* can end up in Hell (an idea Protestants dug). Condemned people are popping in the flames like lottery balls. Notice the humorous details in the commotion of people heading to hell (especially what the little green devil is doing to the sinful monk).

Cathedral entrance is free (April–Oct Tue–Sat 10:00–17:00, Sun 11:30–17:00, closed Mon; Nov–March Tue–Fri 11:00–13:00 & 14:00–16:00, Sat until 17:00, Sun 11:30–14:00, closed Mon; tel. 031-312-0462). Climb the spiral staircase 210 feet above the town for the view and the exercise (choose between two stairways: 312 or 354 steps). Elisabeth Bissig lives way up there, watching over the church, answering questions, and charging tourists 3 SF for the city view and a chance to peek at her bells.

Behind the cathedral is a terrace overlooking the river. Go towards the terrace, walking by free public WCs (industrial strength, pop in and push the buttons). Like the United States, Switzerland is dealing with a persistent drug abuse problem. Rather than fill its jails, it has tried a more compassionate approach (which hasn't worked well either): People shooting up have been such a problem that public toilets like this one are lit by blue lights, so junkies can't locate their veins.

Continue on to the...

Münsterplattform: This terrace was built, starting in the 14th century, from all kinds of "recycled" stones from older buildings. Archaeologists even unearthed some heads of statues that were victims of Reformation iconoclasts. Look down on the Aare (find the bear out on the breakwater). Notice the security nets below you. The platform used to be the favorite place for suicides—to the terror of the people living below. The Pavilion Café offers a scenic spot for a bite or drink on a sunny day.

With your back to the river, return to the main drag, Kramgasse. On the Fountain of Justice, a blindfolded figure of Justice triumphs over the mayor, pope, sultan, and emperor. A few steps above the fountain, a grate reveals a bit of the stream that used to flow open down the middle of the peninsula, providing people with a handy disposal system.

From here, it's a straight stretch to the bridge at the end of the old town...

Nydegg Bridge: Look downstream from the Nydegg Bridge. To your left is the site of the original town castle (now a church). The small bridge below is the oldest in Bern (once the only bridge crossing the Aare here). Above on the ridge (just behind and to the right of the pointy spire) is the Rose Garden, a restaurant capping the ridge with fine views. And just upstream stands the site of the original Lindt Chocolate factory.

Continue across the bridge to reach the...

Bear Pits (Bärengraben): The symbol of Bern is the bear, and some lively ones frolic in these big, barren, concrete pits, to the

delight of locals and tourists alike (daily 9:00–16:00). You may see graffiti from the B.L.M. (Bear Liberation Movement), which, through its terrorist acts, has forced a reluctant city government to give the sad-eyed bears better living conditions.

Behind the pits is the...

Old Tram Depot: This depot hosts a tourist center (TI, free video on the city, brewery restaurant/café with terrace). Its excellent multimedia show, complete with an animated town model and marching Napoleonic-era soldiers, illustrates the history and wonders of Bern. Worth the time, the 20-minute show is more interesting than the bears. You can enter late, as the last half is only beauty shots of the town, with no language barrier (free, uncomfortable benches, show in English once hourly—see schedule—or ask for a printed script, daily June-Sept 9:00–18:00, March–May and Oct 10:00–16:00, shorter hours in winter).

Up the pathway is the **Rose Garden** (Rosengarten), a restaurant offering basic, reasonably priced food and a great city view (for this option and more, see "Eating," page 95).

From the Old Tram Depot, it's an easy trip on tram #12 back to the station. If wandering back through town, be sure to get off into the quieter side lanes, which have a fascinating and entertaining array of shops and little eateries.

SIGHTS AND ACTIVITIES

▲▲**The Berner Swim**—For something to write home about, join the local merchants, students, and carp in a float down the Aare River. The Bernese, proud of their very clean river and their basic ruddiness, have a tradition—sort of a wet, urban *paseo*. On summer days, they hike upstream five to 30 minutes, then float back down to the excellent (and free) riverside baths and pools (Marzilibad) just

Bern Hotels and Restaurants

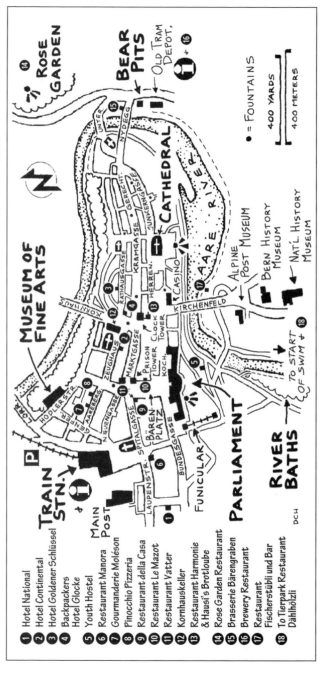

1. Hotel National
2. Hotel Continental
3. Hotel Goldener Schlüssel
4. Backpackers
   Hotel Glocke
5. Youth Hostel
6. Restaurant Manora
7. Gourmanderie Moléson
8. Pinocchio Pizzeria
9. Restaurant della Casa
10. Restaurant Le Mazot
11. Restaurant Vatter
12. Kornhauskeller
13. Restaurant Harmonie
    & Hausi's Brotloube
14. Rose Garden Restaurant
15. Brasserie Bärengraben
16. Brewery Restaurant
17. Restaurant
    Fischerstübli und Bar
18. To Tierpark Restaurant
    Dählhölzli

below the Parliament building. While the locals make it look easy, this can be dangerous—the current is swift. If you miss the last pole, you're history (start stroking over to it well in advance).

If a float down the river is a bit much, you're welcome to enjoy just the Marzilibad, or you can try the other popular free pool, Lorrainebad (downstream, on the other side of town, where the Aare flows much slower—a good spot for beginners). If a quick taste of the river is not enough, you can raft all the way from Thun (near Interlaken) to Bern (details at TI).

▲▲Museum of Fine Arts (Kunstmuseum)—While it features 1,000 years of local art and some Impressionism, the museum's real hit is its fabulous collection of Paul Klee's playful paintings. If you don't know Klee, I'd love to introduce you (7 SF, covered by Swiss Museum Passport—see page 15, no English inside but pick up free English map/brochure, Tue 10:00–21:00, Wed–Sun 10:00–17:00, closed Mon, 4 blocks north of station, Holdergasse 12, tel. 031-328-0944).

Paul Klee Center (Zentrum Paul Klee)—This new museum, dedicated solely to the art of Paul Klee, is in the works...and promises to be fabulous. It's scheduled to open in June 2005. Ask the TI for the latest, or check www.paulkleezentrum.ch.

Other Bern Museums—Across the bridge from the Parliament building on Helvetiaplatz are several museums (Alpine, Berner History, Postal, Natural History, Rifle, and Kunsthalle contemporary art) that sound more interesting than they are (most open Tue–Sun 10:00–17:00, closed Mon, www.museen-bern.ch). The TI produces a pamphlet explaining all the museums.

SLEEPING

These places are listed in geographical order from the train station. The first is a block south of it, and the rest are in the old town just past Bärenplatz, about a five-minute walk away.

$$$ Hotel National is well-located, with 45 fine rooms—some with street noise, so request a quiet room (S-80 SF, Sb-110 SF, D-110 SF, Db-150 SF, smaller fifth floor rooms—which are just fine—are about 20 SF less, apartment-180–260 SF, extra bed-40 SF, elevator, free Internet access, Hirschengraben 24, tel. 031-381-1988, fax 031-381-6878, www.nationalbern.ch, info@nationalbern.ch).

$$$ Hotel Continental has 40 bright and comfy, Nordic-flavored rooms and a cheery breakfast room with a sun terrace (Sb-130 SF, Db-180 SF, Tb-210 SF; cheaper Fri–Sun: Sb-110 SF, Db-150 SF, Tb-180 SF, elevator, Zeughausgasse 27, tel. 031-329-2121, fax 031-329-2199, www.hotel-continental.ch, continental@hotelbern.ch).

$$$ Hotel Goldener Schlüssel is an old, basic, crank-'em-out

Sleep Code

(1.30 SF = about $1, country code: 41)
S = Single, **D** = Double/Twin, **T** = Triple, **Q** = Quad,
b = bathroom, **s** = shower only, **no CC** = Credit Cards not
accepted, **SE** = Speaks English, **NSE** = No English. Unless otherwise noted, credit cards are accepted, English is spoken, and
breakfast is included.

   To help you sort easily through these listings, I've divided
the rooms into three categories, based on the price for a standard
double room with bath:

   $$$ **Higher Priced**—Most rooms 150 SF or more.
    $$ **Moderately Priced**—Most rooms between 90–150 SF.
     $ **Lower Priced**—Most rooms 90 SF or less.

hotel with 29 rooms, right in the city center (S-90 SF, Sb-115 SF, D-130 SF, Db-155 SF, Tb-205 SF, extra bed-50 SF, elevator, Rathausgasse 72, tel. 031-311-0216, fax 031-311-5688, www.goldener -schluessel.ch, info@goldener-schluessel.ch).

   $ Backpackers Hotel Glocke rents the cheapest beds in the old town (dorms: 29 SF in 4- to 6-bed room, D-78 SF, includes sheets, cheaper off-season; no breakfast, but kitchen available, non-smoking, Internet access, laundry, kitchen, reception open 8:00–11:00 & 15:00–22:00, Rathausgasse 75, tel. 031-311-3771, fax 031-311-1008, www.bernbackpackers.com, info@bernbackpackers.com).

   $ Bern Youth Hostel is a big, institutional place below the Parliament building near the river (32-SF dorm beds, D-80 SF, reception open 7:00–10:00 & 15:00–24:00, Weihergasse 4, tel. 031-311-6316, www.jugibern.ch, info@jugibern.ch).

EATING

Between the Station and Bärenplatz

Restaurant Manora is a modern, self-service chain with a quick and healthy series of buffet lines where you grab what looks good—hot plates, salads (4-SF, 7-SF, and 9-SF plates), fancy fruit juices, desserts, and so on (daily 6:30–22:30, across the square and trolley tracks in front of the train station at Bubenbergplatz 5).

   Gourmanderie Moléson is a long, skinny, bistro-type place serving traditional Swiss dishes, *tartes flambées* (Alsatian pizzas-25 SF), vegetarian meals, and 2-course lunch deals for 25 SF. The dressy and very Swiss interior can be a bit smoky, but tables tumble into the street (closed Sun, Aarbergergasse 24, tel. 031-311-4463).

   Pinocchio Pizzeria is dressy for a pizza place, with decent indoor and outdoor seating (daily until 23:00, pasta and pizza for

15–20 SF, pricier main dishes, Aarbergergasse 6, tel. 031-311-3362).

Restaurant della Casa, a traditional Swiss place with Old World ambience inside and a few tables on the sidewalk outside, has daily specials scrawled on chalkboards throughout. While not cheap, it's been a neighborhood favorite for generations (25– to 35–SF plates, closed Sun, between Parliament and the station at Schauplatzgasse 16, tel. 031-311-2142).

Around Bärenplatz

Restaurant le Mazot is popular with locals enjoying the mountain cuisine of French Switzerland. It offers a huge selection of *Rösti* (20 SF), fondues (25 SF), raclette, and other hearty alpine dishes from a user-friendly menu. You can sit inside (woody, mountain-hut ambience, with the smell of melted cheese and tobacco) or enjoy some fine people-watching on the traffic-free square outside (daily, Bärenplatz 5, tel. 031-311-7088).

Restaurant Vatter is exclusively organic—serving mostly vegetarian, lots of Indian cuisine, and some meat dishes. It's a fresh, mod place with a terrace overlooking the lively Bärenplatz. The restaurant is above an organic produce store (25-SF plates, closed Sun, Bärenplatz 2, tel. 031-312-5171).

Around Kornhausplatz

Kornhauskeller, decorated with colorful mural paintings (see description on page 89), is a splurge. It's in the cellar of the old granary, originally built to house the state's wine cellar. This dressy, pricey Italian place offers lunch specials and a fine antipasto bar for those on a budget. Make a meal out of the 16-SF or 24-SF plate, telling the waiter exactly what you'd like (30-SF plates, Mon–Sat 11:45–14:30 & 18:00–24:00, Sun 18:00–23:30, Kornhausplatz 18, tel. 031-327-7272).

Near the Cathedral

Restaurant Harmonie, owned by the Gyger family since 1915, is one of the oldest and most traditional places in town. It offers filling Swiss cuisine and is the favorite lunch spot for Swiss politicians (daily specials, 30-SF plates, closed Sat–Sun, Hotelgasse 3, tel. 031-311-3840).

Hausi's Brotloube is a bakery stocked with everything you need—sandwiches, salads, fruit, drinks, and pastries—to put together a first-class picnic for the nearby Münsterplattform (closed Sun, next to Café Harmonie at Münstergasse 74).

Near the Bear Pits

Many finish their town walk at the bear pits, and have worked up an appetite. You have three fine options here: For a light meal, salad, or tea and cakes with local grannies (and a grand view over the city), walk up Aargauerstalden to the **Rose Garden Restaurant** (March–Oct daily 9:00–22:00, tel. 031-331-3206). For a dressy lunch with local businesspeople, pop into the tight and dressy **Brasserie Bärengraben** (18-SF lunch specials, immediately over the bridge opposite the bears). Or, for something quick and not too expensive in a big, bright, and boisterous brewery setting (or on its leafy terrace overlooking the town and river), consider the **Brewery Restaurant** (fast and healthy 18-SF lunch plates, in the Old Tram Depot behind the bears).

At the Aare River

Restaurant Fischerstübli und Bar, specializing in fish, is the perfect place to be on a hot summer day (daily, weekends only in evening, Gerberngasse 41, tel. 031-311-5367).

   Tierpark Restaurant Dählhölzli is probably the most popular family hangout around when it's sunny. The huge outdoor terrace is divided into a full-service restaurant (marked with tablecloths) and a cheaper self-service section. Next to it is the Dählhölzli Zoo, where children can ride ponies and pet all kinds of animals while parents rest. Before you sit down, check if the chair is dry—this is also a favorite stop for the Aare swimmers to warm up with a cup of coffee. Don't be surprised to find guests in swimsuits and waiters who gracefully accept wet bills (daily, Dalmaziquai 151a, tel. 031-351-1894).

TRANSPORTATION CONNECTIONS

From Bern by train to: Murten (hrly, 30 min, most transfer in Kerzers), **Lausanne** (2/hr, 70 min), **Interlaken** (hrly, 50 min), **Luzern** (every 2 hrs direct, 1.5 hrs; more with transfer in Olten or Zürich, 1.5–2 hrs), **Zürich** (2/hr, 70 min), **Fribourg** in Switzerland (2/hr, 30 min), **Freiburg** in Germany (at least hrly, 2 hrs, some direct, some with transfer in Basel), **Zermatt** (hrly, 3.5 hrs, transfer in Brig), **Lugano** (hrly, 4.25 hrs, transfer in Olten or Zürich), **Appenzell** (hrly, 3.25 hrs, transfer in Gossau), **Munich** (4/day, 5.5 hrs), **Frankfurt** (hrly, 4.5 hrs), **Salzburg** (4/day, 7.25 hrs, transfer in Zürich), **Paris** (4/day, 4.5 hrs). Train info: toll tel. 0900-300-3004 or www.rail.ch.

Route Tips for Drivers

Interlaken to Bern: From Interlaken, catch the autobahn (direction: Spiez, Thun, then Bern). Circle Bern on the autobahn, taking the fourth Bern exit, Neufeld Bern. Signs to *Zentrum* take you to Bern Bahnhof. Turn right just before the station into the Bahnhof Parkplatz (45-min meter parking outside, all-day lot inside,

2–4 SF/hr, depending on time of entry). You're just an escalator ride away from a great TI and Switzerland's capital.

Heading to Murten from Bern: From the station, drive out of Bern following signs for Lausanne, then follow the green signs to Neuchâtel and Murten. The autobahn ends 20 miles later in Murten.

Murten

The finest medieval ramparts in Switzerland surround the 5,000 people
of Murten (or Morat, if you're speak-
ing French). We're on the linguistic
cusp of Switzerland: 25 percent of
Murten speaks French; a few miles to
the southwest, nearly everyone does.

Murten is a totally charming
mini-Bern with lively streets, the
middle one nicely arcaded with breezy
outdoor cafés and elegant shops
(many closed Mon). Its castle is
romantically set, overlooking the Lake
Murten and the rolling vineyards of
gentle Mount Vully in the distance.
Spend a night here and have dinner
with a local Vully wine, white or rosé.

Murten is touristic, but seems to be enjoyed mostly by its own people.

Make time for nearby Avenches. While quaint today, the town was once a powerful Roman capital—as its ruins attest.

ORIENTATION

Tourist Information

Murten's TI is just inside the city walls at the eastern end of town (opposite end from station; May–Sept Mon–Fri 9:00–12:00 & 14:00–18:00, Sat 10:00–14:00, July–Aug also Sun 10:00–14:00, shorter hours and closed weekends Oct–April, Französische Kirchgasse 6, tel. 026-670-5112, www.murtentourismus.ch). Get a free map and ask about sights, biking, and boat trips.

Arrival in Murten

By Train: To reach the town from the station (a 5-min walk), exit to the right, take the first left, walk up Bahnhofstrasse, then turn right through the town gate. Murten is a tiny town...a delight on foot.

By Car: You can park overnight in the old town for free (18:00–10:00). During the day, don't park inside the gates; Murten's brown-shirted parking cops are infamous. Park in the lot near the castle and Co-op supermarket (8 SF/day includes in-and-out privilege, 15 SF for your entire stay if you don't move car, 30 SF/1 wk in-and-out, take ticket and pay at hotel or police station). Get the latest advice on parking from your hotelier.

Helpful Hints

Internet Access: Try A&A Computer (Mon–Fri 9:00–12:00 & 14:00–22:00, Sat 9:00–17:00, closed Sun, behind station at Engelhardstrasse 6, tel. 026-670-0520).

Post Office: It's across the street from the train station.

Launderette: None in town.

Local Guide: Mary Brunisholz, an American who married into this part of Switzerland, is an excellent guide with a car (150–200 SF/half-day, mary.brunisholz@mcnet.ch).

Introductory Murten Walk

This introductory walk will give you the lay of the land, and a lesson on the historic 15th-century Battle of Murten. Start your walk just below the town's main gate at the public school, where you see a statue of the feisty local leader...

Adrian von Bubenberg: This Murten native stopped the Burgundian power grab of the 15th century by beating Charles the Bold. Burgundy was the aggressive power of the day. Adrian von Bubenberg stood here and looked across the lake at the distant peaks of the

Jura Mountains—the historic border between the Swiss and those French bastards. (More on the battle a little later.)

The earliest Swiss clockmakers were from those Jura Mountains. Look at the **clock tower**—where's the little hand? With its lease, the restaurant below takes responsibility for hand-winding the clock each day, as it has since 1712. That's the Bern gate—so called because it opens up onto the road to Bern. The tiny grated window in the mighty door is a security window.

But, rather than enter the gate, go right instead. Head along the outside of the wall, around the first turret, and find the **balls** of Murten. Those balls are left in the wall to remind townsfolk of their incredible victory over the Burgundians—like an Alamo with a happy ending.

Belly up to the lakeview terrace. Across the way is **Mount Vully** (rhymes with gooey)—one big vineyard, and a mecca for lovers of Swiss white wine. The lowlands to the right—a rich former lakebed—is the heart of the fertile Three Lakes Region (lakes Biel,

Murten

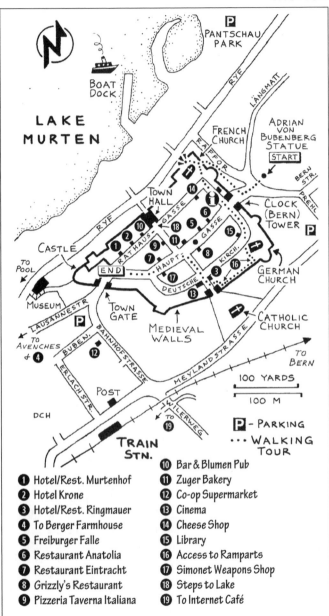

Map labels:

- PANTSCHAU PARK
- RYF
- LÄNGMATT
- BOAT DOCK
- LAKE MURTEN
- FRENCH CHURCH
- FAPFOR
- ADRIAN VON BUBENBERG STATUE
- START
- BERN STR.
- PREHL
- TOWN HALL
- GASSE
- CLOCK (BERN) TOWER
- RATHAUS
- CASTLE
- GASSE
- KIRCH.
- GERMAN CHURCH
- TO POOL
- HAUPT.
- DEUTSCHE
- END
- MUSEUM
- LAUSANNESTR.
- TOWN GATE
- MEDIEVAL WALLS
- CATHOLIC CHURCH
- TO AVENCHES
- BUBEN.
- BAHNHOFSTRASSE
- ERLACH STR.
- POST
- MEYLANDSTRASSE
- TO BERN
- DCH
- WILERWEG
- TO
- TRAIN STN.
- 100 YARDS
- 100 M
- P – PARKING
- ⋯ WALKING TOUR

1. Hotel/Rest. Murtenhof
2. Hotel Krone
3. Hotel/Rest. Ringmauer
4. To Berger Farmhouse
5. Freiburger Falle
6. Restaurant Anatolia
7. Restaurant Eintracht
8. Grizzly's Restaurant
9. Pizzeria Taverna Italiana
10. Bar & Blumen Pub
11. Zuger Bakery
12. Co-op Supermarket
13. Cinema
14. Cheese Shop
15. Library
16. Access to Ramparts
17. Simonet Weapons Shop
18. Steps to Lake
19. To Internet Café

Neuchâtel, and Murten). The lush farmland is called the "vegetable garden of Switzerland" for its soil, which yields more than 60 varieties of produce.

The ancient Celtic "Helvet" tribe recognized the fertility of this land and settled here. The Romans likewise made this land a priority in establishing their colony of Helvetia. (Today, Switzerland is officially known as Confederation Helvetia—the "CH" you see on bumper stickers.)

Check out the small **church**. Foreseeing a showdown with Burgundy, Adrian von Bubenberg had the town walls strengthened. As three-quarters of the town were German-speaking, they took a vote and decided to tear down the French church to get more stones. This little church was rebuilt for the French-speaking community six years after its big one was demolished. As the Calvinist Reformation swept through Catholic Switzerland in the early 16th century, churches like this were stripped of their rich paintings, sculptures, and stained glass. The altar became a Bible on a table, and pulpits became the focus. The emphasis was teaching the word of God. In this church, about the only exception to the "no distractions" rule are tiny stained-glass coats of arms—heraldry of the wealthy families who helped fund its construction.

From here, you'll walk across town (past the TI, Bern tower, and to the German church on the far corner). But first, across the street from the French church, is a cool...

Cheese Shop (Käserei): This farmers' co-op offers a fragrant cheese experience within the walls of Murten. Cheese is made early—around 7:00—but you can peek into the room and imagine the action anytime. Inside is a stunning array of cheeses, from local Murten and Gruyère varieties (on the left) to more exotic and stinky French types (on the right). Left of the counter, a drawer contains a farmer's can of raw milk—the local favorite. Murteners drop by to fill their own containers. The retail shelves are lined with yogurt bottled right here (in cute "mini-milk cans")—a delightful and drinkable treat (daily 7:30–12:00 & 14:00–16:30).

Walk past the TI, the Bern Tower, and up the lane to the **library** (on right, #31). Notice that along with being a "Bibliothek," it's also a "Ludothek." This means parents can check out toys and games for their children, rather than spend their hard-earned money keeping massive places like "Toys R Us" in business. Across the street, the typically Bernese little **Web Husli** shows off its old-time loom. The door is perfect for short people—if you're 5'5", stand tall on the threshold. After a 14th-century fire burned down the wooden town, future building was limited to the characteristic yellow Jura stone (like the library). Around the corner (left) just past the town's morgue, is the public WC.

Continue straight ahead to the...

German Church: Murten's German church, built in 1710, is also post-Reformation-Protestant simple. As the town is on the border between two cantons (Bern and Fribourg), for 400 years its rule was shared: Every five years, it would flip between cantons. Arrangements like this didn't sit well with Napoleon, and around 1800, he made it firmly a part of nearby Fribourg.

Inside, notice the big stucco relief (center of ceiling) with two seals: the bear for Bern and the three castles for Fribourg. The Protestant passion for Bible study is also evident in this church. The pulpit was carved from a single trunk of oak in 1460. Explore the choir (circle of seats for big shots) behind the altar. Find Adrian's seat (hint: The window above shows the war hero in red, with his victorious local yokels in their Alpine red-knit hats...underdogs whupping the Burgundians). Pull up the seat and rest on the miseri-cord—a lazy but permissible alternative when everyone stands during a long service. Notice that the two prime seats do double duty (on the right hand of the preacher sat the leader of Bern or Fribourg—depending on who happened to be ruling that year). To computer gamers, the stained-glass depiction of the crucifixion feels proto-Tetris (c. 1926).

Leaving the church, hook left around the back. Finger the lime-stone and sandstone tombstones, quarried from Mount Vully for noble families. Then climb the creaky stairs onto the ramparts and walk about 50 yards.

Rampart Ramble: Murten's only required sightseeing is to scramble the ramparts (free, open daily, closed at night). Survey the town. Note the uniformity of Murten. Paint your place the wrong color, and you may be instructed to redo it—at your own expense. Scanning the countless chimneys, think of the enforced conformity that comes with living in a small town (and find the one oddball). Telephone and electricity wires are all underground. Look back at the roof of the German church. A color-blindness test is built into its tiles. (If you can find the six-sided "star of David"—not a Jewish symbol in this case, but recalling the star that guided the wise men to Bethlehem on the first Christmas—you're okay.)

Continue to the tower. Climb the steps for a commanding town and lake view. With your back to the lake, look inland and imagine the action on June 22, 1476.

Mighty Charles the Bold, with his 20,000 well-armed Burgundians, was camped on the hill (with the divided forest) for 10 days, laying siege to the town of 2,000. Runners were sent out to gather help. A makeshift army of about 10,000 villagers gathered on the hills to the left. Just as George Washington attacked when the Redcoats were celebrating Christmas, the Swiss swooped in as the Burgundians were still hungover from a big midsummer night's eve bash. It was pouring rain—a muddy, bloody mess. Almost all 20,000

Burgundians were slaughtered—many driven into the lake with their armor to drown (try swimming in a coat of mail). For centuries, French bones would wash ashore. Charles the (no-longer-so-) Bold barely got away on a very fast horse.

This victory demonstrated to the Swiss the advantages of *E Pluribus Unum,* and the assemblage of the many still-fiercely-independent Swiss cantons into the Confederation Helvetica snowballed. In this sweet little corner, an influential battle in European history had been fought. Burgundian power ebbed, and Europe got to know a new nation...Switzerland.

Walk a bit farther along the wall and descend at the next tower (across from Café-Pension Ringmauer). The stairs lead to a fine old clock mechanism from 1816. Once powering the big clock in the City Hall tower, it spent decades in an Ikea-like pile—gathering dust in an attic. An old local, recognizing a good challenge, reassembled it into perfect working order (1991). Notice how the gearbox powers three different clock faces, and how the old hand crank raises the stones that power the clock. The white face determines the clock's time—which rings on the quarter hour.

Step outside the wall, where you'll see the Catholic church (1886), private gardens along the wall, and the different stages of the wall's construction. The first phase was built with large river stones, some arranged in a neat fishbone pattern. Later, the town ran out of money, and the next stage shows pebbles and rubble mixed with a rough concrete. And finally, when the town prospered again, they finished the wall with finely cut sandstone.

Walk back into town, stopping on the first corner at the fire station-turned-community-cinema. Local shareholders are thanked with their names on the door. Pop into the charming theater—80 plush, red seats. Notice what's playing tonight (see "Nightlife," page 105). At this corner, spin slowly, admiring the town's fine shutters, and think of something tour guide-ish to say about them.

Then, continue a block to the...

Main Street: In the 19th century, Murten's townsfolk used one of three water fountains on this street. Enjoy the colorful store signs as they still hang out their shingles in the traditional fashion. Bakery and *pâtisserie* competition on this street is fierce. Drop into one for the local specialties: *Nidlechueche,* a sweet, doughy cream tart (3.20 SF per slice); and *Seelander Zwetschen,* a chocolate-covered prune truffle with liqueur.

Near the top of the main street, **Simonet Weapons** sells all the latest knives by Victor Inox. There's the green stay-glow, and even a model with a memory stick for the outdoorsman with a laptop. At the top of the street (#16), Murten's oldest house has fine paintings under its eaves. There's some nice *Schmuck* (jewelry)

two doors to the right. Farther to the right, at the top of town, step into...

Murten Castle: The town castle, which houses the police station in a former prison (closed to the public), shows off an impressive gun from 1882 and a fine lake view. The nearby museum is not worth your time or money, but steps lead from there down to the lake.

ACTIVITIES

Lake Activities—To get down to Murten's lazy lakefront, find the access just past the castle, or, more centrally, at Rathausstrasse 17 (a block from Hotel Murtenhof). Just past the grassy breakwater is Pantschau, a big park. The park is flanked by cheap self-service eateries (such as La Chaloupe, with salad bar and crêpes) and the Beach House (with better lakeside seating). There's mini-golf,

windsurfing gear rental and instruction, a summer open-air film fest, and a fine lakeside promenade.

One-Hour Cruise (with Hiking Option): Promenade Tour du Lac trips go about six times a day through the summer (12 SF without stops, 16 SF with stopover privileges, 4/day Oct–April, call to confirm off-season, tel. 079-408-6635; TI can help).

Consider stopping in the small town of Praz on the French-speaking shore. From there, you have two good options: You could hike through vineyards up Mount Vully—where a bench and fine lake and Alp views await—and return on the lake with your same ticket. Or you can walk from Praz back to Murten, clockwise around the lake (2 hrs, 4 SF for boat from Murten to Praz).

Half-Day Three Lakes Cruise: Consider sailing on all three lakes of the region on a one-way, three-hour trip (involving one train connection). Boats leave the town of Biel (an easy train ride from Murten) daily at 9:30, cruise through Lake Biel, connect with canals to Lakes Neuchâtel and Murten, and stop at several small medieval villages along the way. The boat arrives in Murten at 12:40, then turns around and heads back along the same route at 14:15, arriving in Biel at 18:00 (one-way-38 SF, round-trip-74 SF but a 64 SF "day card" covers the trip, details at TI or call BSG, tel. 032-329-8811, www.bielersee.ch). There are two trips per day in each direction, each involving a Murten–Biel train connection (1/hr, 1-hr trip).

Swimming Pool—The Olympic-size public swimming pool is outside of town next to the lake, just past the castle (6 SF, daily July–Aug 9:00–19:00, early summer and fall 9:30–19:00).

Biking—The Three Lakes region has 100 miles of signposted bike paths (well described in TI's brochures). Pick up a free map or buy a top-notch one. The best easy ride circles the lake and Mount Vully (through vineyards and, if you like, to the summit for a good view). You can rent **bikes** at train station ticket counters (23 SF/half day, 30 SF/full day, with helmets, daily 6:30–23:00). Ask about being dropped off at the next station, which opens up a world of interesting options.

NIGHTLIFE

Movies—Murten's cute little community co-op theater plays movies nightly (15 SF, Schulgasse 18). Movies are shown in their original language (capital letter indicates the soundtrack language, small letters indicate subtitles—e.g., "Efd" means "English with French and *Deutsch* subtitles").

Theater am See hosts a summer lakeside cinema festival with outdoor screenings of a different movie each night (early July–early Aug, details at TI).

Pubs—There are plenty of inviting pubs and nightclubs in town. **Bar and Blumen** sells flowers by day (check out the Edelweiss), and drinks with a lake view by night (next to Town Hall and Hotel Murtenhof). The main street has an Irish bar and several other nightspots. The bar just outside the Bern Tower is popular with locals.

SLEEPING

(1.30 SF = about $1, country code: 41)
This adorable town is no secret. July through mid-September (especially on weekends) is peak time—make a reservation and expect maximum prices. When price ranges are given in the hotel listings, it means that prices vary depending on the season, type of room, or view.

For a youth hostel, you'll have to sleep in nearby Avenches (see page 108).

$$$ **Hotel Murtenhof,** a worthwhile splurge, has 21 nicely appointed rooms—each a stylish mix of old and new. This place is well run by the Joachim family—Theodore, Jutta, and their son Mark (Sb-110 SF, small Db-140, big Db-230 SF, Tb-200 SF, family rooms, mid-Sept–May ask for a 10 percent discount with this book through 2005, elevator, next to castle at Rathausgasse 1-3, tel. 026-672-9030, fax 026-672-9039, www.murtenhof.ch, info @murtenhof.ch). They have the best lakeview restaurant in town (see below).

$$$ **Hotel Krone** offers 35 decent rooms in a great location (Sb-90–110 SF, Db-130–140 SF, elevator, next door to Hotel Murtenhof at Rathausgasse 5, tel. 026-670-5252, fax 026-670-3610, www.krone-murten.ch, info@krone-murten.ch).

$$ **Hotel Ringmauer** (German for "Ramparts") is friendly and characteristic, with a fun mix of modern decor in a traditional setting. Showers and toilets are within a dash of all 14 rooms (S-60 SF, D-110 SF, Db-120 SF, T-150 SF, Q-165 SF, attached restaurant, near town wall farthest from lake, Deutsche Kirchgasse 2, tel. 026-670-1101, fax 026-672-2083).

$ **Berger Farmhouse** is the choice if "Green Acres is the place for you." Consider a night in a barn (literally) at the big, traditional Berger-Aegerter family farm. Frau Berger, who speaks German and French, fills a big room with six single beds (and can add up to 4 more). There's no plumbing—you use a bathroom in the family building next door. The place is generally empty, so you're likely to have it all to yourself—surrounded by hay, old farm tools, and the noise of animals (May–Nov only because there's no heat, 30 SF per bed with breakfast, she'll cook dinner for 15 SF by request, family deals, includes sheets but no towels, a third of the way to Avenches, a mile or so south of Murten, on the main road just before Greng, look for the sign, Lindenweg 2, tel. 026-670-1407).

EATING

Eating in Murten is a joy. I'd stroll the main drag up one side and down the other to survey the action before making a choice. For elegance and a lake view, it's the Murtenhof. There are several good options right on the lake a 10-minute walk from the town center. Budget eaters can picnic or find a salad bar. Bakeries make good sandwiches, but close by about 18:00.

Anything called "Seelander" or mentioning "three lakes" is typical of this Three Lakes region. Traditional restaurants serve *Egli-Filets,* the very popular perch "from the lake" (these days actually caught in Bodensee—Lake Constance in English—up by the German border). As this is the "vegetable garden of Switzerland," restaurants pride themselves on offering good veggies. You'll want a glass of wonderfully smooth and refreshing white Vully (voo-lee) wine with your meal (generally 3.20 SF per glass).

Restaurant Murtenhof, with a covered terrace giving diners a comfortable and classy lakeside setting, regardless of the weather, serves "updated Three Lakes cuisine." Sipping a glass of local white wine with the right travel partner, while gazing across the lake at hillside vineyards as the sun sets, is one of Europe's fine moments. Their fresh and tasty "catch of the day" (while not *Egli*) actually *is* from the lake (19 SF). To be sure you get the limited lakeside seating, call in a reservation at 026-672-9030 (has salad bar, March–Nov Tue–Sun 11:00–23:00, closed Mon and Dec–Feb). The recorded sheep baaah-ing on the soundtrack adds to the place's rustic elegance.

Ringmauer Restaurant is a good bet for French cuisine and deca-dent desserts, offering a dressy section (40-SF plates, 70-SF 5-course tasting *menu*) and a cheaper zone (30-SF plates). It has fine outdoor seating on a quiet, picturesque lane, but the indoor section can be smoky—a good sign, indicating it's a local favorite. They serve top-end local wine by the glass (Deutsche Kirchgasse 2, tel. 026-670-1101).

Fun-loving **Freiburger Falle** serves all the old *Fribourgeoise* traditions, such as meat on a hot stone (36 SF), fondue, and so on—in a characteristic cellar under the main street. You'll eat under an alphorn and castle-style chandeliers (it hides under the Irish pub at Hauptgasse 43, tel. 026-672-1222, Bruno Luscher).

Restaurant Anatolia is a Turkish place with crayon-quality menus posted everywhere and rather high prices for ethnic food. Still, it's much loved by locals for its fresh ingredients, good cooking, and charming owner, Mehmet. Eat indoors or out, with a fine main-drag view (20–25 SF, Hauptgasse 45, tel. 026-670-2868).

Restaurant Eintracht serves local cuisine from a fun menu, including old-time chef specials. If there is a down-and-dirty, horse-meat-cookin' local hangout in town, this is it (15- to 25-SF plates, half portions available, healthy specials, vineyard ambience or street-side seating, closed Wed, Hauptgasse 19, tel. 026-670-2240).

Grizzly's Restaurant, perfect for those in need of a quick trip back home, is a playful, enthusiastic place with an enticing menu of North American delicacies. The Yukon-chic interior comes with totem poles, buckskins, and rock and roll. The outside offers the finest seats on the main street (fresh salads, trappers' spare ribs, veg-etarian options, Tue–Sun 11:00–23:00, closed Mon, reservations smart, Hauptgasse 24, tel. 026-670-0787). As the menu says, "If the meal's not ready in 10 minutes, it will be in 15. If it's not on the table in 15 minutes, have another beer."

Pizza: Murten has two pizzerias. The one on the main street has better views, but locals prefer **Pizzeria Taverna Italiana** as a better value (17-SF daily specials, 20-SF pizza and pasta, 15-SF pizzas to go, daily 10:00–14:00 & 17:00–23:00, near Hotel Murtenhof at Kreuzgasse 4, tel. 026-670-2122).

Bakeries: The main street has four bakeries, all with ample charm. **Zuger** (at Hauptgasse 33) has a tea room and offers doily indoor seat-ing and pleasant outside seats. They have a reasonable salad bar (8-SF take-away, 10 SF for a plate at a table) as well as delicate, local-style, open-face sandwiches (Wed–Mon 7:00–18:30, closed Tue).

Supermarket: The giant **Co-op** (with a cafeteria) towers between the train station and city center (Mon–Thu 8:00–19:00, Fri 8:00–20:00, Sat 7:30–16:00, closed Sun).

TRANSPORTATION CONNECTIONS

From Murten by train to: Avenches (hrly, 10 min, direction: Payern), **Bern** (hrly, 30 min, most require a transfer in Kerzers), **Fribourg** in Switzerland (hrly, 30 min), **Lausanne** (hrly, 90 min, generally transfer in Fribourg). Train info: toll tel. 0900-300-3004.

Route Tips for Drivers

Murten to Lake Geneva (50 miles): The autobahn from Bern to Lausanne/Lake Geneva makes everything speedy (see Lake Geneva chapter). Murten and Avenches are 10 minutes off the autobahn. Broc, Bulle, and Gruyères are within sight of each other and the autobahn. It takes about an hour to drive from Murten to Montreux. The autobahn (direction: Simplon) takes you high above Montreux (pull off at great viewpoint rest stop) and Château de Chillon. For the castle, take the first exit east of the castle (Villeneuve). Signs direct you along the lake back to the castle.

Near Murten: Avenches

Avenches, four miles south of Murten, was once Aventicum, the Roman capital of Helvetica. Today, it's a quaint little town with an ancient theater taking a bite out of it. From the town spreads a vast field of sparse Roman ruins.

With a pleasant, small-town French ambience, Avenches (ah-vahnsh) is a quieter, less expensive place to stay than Murten. Just a few minutes away by train, it also makes an easy day trip. The **TI** (Mon–Fri 8:30–17:30, closed Sat afternoon and Sun, tel. 026-676-9922, www.avenches.ch) and the town are a seven-minute uphill walk from the station.

Roman Avenches

Aventicum was a Roman capital, with a population of 20,000. The Romans appreciated its strategic crossroads location, fertile land, and comfortable climate (several times voted "most livable place to retire"). While the population of today's Avenches could barely fill the well-worn ruins of their Roman amphitheater, Aventicum was once one of the largest cities of the Roman Empire. Everything sits on Roman ruins, which were nearly quarried to oblivion until the 19th century, when its scant remains were saved. Today, things are carefully preserved. Metal detectors must be registered here. Mothers, knowing that turning up

anything ancient will bring on the archaeologists, scream at their kids, "Don't dig!" Even the benches on the main street are bits of a 2,000-year-old temple cornice.

There are five Roman sights: the amphitheater, the museum, a sanctuary and a theater in a field outside of town, and a lone tower.

The **amphitheater,** or arena, which once seated 18,000, is the largest Roman ruin in Switzerland (free, always open). While the gladiator action is no more, it's still busy with an annual opera festival and other musical events. At the top of the amphitheater (just past the museum entrance), scan the surrounding countryside. All the farmland was once a walled Roman town of about 20,000 people. The **tower** on the ridge (on left)—the only one remaining of the original 73 towers—marks where the wall once stood. In the middle, past the lone standing column of the sanctuary, you can see the small theater ruins (see below).

The **Roman museum** fills a medieval tower attached to the amphitheater in town with three fascinating floors of Roman artifacts. Good students borrow the extensive English catalog, which affords a fairly intimate look at domestic life here back then. Don't miss the glass, mosaics, and a gold bust of Marcus Aurelius (A.D. 80) found in an old Roman sewer in 1939 (4 SF, covered by Swiss Museum Passport—see page 15, April–Sept Tue–Sun 10:00–12:00 & 13:00–17:00, closed Mon; Oct–March Tue–Sun 14:00–17:00, closed Mon).

Perhaps the best Aventicum experience is to spend some quiet time at sunset pondering the evocative **Roman theater** (Théâtre Romaine) and **sanctuary** in the fields, a half-mile walk out of town (free, always open, tiny free car park at the site). The single column marks "Du Cigognier"—nicknamed the "stork sanctuary" (c. 1700) for the stork nest it supported. As the site was a quarry until the 19th century, almost nothing remains.

SLEEPING

(1.30 SF = about $1, country code: 41)
$$$ **Hotel Couronne**—This Old World, three-star place with a modern interior sits grandly on the main square of little Avenches, where Yves and Isabelle Faivre rent 12 charming, bright rooms (Db-160–210 SF depending on size, next to TI, tel. 026-675-5414, www.lacouronne.ch).

$ Friendly **Elisabeth Clement-Arnold** rents a room in her house (D-50 SF first night, then 40 SF per night, no CC, bathroom is yours alone but down the hall, often nobody home until 19:00, reserve by e-mail, rue Centrale 5, tel. & fax 026-675-3031, eckadima@hotmail.com).

$ The Avenches **IYHF hostel,** the only hostel in the area, is a beauty. It's run by the Dhyaf family, has 4- to 10-bed rooms, and includes breakfast, a homey TV room, table tennis, a big backyard, and a very quiet setting near the Roman theater (32 SF for dorm bed in 4-bed room, 29 SF in 6- to 10-bed room, 36 SF per person for S or D and 34 SF per person for T when available, non-members pay 6 SF extra, office open 7:00–9:30 & 17:00–22:00, no curfew, 3 blocks from center at medieval *lavoir,* or laundry, Rue du Lavoir 5, tel. 026-675-2666, fax 026-675-2717, avenches@youthhostel.ch). If you're on a tight budget and have a car, this place is a great option.

GIMMELWALD
and the BERNER OBERLAND

Frolic and hike high above the stress and clouds of the real world. Take a vacation from your busy vacation. Recharge your touristic batteries high in the Alps, where distant avalanches, cowbells, the fluff of a down comforter, the screech of marmots, and the crunchy footsteps of happy hikers are the dominant sounds. If the weather's good (and your budget's healthy), ride a gondola from the traffic-free village of Gimmelwald to a hearty breakfast at Schilthorn's 10,000-foot-elevation, revolving Piz Gloria restaurant. Linger among Alpine whitecaps before riding, hiking, or parasailing down 5,000 feet to Mürren and home to Gimmelwald.

Your gateway to the rugged Berner Oberland is the grand old resort town of Interlaken. Near Interlaken is Switzerland's open-air folk museum, Ballenberg, where you can climb through traditional houses from every corner of this diverse country.

Ah, but the weather's fine and the Alps beckon. Head deep into the heart of the Alps and ride the gondola to the stop just this side of heaven—Gimmelwald.

Planning Your Time

Rather than tackle a checklist of famous Swiss mountains and resorts, choose one region to savor: the Berner Oberland.

Interlaken is the administrative headquarters and a fine trans-portation hub. Use it for business—banking, post office, laundry, shopping—and as a springboard for Alpine thrills. (Note that at higher altitudes, many hotels, restaurants, and shops are closed between Easter and late May.)

With decent weather, explore the two areas that tower above either side of the Lauterbrunnen Valley, south of Interlaken: Kleine Scheidegg/Jungfrau and Mürren/Schilthorn. To check the weather, call the Interlaken TI (tel. 033-826-5300), ask a local, or visit

www.swisspanorama.com (entire area), www.jungfraubahn.ch (for icy Jungfraujoch, accessed by train), and www.schilthorn.ch (for Schilthorn peak, accessed by lift).

The best overnight options are the rustic hamlet of Gimmelwald, the resort town of Mürren, or (for accommodations without the expense and headache of mountain lifts) the village of Lauterbrunnen, on the valley floor. Ideally, spend three nights, with a day exploring each side of the valley.

For the fastest look, consider a night in Gimmelwald, breakfast at the Schilthorn, an afternoon doing the Männlichen-Wengen hike, and an evening or night train out. What? A nature lover not spending the night high in the Alps? Alpus interruptus.

Getting Around the Berner Oberland

For more than 100 years, this region has been the target of nature-worshiping pilgrims. And Swiss engineers and visionaries have made the most exciting alpine perches accessible…

By Lifts and Trains: Part of the fun (and most of the expense) here is riding the many lifts. Generally, scenic trains and lifts are not covered by train passes, but a Eurailpass or Swiss railpass gives you a 25 percent discount on even the highest lifts (without the loss of a flexi-day of your pass). Ask about discounts for early-morning and late-afternoon trips, youths, seniors, families, groups, and those staying a while. The Junior Card for families pays for itself in the first hour of trains and lifts: Children under 16 travel free with parents (20 SF/1 child, 40 SF/2 or more children; available at Swiss train stations). Get a list of discounts and the free fare and time schedule at any Swiss train station. If you're staying a week, you can save money with the **Berner Oberland Pass** (includes all trains, buses, and lifts for 7 days, 220 SF).

Study the "Alpine Lifts in the Berner Oberland" chart on page 144. Lifts generally go at least twice hourly, from about 7:00 until about 20:00 (sneak preview: www.jungfrau.ch). For a complete schedule of all trains, lifts, buses, and boats, pick up the regional timetable (2 SF at any station).

By Car: Lauterbrunnen, Stechelberg, Isenfluh, and Interlaken are all accessible by car. You can't drive to Gimmelwald, Mürren, Wengen, or Kleine Scheidegg—but don't let that stop you from staying up in the mountains; park the car and zip up on a lift. To catch the lift to Gimmelwald, Mürren, and the Schilthorn, park at the gondola station in Stechelberg (2 SF/2 hrs, 6 SF/day, see page 126 for more information). To catch the train to Wengen or Kleine Scheidegg, park at the train station in Lauterbrunnen (2 SF/2 hrs, 9 SF/day).

Interlaken

When the 19th-century Romantics redefined mountains as something more than cold and troublesome obstacles, Interlaken became the original Alpine resort. Ever since, tourists have flocked to the Alps "because they're there." Interlaken's glory days are long gone, its elegant old hotels eclipsed by the new, more jet-setty Alpine resorts. Today, its shops are filled with chocolate bars, Swiss Army knives, and sunburned backpackers.

ORIENTATION

Efficient Interlaken (pop. 5,500) is a good administrative and shopping center. Take care of business, give the town a quick look, and view the live TV coverage of the Jungfrau and Schilthorn weather in the window of the Schilthornbahn office on the main street (at Höheweg 2). Then head for the hills. Stay in Interlaken only if you suffer from Alptitude sickness.

Tourist Information: The **TI** has good information for the region, advice on Alpine lift discounts, and a room-finding service (July–Sept Mon–Fri 8:00–18:30, Sat 8:00–17:00, Sun 10:00–12:00 & 16:00–18:00; Oct–June Mon–Fri 8:00–12:00 & 13:30–18:00, Sat 9:00–12:00, closed Sun; Höheweg 37, tel. 033-826-5300, www .interlakentourism.ch; attached to Hotel Metropole on the main street between West and East stations, a 10-min stroll from either). While the Interlaken/Jungfrau region map costs 2 SF, good mini-versions are included in the many free transportation and hiking brochures. Pick up a Bern map if that's your next destination. The TI organizes free daily walks at 17:00 in the summer (call to confirm).

Arrival in Interlaken

Interlaken has two train stations: East (Ost) and West. All trains stop at both the Ost and West stations. If heading for higher villages, get off at the Ost station. For hotels in Interlaken, get off at the West station. The West station also has a helpful and friendly train information desk (travel center for in-depth rail questions: Mon–Fri 8:00–18:00, Sat–Sun 8:00–12:00 & 14:00–18:00, Nov–March closed Mon–Fri 12:00–14:00; ticket windows open daily 6:00–20:45; tel. 033-826-4750). Ask about discount passes, special fares, railpass discounts, and schedules for the scenic mountain trains. There's a fair exchange booth next to the ticket windows (daily 6:30–20:00).

It's a pleasant 20-minute walk between the West and East stations, or there's an easy, frequent train connection (2/hr, 3.20 SF). From the Interlaken-Ost station, private trains take you deep into the mountainous Jungfrau region (see "Transportation Connections," page 125).

What's What in the Berner Oberland

Allmendhubel (AHL-mehnd-hoo-behl): Funicular from Mürren, leading to good hikes at the top (see page 137).

Ballenberg: Swiss Open-Air Folk Museum, on Lake Brienz (see page 120).

Berner Oberland: The mountainous part of the canton of Bern, sometimes referred to as "Jungfrau region." Everything else on this list is in the Berner Oberland.

Birg (beerg): Cable-car stop between Mürren and the Schilthorn, with a trail leading steeply down to Gimmelwald and more (see page 148).

Brienz (bree-ENTS): Lake on the east side of Interlaken (Brienzersee); also the name of a town on that lake.

Eiger (EYE-gehr): "Ogre," one of the three big mountains in the area (with the Mönch and Jungfrau); famous as a treacherous climbing destination.

First: Overlook point accessible by lift from Grindelwald; endpoint of hike from Schynige Platte (see page 154).

Gimmelwald (GIM-mehl-vahlt): Wonderfully rustic time-warp village overlooking the Lauterbrunnen Valley; good home-base option (see page 126).

Grindelwald (GRIN-dehl-vahlt): Expensive resort town, not to be confused with Gimmelwald.

Grütschalp (GREWTSH-alp): Station at the top of the funicular from Lauterbrunnen. It's connected by train and a trail to Mürren (see page 152).

Interlaken (IN-tehr-lah-kehn): Big town at the "entrance" to the Berner Oberland; you'll go through here to get anywhere else in this chapter (see page 113).

Jungfrau (YOONG-frow): "Maiden," the region's highest peak (13,642 feet).

Jungfraubahnen (YOONG-frow-bah-nehn): Company that runs all of the trains and lifts in the area (except for the Schilthorn).

Jungfraujoch (YOONG-frow-yoke): High-altitude (11,300 feet) observation deck near the Jungfrau peak, accessible by train from Kleine Scheidegg.

Kleine Scheidegg (KLY-neh SHY-dehk): Viewpoint with breathtaking Eiger, Mönch, and Jungfrau views; has several hotels and restaurants (see page 158), plus the train station that offers pricey rides to the Jungfraujoch (page 146).

Lauterbrunnen (LOUT-ehr-broo-nehn): Small town in the middle of the Lauterbrunnen Valley. From here, a funicular goes up to Grütschalp (with connections to Mürren and Gimmelwald) and the train runs up to Wengen and Kleine Scheidegg. For hotels and restaurants, see page 140.

Lauterbrunnen Valley: Valley at the heart of the Berner Oberland; most towns and activities in this chapter overlook this valley.

Männlichen (MAYN-likh-ehn): Overlook point with pastoral meadow and dramatic views, connected to Wengen and also to Grund (near Grindelwald) by lifts; also the starting point of an easy hike to Kleine Scheidegg with nonstop mountain views (see page 152).

Mönch (munkh): "Monk," one of the three major peaks of the region (along with Eiger and Jungfrau).

Mürren (MEW-rehn): Pleasant resort town near Gimmelwald, midway up the Schilthorn cable-car line; a good high-mountain home base for those who find Gimmelwald too small and rustic (see page 134).

Schilthorn (SHILT-horn): The 10,000-foot peak across the Lauterbrunnen Valley from the Jungfrau, reached by cable car from Stechelberg (in the valley), Mürren, and Gimmelwald; features spectacular views and the Piz Gloria revolving restaurant made famous by James Bond (see page 142).

Schilthornbahn: Cable-car company that operates the lift on the west side of the Lauterbrunnen Valley, connecting Stechelberg (on the valley floor) with Gimmelwald, Mürren, Birg, and the Schilthorn.

Schynige Platte (SHIH-nih-geh PLAH-teh): High-altitude observation point near the entrance to Lauterbrunnen Valley, reached by funicular from Wilderswil; starting point of a long but scenic hike to First (see page 154).

Sefinen Valley (seh-FEE-nehn): Branches off the Lauterbrunnen Valley beyond Stechelberg and Gimmelwald; good for a hike (see page 149).

Stechelberg (SHTEH-khehl-behrk): At the end of the Lauterbrunnen Valley, it's the starting point of the cable car leading up to Gimmelwald, Mürren, and on to the Schilthorn (for accommodations, see page 126).

Thun (toon): Lake to the west of Interlaken (Thunersee), and the name of a town on that lake.

Trümmelbach (TREW-mehl-bahkh): Striking series of waterfalls near Lauterbrunnen (see page 156).

Wengen (VAYNG-ehn): Resort town on Jungfrau side of Lauterbrunnen Valley; on the train line between Lauterbrunnen and Kleine Scheidegg (for hotels, see page 157).

Wilderswil (VIHL-dehrs-vihl): Village near entrance of the Lauterbrunnen Valley; home of lackluster Mystery Park; on the train line between Interlaken and Lauterbrunnen; has funicular to Schynige Platte and trailhead to First (see page 154).

Interlaken

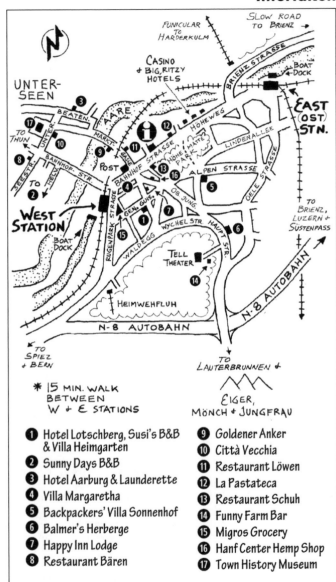

* 15 MIN. WALK
  BETWEEN
  W + E STATIONS

1 Hotel Lotschberg, Susi's B&B & Villa Heimgarten
2 Sunny Days B&B
3 Hotel Aarburg & Launderette
4 Villa Margaretha
5 Backpackers' Villa Sonnenhof
6 Balmer's Herberge
7 Happy Inn Lodge
8 Restaurant Bären
9 Goldener Anker
10 Città Vecchia
11 Restaurant Löwen
12 La Pastateca
13 Restaurant Schuh
14 Funny Farm Bar
15 Migros Grocery
16 Hanf Center Hemp Shop
17 Town History Museum

Helpful Hints

Warning: On Sundays and holidays, small-town Switzerland is quiet. Hotels are open, and lifts and trains run, but many stores are closed.

Telephone: Phone booths cluster outside the post office near the West station. For efficiency, buy a phone card from a newsstand or train station ticket window. (Gimmelwald's sole public phone—at the gondola station—takes only cards, not coins.)

Laundry: Friendly Helen Schmocker's *Wäscherei* has a change machine, soap, English instructions, and a riverside location (open daily 7:00–22:00 for self-service; for full service: Mon–Fri 8:00–12:00 & 13:30–18:00, Sat 8:00–16:00, closed Sun, drop off in the morning and pick up that afternoon, from the main street take Marktgasse over 2 bridges to Beatenbergstrasse 5, tel. 033-822-1566).

Local Guidebook: Don Chmura's Lauterbrunnen guidebook gives history, folk life, flora, fauna, and hiking information (sold throughout the Lauterbrunnen Valley, 8 SF).

Stores: The Migros supermarket is across the street from Interlaken-West train station (Mon–Thu 8:00–18:30, Fri 8:00–21:00, Sat 7:30–16:00, closed Sun). The **Co-op Pronto** mini-market has longer hours (daily 6:00–22:00, across from TI). As Switzerland attempts to buck American pressure and decriminalize pot, there's a buzz surrounding Interlaken's **Hanf Center,** a small shop selling a wide selection of products made from hemp, including clothes, paper, noodles, tea, and beer (Mon 13:30–18:30, Tue–Fri 10:00–12:00 & 13:30–18:30, Sat 10:00–16:00, closed Sun, Rosenstrasse 5, near end of Höhematte Park closest to West station, tel. 033-823-1552).

Interlaken Town Walk

Most visitors use Interlaken as a springboard for high-altitude thrills (and rightly so). But the town itself has history and scenic charm, and is worth a short walk. This 45-minute stroll circles from the West train station down the main drag to the big meadow, past the casino, along the river to the oldest part of town (historically a neighboring town called Unterseen), and back to the station.

Bahnhofstrasse: This main drag, which turns into Höheweg as it continues east, cuts straight through the town center from the West train station to the East. The best Swiss souvenir shopping is along this Bahnhofstrasse stretch (things get more expensive on the Höheweg stretch, near the fancy hotels). Tchibo makes the best take-away coffee in town (Starbucks-style). At the roundabout is the handy post office and Loeb, Interlaken's only department store. Just behind the post office on Marktgasse, the hardware store stocks real cowbells (both ornate and plain). At Höheweg 2, the TV in the window of the Schilthornbahn office shows the weather up top.

Höhematte Park: This "high meadow," or Höhematte (but generally referred to simply as "the park"), marks the beginning of Interlaken's fancy hotel row. Hotels like the Victoria-Jungfrau hearken back to the days when Interlaken was *the* original Alpine resort. The first grand hotels were built here to enjoy the views of the Jungfrau in the distance. (Today, the Jungfraus getting the most attention are next door, at Hooters.)

The park originated as farmland of the monastery that predated the town (marked today by the steeples of both the Catholic and Protestant churches—neither of any sightseeing interest). The actual **monastery site** is now home to the City Hall, courthouse, and city administration building. With the Reformation in 1528, the monastery was shut down and its land was taken by the state. Later, when the land was being eyed by developers, the town's leading hotels and business families bought it and established that it would never be used for commercial buildings (a very early example of smart town planning). There was talk of building a parking lot under it, but the water table here, between the two lakes, is too high. Today, this is a fine place to stroll, hang out on the park benches or at Restaurant Schuh, and watch the parasailors gracefully land.

From the park, turn left into the grounds of **Casino Kursaal** where, at the top of each hour, dwarfs ring the toadstools on the flower clock. The Kursaal, originally a kind of 19th-century fat farm, is now both a casino (passport but no tie required) and a convention center that hosts musical events and nightly folklore shows through the summer (fun yodeling with lots of audience participation, details at the TI).

Follow the path left of the Kursaal to the river (huge public swimming pool just over the river). Walk downstream under the train track and cross the pedestrian bridge, stopping in the middle to enjoy the view.

Aare River: The Aare River is Switzerland's longest. It connects Lake Brienz and Lake Thun (with an 18-foot altitude difference—this short stretch has quite a flow). Then it tumbles out of Lake Thun, heading for Bern and ultimately into the Rhine. Its level is controlled by several sluices. In the distance, a church bell tower marks a different parish and the neighborhood of Unterseen, which shares the town's name, but in German: "Unterseen" is German for "Interlaken" (which is Latin for "between the lakes"). Behind the spire is the pointy summit of the Niesen (like so many Swiss peaks, capped with a restaurant and accessible by a lift). Stroll downstream along the far side of the river to the church spire. The delightful riverside walk is lined by fine residences. Notice that now your Jungfrau view includes the Jungfraujoch observation deck (the little brown bump in the ridge just left of the peak).

Unterseen: At the next bridge, turn right to the town square lined with 17th-century houses on one side and a modern strip on the other. Unterseen was a town when Interlaken was only a monastery. The church is not worth touring. A block away, the (generally empty) **Town History Museum** shows off classic posters, fascinating photos of the construction of the Jungfraujoch, and exhibits on folk life, crafts, and winter sports—all well-described in English (5 SF, May–mid-Oct Tue–Sun 14:00–17:00, closed Mon and mid-Oct–April, Obergasse 26).

Return to Station: From Unterseen, cross the river on Spielmatte, and you're a few minutes' walk from your starting point. On the second bridge, notice the border between the two towns, or parishes, marked by their respective heraldic emblems (each with an ibex, or wild mountain goat). A block or so later, on the left, is the Marktplatz. The river originally ran through this square. The town used to be called "Aaremühle" ("Aare mill") for the mill that was here. But in the 19th century, town fathers made a key marketing decision: Since "Aaremühle" was too difficult for English tourists to pronounce, they changed the name to "Interlaken."

SIGHTS AND ACTIVITIES

Near Interlaken

Boat Trips—"Interlaken" is literally "between the lakes" of Thun and Brienz. You can explore these lakes on a lazy boat trip (8/day mid-June–mid-Sept, fewer off-season, free with Eurail/Eurail Selectpass but uses a flexi-day, schedules at TI or at BLS Travel Center in West station, tel. 033-826-4750 or 033-334-5211). The boats on **Lake Thun** (10/day, 2 hrs to Thun, 4 hrs return, 40 SF round-trip) stop at the St. Beatus Höhlen caves (30 min away, see below) and two visit-worthy towns: Spiez (1 hr) and Thun (1.75 hrs). The boats on **Lake Brienz** (3 hrs, 32 SF round-trip) stop at the super-cute village of Iseltwald (45 min away) and at Brienz (1.25 hrs away, near Ballenberg Open-Air Folk Museum—described below).

St. Beatus Höhlen caves on Lake Thun can be visited with a guided tour (2/hr, 60-min tours, 16 SF, April–mid-Oct daily 10:30–17:00, closed mid-Oct–March, tel. 033-841-1643, www .beatushoehlen.ch). The best excursion plan: Ride the bus from Interlaken (20-min ride, line #21, depart West station at :45 past the hour); tour the caves; take the short, steep hike down to lake; and return by boat (30 min to Interlaken, see above).

Adventure Trips—For the adventurer with money and little concern for personal safety, several companies offer high-adrenaline trips such as rafting, canyoning (rappelling down watery gorges), bungee jumping, and paragliding. Costs range from 90 SF to 190 SF (river rafting-95 SF, paragliding-160 SF, hang gliding-185 SF). Interlaken companies include Alpin Raft (tel. 033-823-4100, www.alpinraft.ch), Alpin Center (at Wilderswil station and across from Balmer's youth hostel, tel. 033-823-5523, www.alpincenter.ch), and Outdoor Interlaken (tel. 033-826-7719, www.outdoor-interlaken.ch). For an overview of your options, visit www.interlakenadventure.com or study the racks of brochures at most TIs and hotels (everyone's getting a cut of this lucrative industry).

Recent fatal accidents jolted the adventure-sport business in the Berner Oberland, leading to a more professional respect for the risks involved. In May 2000, an American died bungee jumping from the Stechelberg-Mürren gondola (the operator used a 180-meter rope for a 100-meter jump). In July 1999, 21 tourists died canyoning on the Saxetenbach River, 10 miles from Interlaken; they were battered and drowned by a flash flood filled with debris. (The monument just outside Wilderswil on the Saxeten Road is stirring.) Enjoying nature up close comes with risks. Adventure sports increase those risks dramatically. Use good judgment.

River Rafting: The three-hour Grindelwald-to-Zweilutschinen rafting trips (offered by all the adventure companies) are most exciting. Swiss Adventures is the only outfit leading raft tours down the Aare River from Thun to Bern (2–3 hrs, no white water, tel. 033-773-7373, www.swissadventures.ch).

Helicopter Touring: Air-Glaciers of Lauterbrunnen offers short and pricey tours with landings on glaciers. If you have more money than time, or can assemble a group of four to six tourists to split the cost and lower the price, this might be worth considering. Trips cost 100 SF to 400 SF, depending on the duration and number of people (tel. 033-856-0560, www.airglaciers.ch).

▲▲**Swiss Open-Air Folk Museum at Ballenberg**—Across Lake Brienz from Interlaken, the Swiss Open-Air Museum of Vernacular Architecture, Country Life, and Crafts in the Bernese Oberland is a rich collection of traditional and historic farmhouses from every region of the country. Each house is carefully furnished, and many feature traditional craftspeople at work. The sprawling 50-acre park, laid out roughly as a huge Swiss map (Italian Swiss in the south, Appenzell in the east, and so on), is a natural preserve providing a wonderful setting for this culture-on-a-lazy-Susan look at Switzerland.

The Thurgau house (#621) has an interesting wattle-and-daub (half-timbered construction) display, and house #331 has a fun bread museum and farmers' shop. There's cheesemaking (near the east entry), traditional farm animals (like very furry-legged roosters, near the merry-go-round in the center), and a chocolate shop (under the restaurant on the east side).

An outdoor cafeteria with reasonable prices is inside the west entrance, and fresh bread, sausage, mountain cheese, and other goodies are on sale in several houses. Picnic tables and grills with free firewood are scattered throughout the park.

The little wooden village of Brienzwiler (near the east entrance) is a museum in itself, with a lovely pint-sized church.

Cost, Hours, Information: 16 SF, half price after 16:00, covered by Swiss Museum Passport—see page 15. A RailAway combo-ticket, available at either Interlaken station, includes transportation to and from Ballenberg and your admission (32 SF from West, 30.40 SF from Ost, add 9.40 SF to return by boat instead). The houses are open May–Oct daily 10:00–17:00, but the park stays open later. Craft demonstration schedules are listed just inside entry. Use the 2-SF map/guide. The more expensive picture book is a better souvenir than guide. Tel. 033-952-1030, www.ballenberg.ch.

Getting There from Interlaken: Take the train from Interlaken to Brienz (hrly, 30 min, 7.20 SF one-way from West station). From Brienz, catch a bus to Ballenberg (10 min, 3 SF one-way) or hike (45 min, slightly uphill). Consider returning by boat (Brienz boat dock next to train station, one-way to Interlaken-16 SF). Trains also run occasionally from Interlaken to Brienzwiler, a 20-min uphill walk to the museum (every 2 hrs, 30 min, 9.20 SF one-way from West station).

Castles and Forts—There are a few impressively well-kept and welcoming old castles in the Interlaken area, worth considering for day trips by boat, bus, or car.

Thun Castle (Schloss Thun), built between 1180 and 1190 by the Dukes of Zähringer, has a five-floor historical museum offering insights into the cultural development of the region over a period of some 4,000 years. From the corner turrets of the castle, you are rewarded with a spectacular view of the city of Thun, the lake, and the Alps (7 SF, April–Oct daily 10:00–17:00, Feb–March daily 13:00–16:00, Nov–Jan Sun only 13:00–16:00, www.schlossthun.ch).

Hünegg Castle (Schloss Hünegg) in Hilterfingen (further along Lake Thun, towards Interlaken) contains a museum exhibiting furnished rooms from the second half of the 19th century. The castle is situated in a beautiful wooded park (mid-May–mid-Oct Mon–Sat 14:00–17:00, Sun 10:00–12:00 & 14:00–17:00, closed off-season, www.schlosshuenegg.ch).

Oberhofen Castle (Schloss Oberhofen) is for those interested in gardens. Its beautifully landscaped park with exotic trees is a delight (free, open mid-March–mid-Nov daily from 9:00 until dusk, closed in winter). The museum in the castle depicts domestic life in the 16th through 19th centuries, including a Turkish smoking room and a medieval chapel (7 SF, open mid-May–mid-Oct Mon 14:00–17:00, Tue–Sun 11:00–17:00, closed off-season).

For a more modern fort, consider visiting the **World War II Swiss Infantry Bunker** in Beatenbucht. From the cable car station there, walk uphill for five minutes to the first bend, keep straight for 10 yards, and walk behind the camouflage at the first right turn.

Mystery Park—This theme park in Wilderswil (just south of Interlaken) ranks as a low sightseeing priority, even in bad weather. The park has modest exhibits on seven themes that explore the world's mysteries, from the construction of Stonehenge (with an impressive laser-light show that is the park's highlight) to the challenge of maintaining a space station on Mars (48 SF, daily 10:00–18:00, tel. 033-827-5757, www.mysterypark.ch). A free shuttle bus takes you to the park from Interlaken's Ost station every 30 minutes.

NIGHTLIFE

For counterculture with a reggae beat, check out **Funny Farm** (past Balmer's Youth Hostel, in Matten). The young frat-party dance scene rages at **Balmer's Metro Bar** (their bomb-shelter disco bar thrives, with cheap drinks and a friendly if loud atmosphere). For a stylish wine bar with local yuppies, check in at the **Vinothek,** across from Città Vecchia in Unterseen (see "Eating," below). If you can't sleep and are waiting for your prunes, try **Restaurant Schuh** on the park.

SLEEPING

I'd head for Gimmelwald, or at least Lauterbrunnen (20 min by train or car). Interlaken is not the Alps. But if you must stay…

$$$ Hotel Lotschberg, with a sun terrace and 21 wonderful rooms, is run by English-speaking Susi and Fritz and is the best real hotel value in town. Happy to dispense information, these gregarious folks pride themselves on a personal touch that sets them apart from other hotels (Sb-112 SF, Db-155 SF, big Db-175 SF, extra bed-25 SF, family deals, rates about 15 percent cheaper mid-Oct–April, closed Nov and Jan, non-smoking, elevator, Internet access, laundry service, bike rental; 5-min walk from West station: leaving station, turn right, after Migros at the circle go left to General Guisanstrasse 31; tel. 033-822-2545, fax 033-822-2579, www.lotschberg.ch, hotel@lotschberg.ch). Effervescent Fritz loves organizing guided adventures. He tandem parasails almost every day with one of his guests (guests "Fly with Fritz" at a discount, about 20 SF cheaper than any other deal in town).

$$ Guest House Susi's B&B is Hotel Lotschberg's no-frills, cash-only annex, run by Fritz and Susi, offering nicely furnished, cozy rooms (Sb-95 SF, Db-125 SF, apartments with kitchenettes for 2 people-100 SF; for 4–5 people-180 SF, prices about 20 percent cheaper mid-Oct–April, closed Nov and Jan, same contact information as Hotel Lotschberg, above).

Sleep Code

(1.30 SF = about $1, country code: 41)
S = Single, **D** = Double/Twin, **T** = Triple, **Q** = Quad,
b = bathroom, **s** = shower only, **no CC** = Credit Cards not
accepted, **SE** = Speaks English, **NSE** = No English. Unless otherwise noted, credit cards are accepted, English is spoken, and
breakfast is included.

To help you sort easily through these listings, I've divided
the rooms into three categories, based on the price for a standard
double room with bath:

$$$ **Higher Priced**—Most rooms 150 SF or more.
$$ **Moderately Priced**—Most rooms between 90–150 SF.
$ **Lower Priced**—Most rooms 90 SF or less.

$$ Villa Heimgarten is a fine house from 1902 in a quiet and
handy location, renting seven basic rooms for a good price. While
not particularly warm, it's a fine value (Sb-45–55 SF, Db-90–110
SF, higher prices are for June–Aug, garden, playground, 5 min from
West Station, across from Hotel Lotschberg at Bernastrasse 7, tel.
033-822-7477, fax 033-822-7479, www.villaheimgarten.ch, info
@villaheimgarten.com).

$$ Sunny Days B&B, a homey, nine-room place in a residential neighborhood, is run by Dave from Britain (Sb-98–110 SF, Db-
110–148 SF, prices vary with season and view, extra bed about 40
SF, Nov–March all rooms 100 SF; exit left out of West station and
take first bridge to your left, after crossing the bridges turn left on
Helvetiastrasse and go 3 blocks to #29; tel. 033-822-8343, fax 033-
823-8343, www.sunnydays.ch, mail@sunnydays.ch).

$$ Hotel Aarburg offers 13 plain, peaceful rooms in a beauti-
fully located but run-down old building a 10-minute walk from the
West station (Sb-70 SF, Db-120 SF, next to launderette at Beaten-
bergstrasse 1, tel. 033-822-2615, fax 033-822-6397, hotel-aarburg
@tcnet.ch).

$ Villa Margaretha, run by English-speaking Frau Kunz-
Joerin, offers the best cheap beds in town. It's like grandma's big
Victorian house on a quiet residential street. Keep your room tidy,
and you'll have a friend for life (D-86 SF, T-129 SF, Q-172 SF, the
3 rooms share a big bathroom, 2-night minimum, closed Oct–April,
no CC, no breakfast served but dishes and kitchenette available, lots
of rules to abide by, go up small street directly in front of West sta-
tion to Aarmühlestrasse 13, tel. 033-822-1813).

$ Backpackers' Villa (Sonnenhof) Interlaken is a creative guest
house run by a Methodist church group. It's fun, youthful, and great for
families, without the frat-party ambience of Balmer's (listed below).

Travelers of any age feel comfortable here. Rooms are comfy, and half come with Jungfrau-view balconies (D-88 SF, T-120 SF, Q-144 SF, dorm beds in 5- to 7-bed rooms with lockers and sheets-32 SF per person, 5 SF more per person for rooms with toilets and Jungfrau-view balconies, includes breakfast, kitchen, garden, movies, small game room, Internet access, laundry, bike rental, no curfew, open all day but reception open only 7:00–11:00 & 16:00–22:00, 10-min walk from either station, across the park from TI, Alpenstrasse 16, tel. 033-826-7171, fax 033-826-7172, www.villa.ch, mail@villa.ch).

$ **Balmer's Herberge** is many people's idea of backpacker heaven. This Interlaken institution comes with movies, table tennis, a cheap launderette (4 SF/load), bar, restaurant, swapping library, Internet access, tiny grocery, bike rental, excursions, a shuttle-bus service (which meets important arriving trains), and a friendly, hard-working staff. This little Nebraska is home for those who miss their fraternity. It can be a mob scene, especially on summer weekends (dorm beds-24 SF, S-40 SF; D, T, or Q-30–34 SF per person; includes sheets and breakfast, non-smoking rooms, open year-round, easy Internet reservations recommended 5 days in advance except for dorm beds, Hauptstrasse 23, in Matten, 15-min walk from either Interlaken station, tel. 033-822-1961, fax 033-823-3261, www .balmers.com, balmers@tcnet.ch).

$ **Happy Inn Lodge** has 15 cheap backpacker rooms above a lively, noisy restaurant a five-minute walk from the West station (S-38 SF, D-76 SF, bunk in 4- to 8-bed dorm-22 SF, breakfast-8 SF, Rosenstrasse 17, tel. 033-822-3225, fax 033-822-3268, www .happyinn.com, info@happyinn.com).

EATING

In Unterseen, the Old Town across the River

Restaurant Bären, in a classic low-ceilinged building with cozy indoor and fine outdoor seating, is a great value for *Rösti*, fondue, raclette, fish, traditional sausage, and salads (20-SF plates, open daily except closed Mon off-season, from West station turn left on Bahnhofstrasse and go over the river a block to Seestrasse 2, tel. 033-822-7526).

Goldener Anker is the local hangout—smoky, with a pool table and a few unsavory types. If you thought Interlaken was sterile, you haven't been here. Jeannette serves and Rene cooks, just as they have for 25 years (hearty 20-SF salads, fresh vegetables, 3 courses for 17 SF, Marktgasse 57, tel. 033-822-1672). This place sometimes hosts small concerts, and has launched some of Switzerland's top bands.

Città Vecchia serves the best Italian food in town, with seating indoors or out, on a leafy square (pizza-15 SF, pasta-20 SF, plates-30 SF, Italian wines, open daily except closed Tue off-season, on main square in Unterseen at Untere Gasse 5, tel. 033-822-1754, Rinaldo).

On or near the Main Drag

Restaurant Löwen has an inviting terrace with reasonably priced food. If Goldener Anker, above, has too much character (or too many characters), this is a more relaxing bet—especially when it's hot and you want to sit outside (dinners for 15–20 SF, open daily, a block behind the post office at Marktplatz 10, tel. 033-821-0505).

La Pastateca, at the top hotel in town (Victoria-Jungfrau), is *très* elegant. To sit on its terrace and watch the Jungfrau is one of the great Interlaken treats. To do it affordably, go with the super antipasto buffet (all you like from a huge spread of Italian-style treats, including lots of meat and seafood, 25 SF), or come for the "business lunch" (the buffet, plus a pasta of your choice, great bread and olive oil, bottled water, and coffee for 27 SF, available Mon–Fri 11:30–14:00). The service is formal and can be slow (daily 11:30–23:00, a block past TI, facing the park, tel. 033-828-2620).

Restaurant Schuh, formerly the Grand Café Schuh, retains its grand-café ambience on the best real estate in town (at the corner of the park, across from Hotel Metropole and TI). Meals are disappointing, but desserts are wonderful, and there's no better place to nurse a drink or coffee and watch the parasailors glide into the park (live schmaltzy music, newspapers, elegant indoor and outdoor seating).

TRANSPORTATION CONNECTIONS

If you plan to arrive at the Zürich Airport and want to head straight for Interlaken and the Alps, see the Zürich chapter (page 38). Note that Interlaken is connected to Luzern and Montreux (on Lake Geneva) via the Golden Pass scenic rail route (see Scenic Rail Journeys chapter). Train info: toll tel. 0900-300-3004 (www.rail.ch).

From Interlaken by train to: Lauterbrunnen (hrly, 30 min, 9 SF each way), **Spiez** (2/hr, 20 min), **Brienz** (hrly, 30 min), **Bern** (hrly, 50 min), **Zürich** and **Zürich Airport** (hrly, 2.25 hrs, most direct but some with transfer in Bern), **Luzern** (hrly, 2 hrs). While there are a few long trains from Interlaken, you'll generally connect from Bern.

From Bern by train to: Lausanne (2/hr, 70 min), **Murten** (hrly, 30 min, most transfer in Kerzers), **Zürich** (2/hr, 70 min), **Zermatt** (hrly, 3.5 hrs, transfer in Brig), **Appenzell** (hrly, 3.25 hrs, transfer in Gossau), **Munich** (4/day, 5.5 hrs), **Frankfurt** (hrly, 4.5 hrs), **Salzburg** (4/day, 7.25 hrs, transfer in Zürich), **Paris** (4/day, 4.5 hrs).

From Interlaken to Gimmelwald

By public transportation: Take the train from the Interlaken Ost station to Lauterbrunnen. From here, you have two options.

1. The faster, easier way—best in bad weather or at the end of a long day with lots of luggage—is to ride the post bus from

Lauterbrunnen station (4 SF, hrly bus departure coordinated with arrival of train, stop: Schilthornbahn) to Stechelberg and the base of the Schilthornbahn gondola station, where the gondola will whisk you in five thrilling minutes up to Gimmelwald (7.80 SF, departing at :25 and :55).

2. The more scenic route is to ride the train to Lauterbrunnen and catch the funicular to Mürren (across the street from the train station). Ride up to Grütschalp, where a special scenic train *(Panorama Fahrt)* will roll you along the cliff into Mürren (total trip from Lauterbrunnen to Mürren: 30 min, 9.80 SF). From there, either walk a paved 30 minutes downhill to Gimmelwald, or walk 10 minutes across Mürren to catch the gondola down to Gimmelwald (costs 7.80 SF).

By car: You can drive to Lauterbrunnen and to Stechelberg, but not to Gimmelwald (park in Stechelberg and take the gondola) or to Mürren, Wengen, or Kleine Scheidegg (park in Lauterbrunnen and take the train/funicular). For drivers, the most direct route to Gimmelwald is via the gondola at Stechelberg. It's a 30-minute drive from Interlaken to the Stechelberg gondola station (parking lot: 2 SF/2 hrs, 6 SF/day). Gimmelwald is the first stop above Stechelberg on the Schilthorn gondola (7.80 SF, 2/hr at :25 and :55). Note that for a week in early May and from mid-November through early December, the Schilthornbahn is closed for servicing. During this time, you'll ride the cargo cable car directly from Stechelberg to Mürren, where a small bus shuttles you down to Gimmelwald.

Gimmelwald

Saved from developers by its "avalanche zone" classification, Gimmelwald was (before tourism) one of the poorest places in Switzerland. Its traditional economy was stuck in the hay, and its farmers, unable to make it in their disadvantaged trade, survived only by Swiss government subsidies (and working the ski lifts in the

winter). For some travelers, there's little to see in the village. Others (like me) enjoy a fascinating day sitting on a bench and learning why they say, "If Heaven isn't what it's cracked up to be, send me back to Gimmelwald."

Take a walk through the town. While its population has dropped in the last century from 200 to about 100 residents, traditions survive.

Most Gimmelwalders have one of two last names: von Allmen or Feutz. They are tough and proud. Raising hay in this rugged terrain is labor-intensive. One family harvests enough to feed only about 15 cows. But they'd have it no other way, and, unlike the absentee-landlord town of Mürren, Gimmelwald is locally owned. (When word got out that urban planners wished to develop Gimmelwald into a town of 1,000, locals pulled some strings to secure the town's bogus avalanche-zone building code.) Those same folks are happy the masses go to touristy and commercialized Grindelwald, just over the Kleine Scheidegg ridge. Don't confuse Gimmelwald and Grindelwald—they couldn't be more different.

ORIENTATION

The huge, sheer cliff face that dominates your mountain views from Gimmelwald is the Schwarzmönch ("Black Monk"). The three peaks above (or behind) it are, left to right, the Eiger, Mönch, and Jungfrau.

A Walk Through Gimmelwald

Gimmelwald, though tiny, with one zigzag street, gives a fine look at a traditional mountain Swiss community. Here's a quick walking tour:

Gondola Station: When the lift came in the 1960s, the village's back end became its front door. Gimmelwald was, and still is, a farm village. Stepping off the gondola, you see a sweet little hut. Set on stilts to keep out mice, the hut was used for storing cheese (the rocks on the rooftop keep the shingles on through wild winter winds). Behind the cheese hut stands the village schoolhouse. In Catholic Swiss towns, the biggest building is the church. In Protes-

tant towns, it's the school. Gimmelwald's biggest building is the school (2 teachers share one teaching position, 17 students, and a room that doubles as a chapel when the Protestant pastor makes his monthly visit). Don't let Gimmelwald's low-tech look fool you: In this school, each kid has his or her own Web site. In the opposite direction, just beyond the little playground, is Gimmelwald's Mountain Hostel (listed below).

Walk up the lane 50 yards, past the shower in the phone booth, to Gimmelwald's...

"Times Square": The yellow Alpine "street sign" shows where you are, the altitude (4,470 feet), and how many hours *(Std.)* and minutes it takes to walk to nearby points. Most of the buildings used

Gimmelwald

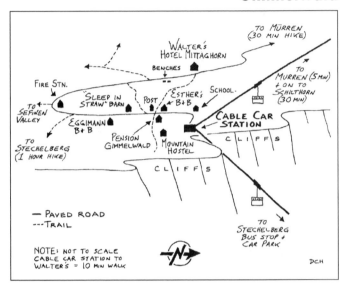

TO MÜRREN
(30 MIN HIKE)

WALTER'S
HOTEL MITTAGHORN

BENCHES

TO
MÜRREN (5MIN)
+ ON TO
SCHILTHORN
(30 MIN)

FIRE STN.

"SLEEP IN
STRAW" BARN

POST

ESTHER'S
B+B

SCHOOL

TO
SEFINEN
VALLEY

EGGIMANN
B+B

CABLE CAR
STATION

C L I F F S

TO
STECHELBERG
(1 HOUR HIKE)

PENSION
GIMMELWALD

MOUNTAIN
HOSTEL

C L I F F S

— PAVED ROAD
--- TRAIL

TO
STECHELBERG
BUS STOP +
CAR PARK

NOTE: NOT TO SCALE
CABLE CAR STATION TO
WALTER'S = 10 MIN WALK

N

DCH

to house two families and are divided vertically right down the middle. The writing on the post office building is a folksy blessing: "Summer brings green, winter brings snow. The sun greets the day, the stars greet the night. This house will keep you warm. May God give us his blessings." The date indicates when it was built or rebuilt (1911). Gimmelwald has a strict building code. For instance, shutters can only be natural, green, or white. Esther's farmer shop (10 yards uphill, always open, buy things on the honor system) is worth a look. From this tiny intersection, we'll follow the town's main street (away from gondola station).

Main Street: Walk up the road. Notice the announcement board: one side for tourist news, the other for local news. Cross the street and peek into the big new barn, dated 1995. This is part of the Sleep in Straw association, which rents out barn spots to travelers when the cows are in the high country. To the left of the door is a cow-scratcher. Swiss cows have legal rights (for example, in the winter, they must be taken out for exercise at least 3 times a week). This big barn is built in a modern style. Traditionally, barns were small (like those on the hillside high above) and closer to the hay. But with trucks and paved roads, hay can be moved more easily, and farm businesses need more cows to be viable. Still, even a well-run big farm hopes just to break even. The industry survives only with government subsidies (see "Swiss Cow Culture" sidebar, page 130). Go just beyond the next barn. On your right is the...

Water Fountain/Trough: This is the site of the town's historic water supply. Local kids love to bathe and wage water wars in this when the cows aren't drinking from it. From here, detour left down a lane about 50 yards (along a wooden fence and past pea-patch gardens) to the next trough and the oldest building in town, Husmättli, from 1658. (The town's 17th-century buildings are mostly on the road zigzagging below town.) Study the log-cabin construction. Many are built without nails. The wood was logged up the valley and cut on the water-powered village mill (also below town). Gimmelwald heats with wood and, since the wood needs to age a couple of years to burn well, it's stacked everywhere.

Back on the paved road, continue uphill. Notice the cute cheese hut on the right (with Alpine cheese for sale). It's full of strong cheese—up to three years old. On the left (at the B&B sign) is the home of Olle and Maria, the village schoolteachers. Maria runs the Lilliput shop (the "smallest shop with the greatest gifts"—handmade delights from the town and region, just ring the bell and meet Maria). Her son does a booming trade in sugar-coated almonds; her daughter competes with cookies. Fifty yards farther along is the...

Alpenrose: At the old schoolhouse, notice the big ceremonial cowbells hanging under the uphill eave. These swing from the necks of cows during the procession from the town to the high Alps (mid-June) and back down (around Sept 20). If the cows are gone, so are the bells—hanging from similar posts under the eves of mountain huts in the high meadows.

Sefinen Valley: At the end of town, notice the dramatic Sefinen Valley. All the old homes in town are made from local wood cut from the left-hand side of this valley (shady side, slow-growing, better timber). The road switches back at the...

Gimmelwald Fire Station: The *Föhnwacht Reglement* sheet, posted on the fire station building, explains rules to keep the village from burning down during the fierce dry wind of the Föhn season. During this time, there's a 24-hour fire watch, and even smoking cigarettes outdoors is forbidden. Mürren was devastated by a Föhn-caused fire in the 1920s. Because villagers in Gimmelwald—mindful of the quality of their volunteer fire department—are particularly careful with fire, this is a rare village to not have had a terrible fire in its history.

Check out the other posted notices. This year's Swiss Army calendar tells reservists when and where to go. Every Swiss male does a year in the military, then a few days a year in the reserves until about age 40. The *Schiessübungen* poster details the shooting exercises required this year. In keeping with the William Tell heritage, each Swiss man does shooting practice annually for the military (or spends 3 days in jail).

Swiss Cow Culture

Traditional Swiss cow farmers could make more money for much easier work in another profession. In a good year, farmers produce enough cheese to break even—they support their families on government subsidies. (The government supports traditional farming as

much for the tourism as for the cheese.) But these farmers have made a lifestyle choice to keep tradition alive and to live high in the mountains. Rather than lose their children to the cities, Swiss farmers have the opposite problem: Kids argue over who gets to take over the family herd.

The cows' grazing ground can range in elevation by as much as 5,000 feet throughout the year. In the summer (usually mid-June), the

farmer straps elaborate ceremonial bells on his cows and takes them up to a hut at high elevations. The cows hate these big bells, which can cost upwards of 2,000 SF apiece—a proud investment for a humble farmer. When the cows arrive at their summer home, the bells are hung under the eaves.

These high-elevation summer stables are called "alps." Try to find some on a Berner Oberland tourist map (e.g., Wengernalp, Grütschalp, Schiltalp). The cows stay at the alps for about 100 days. The farmers hire a team of cheesemakers to work at each alp—

High Road: Follow the high road to Hotel Mittaghorn. The resort town of Mürren hovers in the distance. And high on the left, notice the hay field with terraces. These are from WWII days, when Switzerland, wanting self-sufficiency, required all farmers to grow potatoes. Today, this is a festival of Alpine flowers in season (best at this altitude in May and June). From Hotel Mittaghorn, you can return to Gimmelwald's "Times Square" via the stepped path.

"NIGHTLIFE"

Evening fun in Gimmelwald is found at the hostel (offering a pool table, Internet access, lots of young Alp-aholics, and a good chance to share information on the surrounding mountains) or at **Pension Gimmelwald's** terrace restaurant next door. **Walter's bar** (in Hotel Mittaghorn) is a local farmers' hangout. When they've made their hay, they come here to play. Although they look like what some people would call hicks, they speak some English and can be fun to get to know. Sit outside (benches just below the rails, 100 yards down the lane from Walter's) and watch the sun tuck the mountaintops mostly hippies, students, and city slickers eager to spend three summer months in the mountains. Each morning, the hired hands get up at 5:00 to milk the cows, take them to pasture, and make the cheese—milking the cows again when they come home in the evening. In summer, all the milk makes alp cheese (it's too difficult to get it down to the market). In the winter, with the cows at lower altitudes, the fresh milk is sold as milk.

Every alp also has a resident herd of pigs. Cheesemaking leftovers (*Molke,* or whey) can damage the ecosystem if thrown out—but pigs love the stuff. The pigs parade up with the cows...but no one notices. Cheesemakers claim that bathing in whey improves the complexion...but maybe that's just the altitude talking.

Meanwhile, the farmers—glad to be free of their bovine responsibilities—turn their attention to making hay. The average farmer has a few huts at various altitudes, each surrounded by small hay fields. The farmer follows the seasons up into the mountains, making hay and storing it above the huts. In the fall, the cows come down from the alps and spend the winter moving from hut to hut, eating the hay the farmer spent the summer preparing for them.

Throughout the year, you'll see farmers moving their herds to various elevations. If snow is in the way, farmers sometimes use tourist gondolas to move their cows. Every two months or so, Gimmelwald farmers bring together cows that aren't doing so well and herd them into the gondola to meet the butcher in the valley below.

into bed as the moon rises over the Jungfrau. If this isn't your idea of nightlife, stay in Interlaken.

SLEEPING

(4,593 feet, 1.30 SF = about $1, country code: 41)
Gimmelwald is my home base in the Berner Oberland. To inhale the Alps and really hold them in, you'll sleep high in Gimmelwald, too. Poor but pleasantly stuck in the past, the village has a creaky hotel, happy hostel, decent pension, a couple of B&Bs, and even a Web site (www.gimmelwald.ch). The only bad news is that the lift costs 7.80 SF each way to get here.

$$ Maria and Olle Eggimann rent two rooms—Gimmelwald's most comfortable—in their quirky but Alpine-sleek chalet. Maria and Olle, who job-share the village's only teaching position and raise three kids of their own, offer visitors a rare and intimate peek at this community (D-110 SF, Db with kitchenette-180 SF for 2 or 3 people, optional breakfast-18 SF, no CC, last check-in 19:30, 3-night minimum, from gondola continue straight for 200 yards along the town's only road, B&B on left, tel. 033-855-3575, oeggimann@bluewin.ch, SE fluently).

$$ Pension Restaurant Gimmelwald offers 13 basic rooms under low, creaky ceilings (D-100 SF, Db-120 SF, T-135 SF, Q-170 SF, 10 percent less for 3-night stays; these prices good through 2005 with this book). It also has sheetless backpacker beds (35 SF in small dorm rooms, 6 SF for sheets). The pension has a scenic terrace overlooking the Jungfrau and the hostel (below), and is the village's only restaurant, offering good meals (closed late Oct–Christmas and mid-April–mid-May, non-smoking rooms but restaurant can get smoky, 50 yards from gondola station; reserve by phone, plus obligatory reconfirmation by phone 2–3 days before arrival; tel. 033-855-1730, fax 033-855-1925, pensiongimmelwald@tcnet.ch, Liesi and Mäni).

$ Hotel Mittaghorn, the treasure of Gimmelwald, is run by Walter Mittler, a perfect Swiss gentleman. Walter's hotel is a classic, creaky, Alpine-style place with memorable beds (if too lumpy or short, consider putting mattress on floor), ancient down comforters (short and fat; wear socks and drape the blanket over your feet), and a million-dollar view of the Jungfrau Alps. The loft has a dozen real beds, several sinks, down comforters, and a fire ladder out the back window. The hotel has one shower for 10 rooms (1 SF/5 min). Walter is careful not to let his place get too hectic or big, and he enjoys sensitive Back Door travelers. He runs  the hotel with a little help from Rosemarie, from the village. To some, Hotel Mittaghorn is a fire waiting to happen, with a kitchen that would never pass code, bumpy beds, teeny towels, and minimal plumbing, run by an eccentric old grouch. These people enjoy Mürren, Interlaken, or Wengen, and that's where they should sleep. Be warned, you'll see more of my readers than locals here, but it's a fun crowd—an extended family (D-70 SF, Db-80 SF, T-100 SF, Q-125 SF, loft beds-25 SF, 6-SF surcharge per person for 1-night stays, no CC, closed Nov–March, tel. 033-855-1658, www.ricksteves.com/mittaghorn). Reserve by telephone only, then reconfirm by phone the day before your arrival. Walter usually offers his guests a hearty 15-SF dinner (salad, main course, and dessert, served at 19:30, by reservation only). Hotel Mittaghorn is at the top of Gimmelwald, a five-minute climb up the steps from the village intersection.

$ Mountain Hostel is a beehive of activity, as clean as its guests, cheap, and friendly. Phone ahead, or, to secure one of its 50 dorm beds the same day, call after 9:30 and leave your name. The hostel has low ceilings, a self-service kitchen, a mini-grocery, a free pool table, and healthy plumbing. It's mostly a college-age crowd; families and older travelers will probably feel more comfortable elsewhere. Petra Brunner has lined the porch with flowers. This relaxed hostel survives with the help of its guests. Read the signs (Please Clean the Kitchen), respect Petra's rules, and leave it tidier than you found it. The place is one of those rare spots where a congenial atmosphere spontaneously combusts, and spaghetti becomes communal as it cooks (20 SF per bed in 6- to 15-bed rooms, includes sheets, showers-1 SF, no breakfast, hostel membership not required, no CC, Internet access, laundry, 20 yards from lift station, tel. & fax 033-855-1704, www.mountainhostel.com, mountainhostel@tcnet.ch).

$ **Esther's B&B,** overlooking the main intersection of the village, is like an upscale mini-hostel, with five clean, basic, and comfortable rooms sharing two bathrooms and a great kitchen (S-40 SF, D-80 SF, big D-95 SF, T-100 SF, big T-120 SF, Q-160 SF, family room for up to 5, no CC, 2-night stays preferred, breakfast-12 SF, non-smoking, tel. 033-855-5488, fax 033-855-5492, www.esthersguesthouse.ch, info@esthersguesthouse.ch, some English spoken).

$ **Schlaf im Stroh** ("Sleep in Straw") offers exactly that, in an actual barn. After the cows head for higher ground in the summer, the friendly von Allmen family hoses out their barn and fills it with straw and budget travelers. Blankets are free, but bring your own sheet, sleep sack, or sleeping bag. No beds, no bunks, no mattresses, no kidding. Esther fluffs up your hay each night (21 SF, 10 SF for kids up to 10, thereafter kids pay their age plus 1 SF, no CC, includes breakfast "barn service" and a modern bathroom, showers-2 SF, open late-June–mid-Oct depending on grass and snow levels, almost never full; from lift, continue straight through intersection to big modern barn marked 1995 on the right, run by Esther with same contact information as above).

EATING

Pension Gimmelwald, the only restaurant in town, serves a hearty breakfast buffet for 13.50 SF, good lunches, and dinners (15–20 SF). The menu features cheese fondue, *Rösti*, local organic produce, homemade pies, and unforgettable (no matter how you try) brownies (daily 8:00–23:00).

Other Options: The hostel has a decent members' kitchen and makes great pizzas in the evenings (non-guests welcome). Hotel Mittaghorn serves dinner only to its guests (15 SF). Consider packing in a picnic meal from the larger towns. If you need a few groceries and want to skip the hike to Mürren, you can buy the essentials—noodles, spaghetti sauce, and candy bars—at the Mountain Hostel's reception desk.

The local farmers sell their produce. Esther (at the main intersection of the village) sells cheese, sausage, bread, and Gimmelwald's best yogurt—but only until the cows go up in June.

Mürren

Mürren—pleasant as an Alpine resort can be—is traffic-free and filled with bakeries, cafés, souvenirs, old-timers with walking sticks,  GE employees enjoying incentive trips, and Japanese tourists making movies of each other with a Fujichrome backdrop. Its chalets are prefab-rustic. With help from a gondola, train, and funicular, hiking options are endless from Mürren. Sitting on a ledge 2,000 feet above the Lauterbrunnen Valley, surrounded by a fortissimo chorus of mountains, the town has all the comforts of home (for a price) without the pretentiousness of more famous resorts.

Historic Mürren, which dates from 1384, has been overwhelmed by development. Still, it's a peaceful town. There's no full-time doctor, no police officer (they call Lauterbrunnen if there's a problem), and no resident priest or pastor. (The Protestant church—up by the TI—posts a sign showing where the region's roving pastor preaches each Sunday.) There's not even enough business to keep a bakery open full-time (Mürren's bakery is open mid-June–Sept and Dec–April)—a clear indication that this town is either lively or completely dead, depending on the season. Keep an eye open for the "Milch Express," a tiny cart that delivers fresh milk and eggs to hotels and homes throughout town.

ORIENTATION

Mürren sits high on a ledge, overlooking the Lauterbrunnen Valley. You can walk from one end of town to the other in about 10 minutes.

There are two basic ways to get to Mürren: on the panoramic train from Grütschalp (connects via funicular to Lauterbrunnen); or on the gondola from Stechelberg (in the valley), which stops at Gimmelwald, Mürren, and continues up to the Schilthorn. The train and gondola stations (which both have lockers) are at opposite ends of town.

Tourist Information: Mürren's **TI** can help you find a room and give hiking advice (July–Sept daily 8:30–19:00, Thu until 20:30, less off-season, above the village, follow signs to Sportzentrum, tel. 033-856-8686, www.wengen-muerren.ch). You can change money at the TI, or even better, use the ATM by the Co-op grocery.

Helpful Hints

R & R: The slick **Sportzentrum** (sports center) that houses the TI offers a world of indoor activities (13 SF to use pool and whirlpool; 8 SF for Gimmelwald, Lauterbrunnen, and Interlaken hotel guests; free for guests at Mürren hotels—ask your hotelier for a voucher; pool open Mon–Sat 14:00–18:45, Thu until 20:30, closed Sun, May, and Nov–mid-Dec). In season, they offer squash, mini-golf, table tennis, and a fitness room.

Bike Rental: You can rent mountain bikes and hiking boots at Stäger Sport (bikes with helmets-35 SF/day, boots-12 SF/day, daily 9:00–17:00, closed mid-Sept–mid-June, across from TI/Sportzentrum, tel. 033-855-2355, www.staegersport.ch).

Internet Access: Connect at the TI (see above) or Eiger Guesthouse (daily 8:00–23:00, across from train station, see "Sleeping," below, tel. 033-856-5460).

Laundry: Top Apartments will do your laundry by request (25 SF per load, unreliable hours: Mon–Sat 9:00–11:00 & 15:00–17:00, closed Sun, behind and across from Hotel Bellevue, look for blue triangle, call first to drop off in morning, tel. 033-855-3706).

Mürren Town Walk

Mürren has long been a top ski resort, but a walk across town offers a glimpse into its past. This stroll takes you through town on the main drag, from the train station (where you'll arrive if coming from Lauterbrunnen) to the gondola station, then back up to the Allmendhubel funicular station.

Train Station: The first trains pulled into Mürren in 1891. (A circa-1911 car is permanently parked at the Grütschalp station.) A display case inside the station shows an original car from the narrow-gauge, horse-powered line that rolled fancy visitors from here into town. The current station, built in 1964, comes with impressive engineering for heavy cargo. Look out back, where a small truck can be loaded up and drive away.

Stroll under the Anfi Palace Hotel: Wander into town along the main road. The towering Anfi Palace Hotel was the "Grand Palace Hotel" until it burned in 1928. Its Jugendstil Hall is the finest room in Mürren. The small wooden platform on the left—looking like a suicide springboard—is the place where snow removal trucks dump their loads over the cliff in the winter. Look back at the meadow below the station: This is a favorite grazing

Mürren

1. Anfi Palace Hotel
2. Hotel Alpina & Edelweiss Cafeteria
3. Hotel Bellevue
4. Hotel Jungfrau & Haus Mönch
5. Hotel Blumental
6. Eiger Guesthouse
7. Chalet Fontana
8. To Chalet Helvetia
9. Stägerstübli Restaurant
10. Restaurant Hotel Eiger
11. Top Apartments (Laundry)
12. Co-op Grocery

— PAVED ROAD
--- TRAIL

NOT TO SCALE–
CABLE CAR STN.
TO TRAIN STN. IS
ABOUT 10 MIN. WALK

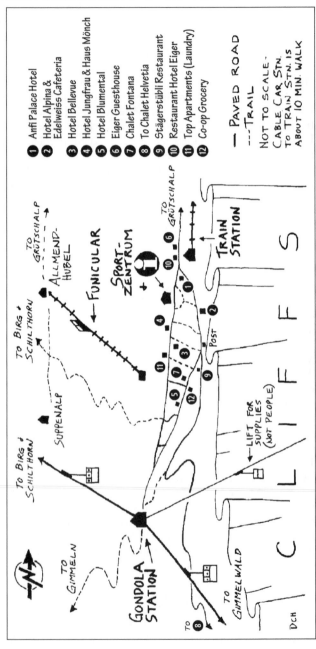

spot for chamois (the animals, not the rags for washing cars). Ahead, at Edelweiss Hotel, step to the far corner of the restaurant terrace for a breathtaking view stretching from the big three (Eiger, Mönch, and Jungfrau) to the lonely cattle farm in the high alp on the right. Then look down.

Next, the Haus Montana was where Kandahar ski boots were first made in 1933 (to give the necessary support to daredevils racing from the Schilthorn to the valley floor in Mürren's infamous Inferno race). Today, the still-respected Kandahar boots are made in nearby Thun.

Downtown Mürren: You'll pass the main intersection (where the small service road leads down to Gimmelwald) and the only grocery store in town (Co-op). The tiny fire barn (Feuerwehr) has a list showing the leaders of the volunteer force and their responsibilities. The old barn behind it on the right evokes the day, not so long ago, when the town's barns housed cows. Imagine Mürren with more cows than people.

Gondola Station: Reaching the far end of Mürren, you come to the gondola station. The first gondola (goes directly to Stechelberg) is for cargo, garbage, and the (reputedly) longest bungee jumping in the world. The other takes hikers and skiers up to the Schilthorn and down to Stechelberg via Gimmelwald.

Upper Mürren: Hiking back along the high road, you pass Mürren's two churches, the mountain bike rental office, the Allmendhubel funicular station, and the Sportzentrum (with swimming pool and TI).

Mürren's Allmendhubel Funicular: A quaint-looking but surprisingly rewarding funicular (1912, renovated in 1999) carries nature lovers from Mürren to a perch offering a Jungfrau view that (while much lower) rivals the Schilthorn. At the station, notice the 1920s bobsled. The restaurants here (full- and self-service) have awesome views.

Allmendhubel is particularly good for families: It's cheaper than the Schilthorn. The restaurant overlooks a great playground. And the entertaining children's hike—with rough and thrilling, kid-friendly Alpine rides along the way—departs from here. This is also the departure point for the North Face hike and walks to Grütschalp (see "Hikes," page 147).

SLEEPING

(5,381 feet, 1.30 SF = about $1, country code: 41)
Prices for accommodations are often higher during the ski season. Many hotels and restaurants close in spring, roughly from Easter to early June, and any time between late September and mid-December.

$$$ **Hotel Alpina** is a simple, modern place with 24 comfortable rooms and a concrete feeling—a good thing, given its cliff-edge position (Sb-85 SF, Db-160 SF, Tb-200 SF, Qb-220 SF with awesome Jungfrau views and balconies, prices less off-season and without a view, outside mid-June–mid-Aug ask for a 10 percent Rick Steves discount in 2005, family rooms, homey lounge, exit left from train station, walk 2 min downhill, tel. 033-855-1361, fax 033-855-1049, www.muerren.ch/alpina, alpina@muerren.ch, Cecilia and her son Roger SE).

$$$ **Hotel Bellevue** has a homey lounge, solid woodsy furniture, a great view terrace, the hunter-themed Jägerstübli restaurant, and 17 great rooms at fair rates, all with balconies and views (Sb-110 SF, Db-190 SF; special deal with this book in 2005: Db-150 SF if staying 2 nights or more except July–Aug; Internet, tel. 033-855-1401, fax 033-855-1490, www.muerren.ch/bellevue, bellevue-crystal@bluewin.ch, Ruth and Othmar Suter).

$$$ **Hotel Jungfrau** offers 29 modern and comfortable rooms (with view: Sb-95–110 SF, Db-190–210 SF; no view: Sb-90–110 SF, Db-170–200 SF; elevator, near TI/Sportzentrum, tel. 033-855-4545, fax 033-855-4549, www.hoteljungfrau.ch, mail@hoteljungfrau.ch, Anne-Marie and Andres).

$$$ **Hotel Blumental** has 16 older but nicely furnished rooms and a fun, woodsy game/TV lounge (Sb-75–80 SF, Db-150–170 SF, higher prices are for July–Aug, plush but smoky lobby, attached restaurant, tel. 033-855-1826, fax 033-855-3686, www.muerren.ch/blumental, blumental@muerren.ch, Rolf and Heidi, fourth generation in the von Allmen family).

$$ **Eiger Guesthouse** offers 14 good budget rooms. This is a friendly, creaky, easygoing home away from home (S-60–65 SF, Sb-80–85 SF, D-100–110 SF, Db-130–140 SF, 39- to 45-SF beds in 2- and 4-bunk rooms, includes sheets and breakfast; special through 2005 with this book: D-85 SF with a 2-night minimum year-round; Internet, closed Nov and for one month after Easter, across from train station, tel. 033-856-5460, fax 033-856-5461, www.muerren.ch/eigerguesthouse, eigerguesthouse@muerren.ch, well run by Scotsman Alan and Swiss Véronique). The restaurant serves good, reasonably priced dinners. Its poolroom—with public Internet access—is a popular local hangout. They have my Switzerland Alps TV show on DVD available in the lobby.

$$ **Haus Mönch,** a basic, blocky lodge run by Hotel Jungfrau, offers 20 woodsy, well-worn, but fine rooms, plus good Jungfrau views (Db-140–144 SF, Tb-180 SF, near TI and Sportzentrum, tel. 033-855-4545, fax 033-855-4549, www.hoteljungfrau.ch, mail@hoteljungfrau.ch).

$ **Chalet Fontana,** run by charming Englishwoman Denise Fussell, is a rare budget option in Mürren, with simple, crispy-clean, and comfortable rooms (35–45 SF per person in small doubles or triples with breakfast and shared bathrooms, price varies with size of room, 5 SF cheaper without breakfast, 1 apartment with kitchen and bathroom-110 SF for 2 people, 145 SF for 4, no CC, closed Nov–April, across street from Stägerstübli restaurant in town center, tel. 033-855-4385, mobile 078-642-3485, chaletfontana@muerren .ch). If no one's home, check at the Ed Abegglen shop next door (tel. 033-855-1245, off-season only).

$ **Chalet Helvetia,** run by Frau Hunziker, offers a homey, clean, two-bedroom apartment with bathroom, kitchen, separate entrance, and balcony for 40 SF per person (up to 5 people, no breakfast, 2-night minimum preferred, more expensive for 1-night stays, 200 yards below cable-car station on path to Gimmelwald, look for red *Zimmer* sign on right, tel. 033-855-4169, mobile 079-234-7867, kurthunziker105@msn.com).

EATING

Many of these restaurants are in or near my recommended hotels. Outside of summer and ski season, it can be hard to find any place that's open (ask around).

Stägerstübli is, hands down, *the* place to eat in town. It's the only real restaurant not associated with a hotel. Located in the town center, this 1902 building was once a tea room for rich tourists, while locals were limited to the room in the back—the nicest dining area today (lunches and dinners for 15–30 SF, daily 11:30–22:00, Lydia SE). Sitting on its terrace, you know just who's out and about in town.

Pasci's Snack Bar Bistro has fun, creative, and inexpensive light meals; a good selection of salads, vegetarian dishes, coffees, teas, and pastries; and impressive views (take-out available, run by a serious chef—Pasci—and Franzi, daily 10:00–18:00, at the Sportzentrum, overlooking the ice rink).

Restaurant Hotel Jungfrau is a dressy ski lodge with a modern octagonal dining room and a fine view terrace (nightly from 18:30, always a 10.50-SF salad bar, 50-SF 4-course meal, vegetarian options, 23-SF cheese fondue, near TI/Sportzentrum, tel. 033-855-4545, see "Sleeping," above).

The **Edelweiss self-serve restaurant** offers lunch with the most cliff-hanging dining in town—incredible views (daily 10:30–18:00, next to Hotel Alpina, see "Sleeping," above).

Restaurant Hotel Eiger is considered one of the better places in town, with a good chef, classy indoor seating, and a terrace with a view obstructed by the station (open daily, 20-SF plates, 29-SF *menu*, an enticing variety of meat fondue dinners for 45 SF, tel. 033-856-5454). Note that this is not the same as **Eiger Guesthouse**— which also serves good, but simpler, food (see "Sleeping," above).

Hotel Bellevue is pricey but atmospheric, with three dining zones: view terrace, elegant indoor, and the Jägerstübli—a cozy, well-antlered hunters' room guaranteed to disgust vegetarians. This is your best bet for game, as they buy chamois and deer direct from local hunters (mid-June–Oct from 18:00, 35-SF meals, tel. 033-855-1401, see "Sleeping," above).

The **Co-op** is the only grocery store in town, with good picnic fixings and sandwiches (Mon–Fri 8:00–12:00 & 14:00–18:00, Sat until 16:00, closed Sun). Given restaurant prices, this place is a godsend for those on a tight budget.

Lauterbrunnen

Lauterbrunnen—with a train station (has lockers), funicular, bank, shops, and lots of hotels—is the valley's commercial center. This is the jumping-off point for Jungfrau and Schilthorn adventures. It's idyllic, in spite of the busy road and big buildings.

ORIENTATION

Tourist Information: Stop by the friendly TI to check the weather forecast, use the Internet, and buy any regional train or lift tickets you need (June–Aug Mon–Sat 10:00–12:00 & 15:00–18:30, closed Sun, shorter hours off-season, 1 block up from station, tel. 033-856-8568, www.wengen-muerren.ch).

Helpful Hints
Bike Rental: You can rent mountain bikes at Imboden Bike on the main street (25-SF/4 hrs, 35-SF/full day, full-suspension—reserve ahead—45-SF/half day, 65-SF/full day, daily 8:00–18:30, tel. 033-855-2114).

Internet and Laundry: The Valley Hostel on the main street runs an Internet café and a small launderette (10-SF/load, don't open dryer door until machine is finished, or you'll have to pay another 5-SF to start it again; both daily 8:00–22:00, shorter hours Nov–April, tel. 033-855-2008).

SLEEPING

(2,612 feet, 1.30 SF = about $1, country code: 41)

$$ Hotel Staubbach, a big, Old World place—one of the first hotels in the valley (1890)—is being lovingly restored by hard-working American Craig and his Swiss wife, Corinne. Its 30 plain, comfortable rooms are family-friendly, there's a kids' play area, and the parking is free. Many rooms have great views. They keep their prices down by cleaning the rooms only after every third night (S-50 SF, Ss-60 SF, Sb-90 SF, D-80 SF, Db-110 SF, figure 40 SF per person in family rooms sleeping up to 6, 10 SF extra per room for 1-night stays, elevator, 4 blocks up from station on the left, tel. 033-855-5454, fax 033-855-5484, www.staubbach.ch, hotel@staubbach.ch). Guests can watch a DVD of my TV show on the region in the lounge.

$ Valley Hostel is practical, friendly, and comfortable, offering 70 inexpensive beds for quieter travelers of all ages, with a pleasant garden and the welcoming Abegglen family: Martha, Alfred, Stefan, and Fränzi (D with bunk beds-56 SF, twin D-64 SF, beds in larger family-friendly rooms-28 SF per person, breakfast-5 SF, kitchen available, no CC, most rooms have no sinks, 16-SF cheese fondue on request for guests 18:00–20:00, non-smoking, Internet access, laundry, 2 blocks up from train station, tel. & fax 033-855-2008, www.valleyhostel.ch, info@valleyhostel.ch).

$ Chalet im Rohr—a creaky, old, woody firetrap of a place—has oodles of character (spiced with lots of Asian groups) and 50 26-SF beds in big one- to four-bed rooms that share six showers (no breakfast, common kitchen, no CC, closed for 3 weeks after Easter, below church on main drag, tel. & fax 033-855-2182).

$ Matratzenlager Stocki is rustic and humble, with the cheapest beds in town (14 SF with sheets in easygoing little 30-bed coed dorm with kitchen, closed Nov–Dec, across river from station, tel. 033-855-1754, Frau Graf SE).

$ *Camping:* Two campgrounds just south of town provide 15- to 35-SF beds (in dorms and 2-, 4-, and 6-bed bungalows, no sheets, kitchen facilities, no CC, big English-speaking tour groups): **Mountain Holiday Park-Camping Jungfrau,** romantically situated beyond Staubbach Falls, is huge and well organized by Hans (tel. 033-856-2010, fax 033-856-2020, www.camping-jungfrau.ch). It also has fancier cabins (25 SF per person). **Schützenbach Retreat,** on the left just past Lauterbrunnen toward Stechelberg, is simpler (tel. 033-855-1268, www.schutzenbach-retreat.ch).

EATING

At **Hotel Restaurant Oberland,** the Nolan family takes pride in serving tasty meals from a fun menu (daily 11:30–16:00 & 17:30–21:00, tel. 033-855-1241).

Hotel Restaurant Jungfrau, along the main street on the right-hand side, offers a wide range of specialties served by a friendly staff (daily 12:00–14:00 & 18:00–20:00, tel. 033-855-3434, run by Brigitte Melliger).

Hotel Restaurant Silberhorn is the local choice for a fancy meal out (fine indoor and outdoor seating, above the funicular station, tel. 033-856-2210).

MORE IN THE BERNER OBERLAND

SIGHTS AND ACTIVITIES

Lifts and Trains
The following lifts are both rated ▲▲▲. Doing at least one of them is an essential Berner Oberland experience.

The Schilthorn and a 10,000-Foot Breakfast
The Schilthornbahn carries skiers, hikers, and sightseers effortlessly

to the 10,000-foot summit of the Schilthorn, where the Piz Gloria station awaits, with a solar-powered revolving restaurant, shop, and panorama terrace. Linger on top. Piz Gloria has a free "touristorama" film room with a multi-screen slide show and explosive highlights from the James Bond thriller that featured the Schilthorn (*On Her Majesty's Secret Service;* if it's not running, press the 007 button on the column in the middle of the room).

Watch paragliders set up, psych up, and take off, flying 45 minutes with the birds to distant Interlaken. (This is a tough launch point, but generally safe in the morning and late in the summer.) Walk along the ridge out back. This is a great place for a photo of you, the mountain-climber.

When you ascend in the gondola, take a look at the altitude meter. (The Gimmelwald-Schilthorn hike is free, if you don't mind a 5,000-foot altitude gain.) Ask at the Schilthorn station for a gondola souvenir decal (Schilthornbahn station in Stechelberg,

tel. 033-856-2141). For another cheap thrill, ask the gondola attendant to crank down the window (easiest on the Mürren-Birg section). Then stick your head out the window...and you're hang-gliding.

You can ride up to the Schilthorn and hike down, but it's tough. For information on **hikes** from lift stations along the Schilthorn cable-car line, see "Hikes," page 147. My favorite "hike" from the Schilthorn is simply along the ridge out back, to get away from the station and be all alone on top of an Alp.

Youth hostelers—not realizing that rocks may hide just under the snow—scream down the ice fields on plastic-bag sleds from the Schilthorn mountaintop. (English-speaking doctor in Lauterbrunnen.)

Cost and Hours: The early-bird and afternoon-special gondola tickets (60 SF round-trip, before 9:00 or after 15:30) take you from Gimmelwald to the Schilthorn and back at a discount (normal rate-80 SF, or 94 SF from the Stechelberg car park; parking-2 SF/2 hrs, 6 SF/day). These same discounted fares are available all day long in the shoulder season (roughly May and Oct). Eurailpass and Swiss railpass holders—who get a 25 percent discount (a better deal than the early/late specials)—might as well go whenever they like, because there's no double discount. Lifts go twice hourly, and the ride (including 2 transfers) to the Schilthorn takes 30 minutes. For more information, including current weather conditions, see www.schilthorn.ch.

Breakfast at 10,000 Feet: There's no à la carte—only a fixed meal for 15 SF (rolls and hot chocolate or coffee) or 22.50 SF (add egg, ham, and champagne; breakfast served 8:00–11:00). If you're going for breakfast before 9:00, consider an early-bird-plus-breakfast combo-ticket to save a few francs (73 SF round-trip from Gimmelwald, 84 SF from Stechelberg). Ask for more hot drinks if necessary. If you're not revolving, ask them to turn it on.

Jungfraujoch

The literal high point of any trip to the Swiss Alps is a train ride through the Eiger to the Jungfraujoch. At 11,300 feet, it's Europe's

Alpine Lifts in the Berner Oberland

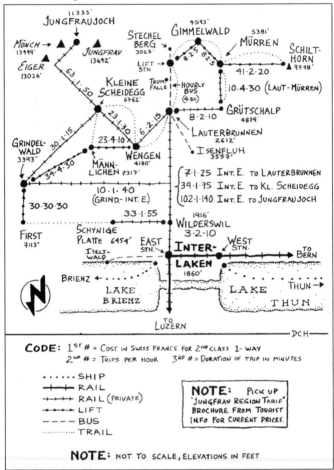

CODE: 1ST # = COST IN SWISS FRANCS FOR 2ND CLASS 1- WAY
2ND # = TRIPS PER HOUR   3RD # = DURATION OF TRIP IN MINUTES

······· SHIP
├──┼──┤ RAIL
├┼┼┼┼┤ RAIL (PRIVATE)
·─•─•─• LIFT
─ ─ ─ ─ BUS
············· TRAIL

NOTE: PICK UP 'JUNGFRAU REGION TARIF' BROCHURE FROM TOURIST INFO FOR CURRENT PRICES.

NOTE: NOT TO SCALE, ELEVATIONS IN FEET

highest train station. The ride from Kleine Scheidegg takes about an hour (sit on right side for better views), including two five-minute stops at stations actually halfway up the notorious North Face of the Eiger. You have time to look out windows and marvel at how people could climb the Eiger—and how the Swiss built this train more than a hundred years ago. The second half of the ride takes you through a tunnel inside the Eiger (some newer train cars run multilingual videos about the history of the train line).

Once you reach the top, study the Jungfraujoch chart to see your options (many of them are weather-dependent). There's a restaurant, history exhibit, ice palace (a cavern with a gallery of ice statues), and

Berner Oberland

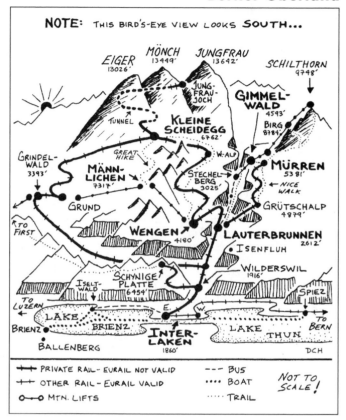

NOTE: THIS BIRD'S-EYE VIEW LOOKS SOUTH...

EIGER 13026'
MÖNCH 13449'
JUNGFRAU 13642'
SCHILTHORN 9748'
JUNG-FRAU-JOCH
TUNNEL
GIMMEL-WALD 4593'
KLEINE SCHEIDEGG 6762'
BIRG 8784'
GRINDEL-WALD 3393'
GREAT HIKE
W. ALP
MÄNN-LICHEN 7317'
STECHEL-BERG 3025'
MÜRREN 5381'
NICE WALK
GRUND
GRÜTSCHALP 4879'
↑ TO FIRST
WENGEN 4180'
LAUTERBRUNNEN 2612'
ISENFLUH
WILDERSWIL 1916'
ISELT-WALD
SCHYNIGE PLATTE 6454'
SPIEZ
TO LUZERN
LAKE BRIENZ
E.
W.
LAKE THUN
TO BERN
BRIENZ
INTER-LAKEN 1860'
BALLENBERG
DCH

┿┿ PRIVATE RAIL – EURAIL NOT VALID	--- BUS
┼┼ OTHER RAIL – EURAIL VALID	•••• BOAT
o—o MTN. LIFTS	····· TRAIL

NOT TO SCALE!

a 20-minute video that plays continuously. A tunnel leads outside, where you can ski (30 SF for gear and lift ticket), sled (free loaner discs with deposit), ride in a dog sled (6 SF, mornings only), or hike 45 minutes across the ice to Mönchsjochhütte (a mountain hut with a small restaurant). An elevator leads to the Sphinx observatory for

the highest viewing point, from which you can see Aletsch Glacier—Europe's longest, at nearly 11 miles—stretch to the south. Remember that your body isn't used to such high altitudes. Signs posted at the top remind you to take it easy.

Hiking in the Berner Oberland

This region is a wonderful place to hike, and I've listed my favorite excursions. The super-scenic walk from Männlichen to Kleine Scheidegg is the best of all worlds: It's both dramatic and relatively easy. The hike from Schynige Platte to First is spectacular, but much more challenging, as is the hike from the Birg cable-car station down to Gimmelwald—don't try either of these in bad weather. In case of rain, the lower hikes (North Face Trail from Allmendhubel; the walk from Mürren or Allmendhubel to Grütschalp; the Sefinen Valley hike from Gimmelwald; and the stroll along the Lauterbrunnen Valley) are better bets.

To do any serious hiking, you should invest in a real hiking map. Hikers can get specifics at the Mürren TI or from hoteliers. For a description of six diverse hikes on the west side of Lauterbrunnen, pick up the fine and free *Mürren-Schilthorn Hikes* brochure. This 3-D map of the Mürren mountainside makes a useful and attractive souvenir. For the other side of the valley, get the *Wandern Jungfraubahnen* brochure, which also has a handy 3-D map of hiking trails (both brochures free at stations, hotels, and TIs).

Once underway, don't mind the fences (although wires can be solar-powered electric); a hiker has the right of way in Switzerland. Don't forget a water bottle and some munchies. Trails are well-marked, with yellow signs listing destinations and the estimated time it'll take you to walk there. Refer to maps (within this chapter) as you read about the hikes.

Weather Concerns: Locals always seem to know the weather report (as much of their income depends on it). Clouds can roll in

One of the best hikes in the region—from Männlichen to Kleine Scheidegg—could be combined with your trip up to the Jungfraujoch (see page 152).

Cost and Hours: The first trip of the day to Jungfraujoch is discounted; ask for a Good Morning Ticket, and return from the top by noon (Nov–April you can get Good Morning rates for the first or second train and stay after noon; train runs all year; round-trip fares to Jungfraujoch: from Kleine Scheidegg-104 SF, 80 SF for first trip of day—about 8:02; from Lauterbrunnen-154 SF, 130 SF for first trip—about 7:08, confirm times and prices, 25 percent discount for Eurailpass and Swiss railpass holders). Pick up a leaflet on the lifts at a local TI, or call 033-828-7233 (www.jungfraubahn.ch). For a tri-lingual weather forecast, call 033-828-7931; if it's cloudy, skip the trip.

anytime, but skies are usually clearest in the morning. All over the region, TV sets are tuned to the local weather station, with real-time views from all the famous peaks. The same station airs a travelogue on the region each evening around 21:30. You can also check the weather at www.swisspanorama.com.

Snow: As late as July, snow can curtail your hiking plans (the Männlichen lift doesn't even open until the first week in June). Before setting out on any hike, get advice from a knowledgeable local. Well into the spring, and sometimes also in early fall, the high trails (Männlichen to Kleine Scheidegg, Schynige Platte to First, and anything from Schilthorn or Birg) are likely to be impassible.

Wildlife: As hunting is not allowed in the vicinity of any lifts, animals find comfort in places you're likely to be. Keep an eye out for chamois (called *Gemse* here)—the sure-footed "goat antelope" that lives at the top of the treeline, and goes a little lower when hungry. Spotting an ibex—a wild goat with horns, scrambling along the rocky terrain—is another Berner Oberland thrill. You'll also encounter marmot, big Alpine mice (like 2 pound squirrels) who get really fat each summer, planning to sleep underground for six months through the winter. These burrowing rodents are fun to watch, and if you sit still, they don't see you. You'll hear them whistle. Your best viewing place is above Allmendhubel, in the meadow above the highest hut in Blumental.

Nordic Walking: You may wonder about the Germans you'll see with their walking sticks *(Alpenstock)*. This is trying to be the next craze: Nordic walking. Enthusiasts claim Nordic walking is an all-body workout, activating 90 percent of your muscles and burning a third more calories than "normal" walking, while cutting way back on the strain on your back and knees when going downhill. To do it right requires proper instruction. Sticks can be rented at some outdoor shops.

Hikes

There are days of possible hikes from Gimmelwald and Mürren. Many are a fun combination of trails, mountain trains, and gondola rides. I've listed them based on which side of the Lauterbrunnen Valley they're on: west (the Gimmelwald/Mürren/Schilthorn side) or east (the Jungfrau side).

On the Gimmelwald (West) Side of the Lauterbrunnen Valley
Hikes from the Schilthorn

While several tough trails lead down from the Schilthorn, most visitors take the cable car round-trip simply for the views (see "Lifts and Trains," above). But if you're a serious hiker, consider walking all the way down (first hike) or part of the way down (second hike) back into Gimmelwald. Don't attempt to hike down from the Schilthorn unless the trail is clear of snow. Adequate shoes and clothing (weather can change quickly) and good knees are required. (If you want to visit the Sprutz Waterfall on your way to Gimmelwald, see page 151.)

From the Top of the Schilthorn—To hike downhill from the Piz Gloria revolving restaurant at the peak, start at the steps to the right of the cable, which lead along a ridge between a cliff and the bowl. As you pass huge rocks and shale fields, keep an eye out for the painted rocks that mark the scant trail. Eventually, you'll hit the service road (a ski run in the winter), which is steep and not very pleasant. Passing a memorial to a woman killed by lightning in 1865, you come to the small lake called Grauseeli. Leave the gravel road and hike along the lake. From there, follow the trail (with the help of cables when necessary) to scamper along the shale in the direction of Rotstockhütte (to Gimmelwald, see next hike) or Schilttal (the valley leading directly to Mürren; follow Mürren/Rotstockhütte sign painted on the rock at the junction).

▲▲Birg to Gimmelwald via Brünli—Rather than the very long hike all the way back down into Gimmelwald, I prefer the easier (but still strenuous) hike from the intermediate cable-car station at Birg. This is efficiently combined with a visit to the Schilthorn (from Schilthorn summit, ride cable car halfway down, get off at Birg, and hike down from there; buy the round-trip excursion early-bird fare—which is cheaper than the Gimmelwald-Schilthorn-Birg ticket—and decide at Birg if you want to hike or ride down).

The most interesting trail from Birg to Gimmelwald is the high one via Grauseeli Lake and Wasenegg Ridge to Brünli, then down to Spielbodenalp and the Sprutz waterfall. Warning: This trail is quite steep and slippery in places, and can take four hours. Locals take their kindergartners on this hike, but it can seem dangerous to Americans unused to Alpine hikes. Do not attempt this hike in snow—which you might find at this altitude, even in the peak of summer. (Get local advice.)

From the Birg lift, hike toward the Schilthorn, taking your first left down and passing along the left side of the little Grauseeli lake. From the lake, a gravelly trail leads down rough switchbacks (including a stretch where the path narrows and you can hang onto a guide cable against the cliff face) until it levels out. When you see a rock painted with arrows pointing to Mürren and Rotstockhütte, follow the path to Rotstockhütte (traditional old farm with light meals and drinks, mattress loft with cheap beds), traversing the cow-grazed mountainside.

For a thrill, follow Wasenegg Ridge. It's more scary than dangerous if you're sure-footed and can handle the 50-foot-long "tightrope" section along an extremely narrow ledge with a thousand-foot drop. This trail gets you to Brünli with the least altitude drop. (The safer, well-signposted approach to Brünli is to drop down to Rotstockhütte, then climb back up to Brünli.) The barbed-wire fence leads to the knobby little summit, where you'll enjoy an incredible 360-degree view and a chance to sign your name on the register stored in the little wooden box.

A steep trail winds directly down from Brünli toward Gimmelwald and soon hits a bigger, easy trail. The trail bends right (just before the farm/restaurant at Spielbodenalp), leading to Sprutz. Walk under the Sprutz waterfall, then follow a steep, wooded trail that deposits you in a meadow of flowers at the top side of Gimmelwald.

Hikes from Gimmelwald

▲**Up Sefinen Valley to Kilchbalm**—An easy trail from Gimmelwald is up the Sefinen Valley (Sefinental). This is a good rainy-weather hike, as you can go as far as you like. After two hours and a gain of only 800 feet, you hit the end of the trail and Kilchbalm, a dramatic bowl of glacier fields. Note that snow can make this trail unsafe, even into the summer (ask locally for information), and there's no food or drink along the way.

From the Gimmelwald fire station, walk about 100 yards down the paved Stechelberg road. Leave it on the dirt Sefinental road, which becomes a lane, then a trail. You'll cross a raging river and pass a firing range where locals practice their marksmanship (Fri and Sat evenings; the "danger of fire" sign refers to live bullets). Follow signs to Kilchbalm into a forest, along a river, and finally to the glacier fields.

▲**Gimmelwald-Tanzbodeli-Obersteinberg-Stechelberg/ Gimmelwald**—This eight-hour, 11-mile hike is extremely rewarding, offering perfect peace, very few people, traditional Alpine culture, and spectacular views. (There's no food or drink for 5 hours, so pack accordingly.) As the trail can be a bit confusing, this is best done with a good map (buy locally).

About 100 yards below the Gimmelwald firehouse, take the Sefinental dirt road (described above). As the dirt road switches back after about 30 minutes, take the right turn across the river and start your ascent, following signs to Obersteinberg. After 90 minutes of hard climbing, you have the option of a side-trip to Busenalp. This is fun if the goat and cow herder is there, as you can watch the traditional cheesemaking in action. (He appreciates a bottle of wine from hikers.) Trail markers are painted onto rocks—watch carefully. After visiting Busenalp, return to the main path.

At the "Obersteinberg 50 min/Tanzbodeli 20 min" signpost, head for Tanzbodeli (literally, "Dancing Floor"). This is everyone's favorite Alpine perch—great for a little romance, or a picnic with breathtaking views of the Obersteinberg valley. From here, you enter

Gimmelwald Area Hikes

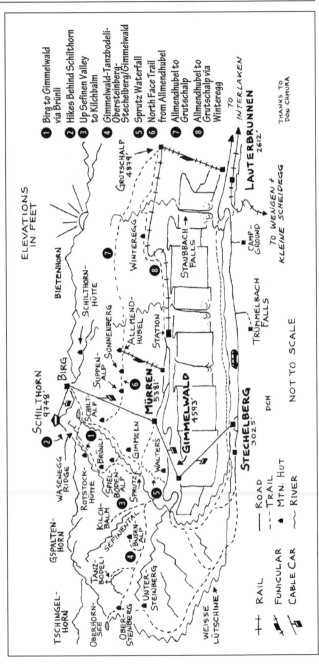

1. Birg to Gimmelwald via Brünli
2. Hikes Behind Schilthorn
3. Up Sefinen Valley to Kilchbalm
4. Gimmelwald-Tanzbodeli-Obersteinberg-Stechelberg/Gimmelwald
5. Sprutz Waterfall
6. North Face Trail from Allmendhubel
7. Allmendhubel to Grütschalp
8. Allmendhubel to Grütschalp via Winteregg

THANKS TO DON CHMURA

ELEVATIONS IN FEET

NOT TO SCALE

RAIL
ROAD
TRAIL
MTN. HUT
RIVER
FUNICULAR
CABLE CAR

a natural reserve, so you're likely to see chamois and other Alpine critters. From Tanzbodeli, you return to the main trail (there's no other way out) and continue to Obersteinberg. You'll eventually hit the Mountain Hotel Obersteinberg (see "Sleeping," page 159; American expat Vickie will serve you a meal or drink).

From there, the trail leads to Hotel Tschingelhorn and back to Gimmelwald (2 hrs total) or Stechelberg (bottom of Schilthorn cable car, 90 min total). About an hour later, you hit a fork in the trail and choose where you'd like your hike to end.

▲**Sprutz Waterfall**—The forest above Gimmelwald hides a powerful waterfall with a trail snaking behind it, offering a fun gorge experience. While the waterfall itself is not well-signed, it's on the Gimmelwald-Spielbodenalp trail. It's steep, through a forest, and can be very slippery when wet, but the actual crossing under the waterfall is just misty.

The hike up to Sprutz from Gimmelwald isn't worth the trip in itself, but it's handy when combined with the hike down from Birg and Brünli (see above) or the North Face Trail (see below). As you descend on either of these two hikes, the trail down to Gimmelwald splits at Spielbodenalp—to the right for the forest and the waterfall; to the left for more meadows, the hamlet of Gimmeln, and more gracefully back into Gimmelwald.

Hikes from Mürren/Allmendhubel

▲▲**North Face Trail from Allmendhubel**—For a pleasant, mainly downhill, two-hour hike (4 miles, from 6,385 feet to 5,375 feet), ride the Allmendhubel funicular up from Mürren (7.40 SF, much cheaper than Schilthorn, good restaurant at top). From there, follow the well-signed route circling around to Mürren (or cut off at Spielbodenalp, near the end, and descend into Gimmelwald via the Sprutz Waterfall). Just follow the blue signs. You'll enjoy great views, flowery meadows, mountain huts, and a dozen information boards along the way, describing the fascinating climbing history of the great peaks around you.

Along the trail, you'll pass four farms (technically "alps," as they are only open in the summer) that serve meals and drinks. Sonnenberg was allowed to break the all-wood code with concrete for protection against avalanches. Suppenalp is quainter. Lean against the house with a salad, soup, or sandwich and enjoy the view.

Notice how older huts are built into the protected side of rocks and outcroppings, in anticipation of avalanches. Above Suppenalp, Blumental ("Flower Valley") is hopping with marmots. Because hunters are not allowed near lifts, animals have learned that these are safe places to hang out—giving tourists a better chance of spotting them.

The trail leads up and over to a group of huts called Schiltalp. If the poles under the eve have bells, the cows are up. If not, the cows are still at the lower farm. Half the cows in Gimmelwald (about 100) spend their summers here. In July, August, and September, you can watch them making cheese and have a snack or drink. Thirty years ago, each family had its own hut. Labor was cheap and available. Today, it's a communal thing, with several families sharing the expense of a single cow herder. Cow herders are master cheesemakers, and have veterinary skills, too.

From Schiltalp, the trail winds gracefully down to Spielbodenalp—a farm with lots going on (open May–mid-Oct Fri–Wed, closed Thu, good menu, 31-SF dorm beds with breakfast). From there, you can finish the North Face trail (continuing down and left through meadows and the hamlet of Gimmeln, then back to Mürren, with more historic signposts); or cut off right (descending steeply through a thick forest and under the dramatic Sprutz Waterfall into Gimmelwald—see Sprutz Waterfall, above, for details).

▲**Allmendhubel/Mürren to Grutschalp**—For a not-too-tough, three-hour walk with great Jungfrau views, ride the funicular from Mürren to Allmendhubel (6,344 feet) and walk to Grütschalp (a drop of about 1,500 feet), where you can catch the panorama train back to Mürren. An easier version is the lower Bergweg from Allmendhubel to Grütschalp via Winteregg and its cheese farm. For a super-easy family stroll with grand views, walk from Mürren just above the train tracks to either Winteregg (40 min, restaurant, playground, train station) or Grütschalp (60 min, train station), then catch the panorama train back to Mürren.

Hikes on the Jungfrau (East) Side of the Lauterbrunnen Valley

▲▲▲**The Männlichen-Kleine Scheidegg Hike**—This is my favorite easy Alpine hike (2.5 miles, 1.5 hours, 900-foot altitude drop to Kleine Scheidegg). It's entertaining all the way, with glorious Jungfrau, Eiger, and Mönch views. That's the Young Maiden being protected from the Ogre by the Monk. (These days, that could be problematic.) Trails may be snowbound into June; ask about conditions at the lift stations or local TIs. If the Männlichen lift is closed, you can take the train straight from Lauterbrunnen to Kleine Scheidegg (see Jungfraujoch under "Lifts and Trains," page 143).

If the weather's good, descend from Gimmelwald bright and early to Stechelberg. From here, get to the Lauterbrunnen train station by post bus (4 SF, bus is synchronized to depart with the arrival of each lift) or by car (parking at the large, multistory pay lot behind the Lauterbrunnen station-2 SF/2 hrs, 9 SF/day). At Lauterbrunnen, buy a train ticket to Männlichen (29 SF one-way). If hiking from Männlichen to Wengen via Kleine Scheidegg (this complete hike), you'll buy a ticket from Lauterbrunnen to Männlichen, then from Wengen back to Lauterbrunnen, for 51 SF. Sit on the right side of the train for great waterfall views on your way up to Wengen. In Wengen, walk across town (buy a picnic, but don't waste time here if it's sunny—you can linger after your hike) and catch the Männlichen lift to the top of the ridge high above you (lift departs every 15 min, beginning the first week of June). Note that the lift can be open even if the trail is closed; confirm that the trail is open before ascending.

From the top of Wengen-Männlichen lift station, turn left and hike uphill 20 minutes to the little peak (Männlichen Gipfel, 7,500 feet) for that king- or queen-of-the-mountain feeling. Then take an easy hour's walk—facing spectacular Alpine panorama views—to

Kleine Scheidegg for a picnic or restaurant lunch. To start the hike, leave the Wengen-Männlichen lift station to the right. Walk past the second Männlichen lift station (this one leads to Grindelwald, the touristy town in the valley to your left). Ahead of you in the distance, left to right, are the north faces of the Eiger, Mönch, and Jungfrau; in the foreground is the Tschuggen peak, and just behind it, the Lauberhorn. This hike takes you around the left (east) side of this ridge. Simply follow the signs for Kleine Scheidegg, and you'll be there in about an hour—a little more for gawkers, picnickers, and photographers. You might have to tiptoe through streams of melted snow—or some small snow banks, even well into the summer—but the path is well-marked, well-maintained, and mostly level all the way to Kleine Scheidegg.

About 35 minutes into the hike, you'll reach a bunch of benches and a shelter with incredible unobstructed views of all three peaks—the perfect picnic spot. Fifteen minutes later on the left, you'll see the first sign of civilization: Restaurant Grindelwaldblick, offering a handy terrace lunch stop with tasty, hearty, and reasonable food (open daily, closed Dec and May, see "Sleeping and Eating in Kleine Scheidegg," page 158). After 10 more minutes, you'll be at the Kleine Scheidegg train station, with plenty of other lunch options (including Bahnhof Buffet, see "Sleeping and Eating in Kleine Scheidegg," page 158).

From Kleine Scheidegg, you can catch the train to "the top of Europe" (see Jungfraujoch information, page 143). Or head downhill, riding the train or hiking (30 gorgeous min to Wengernalp station, a little further to the Allmend stop; 60 more steep min from there into the town of Wengen). The Alpine views might be accompanied by the valley-filling mellow sound of alphorns and distant avalanches.

If the weather turns bad or you run out of steam, catch the train at any of the stations along the way. After Wengernalp, the trail to Wengen is steep and, though not dangerous, requires a good set of knees. Wengen is a good shopping town. (For accommodations, see "Sleeping in Wengen," page 157.) The boring final descent from Wengen to Lauterbrunnen is knee-killer steep—catch the train.

▲▲Schynige Platte to First—The best day I've had hiking in the Berner Oberland was when I made this demanding six-hour ridge walk, with Lake Brienz on one side and all that Jungfrau beauty on the other. Start at Wilderswil train station (just above Interlaken) and catch the little train up to Schynige Platte (6,560 feet). The high point is Faulhorn (8,790 feet, with its famous mountaintop hotel). Hike to a small mini-gondola called "First" (7,110 feet), then ride down to Grindelwald and catch a train back to your starting point, Wilderswil. Or, if you have a regional train pass (or no car but endless money), take the long, scenic return trip to Gimmelwald: From Grindelwald, take the lift up to Männlichen, do the hike to Kleine Scheidegg and Wengen (see above), then head down into Lauterbrunnen and on to Gimmelwald.

For a shorter (3-hr) ridge walk, consider the well-signposted Panoramaweg, a loop from Schynige Platte to Daub Peak.

The Alpine flower park (5 SF, at the Schynige Platte station) offers a delightful stroll through several hundred Alpine flowers (best in summer) including a chance to see Edelweiss growing in the wild.

Lowa, a leading local manufacturer of top-end hiking boots, has a promotional booth at the Schynige Platte station providing free loaner boots to hikers who'd like to give their boots a try. They are already broken in, but bring thick socks (or buy them there).

If hiking here, be mindful of the last lifts (which can be as early as 16:30). Climbing from First (7,113 feet) to Schynige Platte (6,454 feet) gives you a later departure down and less climbing.

Mountain Biking

Mountain biking is popular and accepted, as long as you stay on the clearly marked mountain-bike paths. A good ride is the round-trip Mürren Loop that runs from Mürren to Gimmelwald, down the

Sefinen Valley to Stechelberg, along the dreamy bike path left of the river to Lauterbrunnen, up by funicular to Grütschalp (bike costs same as person-7.80 SF), and back through a working cheese farm to Mürren. You can rent bikes in Mürren (Stäger Sport, 35 SF/day includes helmet, daily 9:00–17:00, closed mid-Sept–mid-June, across from TI/Sportzentrum, tel. 033-855-2355, www.staegersport.ch) or in Lauterbrunnen (Imboden Bike, 25 SF/4 hrs, 35 SF/day; call ahead to reserve a full-suspension bike: 45 SF/half day, 65 SF/full day; daily 8:30–18:30, tel. 033-855-2114). The Lauterbrunnen shop is often open when the Mürren one isn't. It costs 2.50 SF per segment to take a bike onto the gondola.

You can also bike the Lauterbrunnen Valley from Lauterbrunnen to Interlaken. It's a gentle downhill ride via a peaceful bike path across the river from the road (don't bike on the road). Rent a bike at Lauterbrunnen (see above), bike to Interlaken, and return to Lauterbrunnen by train (to take bike on train, pay about 4 SF extra). Or rent a bike at either Interlaken station, take the train to Lauterbrunnen, and ride back.

Rainy-Day Options

When it rains here, locals joke that they're washing the mountains. If clouds roll in, don't despair. They can roll out just as quickly. With good rain gear and the right choice of trail, a hike in the rain can be thoroughly enjoyable, with surprise views popping out all around you as the clouds break. And there are plenty of good bad-weather options.

▲▲Cloudy-Day Lauterbrunnen Valley Walk—Try the easy trails and pleasant walks along the floor of the Lauterbrunnen Valley. For a smell-the-cows-and-flowers lowland walk—ideal for a cloudy day, weary body, or tight budget—follow the riverside trail from Stechelberg's Schilthornbahn station (left of river) for three miles downhill to Lauterbrunnen's Staubbach Falls, near the town church (you can reverse the route, but it's a gradual uphill to Stechelberg). Detour to Trümmelbach Falls (described below) en route. There's a fine, paved, car-free, riverside path all the way (popular with bikers). In this "Valley of Many Waterfalls" (literally), you'll see cone-like mounds piled against the sides of the cliffs, formed by centuries of rocks hurled by tumbling rivers.

If you're staying in Gimmelwald: Take the lift down to Stechelberg (5 min), then walk to Lauterbrunnen, detouring to Trümmelbach Falls shortly after Stechelberg (15 min to falls, another 45 min to Lauterbrunnen). To return to Gimmelwald from Lauterbrunnen, take the funicular up to Grütschalp (10 min), then either walk (90 min to Gimmelwald) or take the panorama train (15 min) to Mürren. From Mürren, it's a downhill walk (30 min) to Gimmelwald. (This loop trip can be reversed.)

Note that this is an El Dorado of base-jumping (parachuting off of cliffs), and each season the bodies of dead thrill-seekers plummet to the valley floor. They hike to the top of a cliff, leap off—falling as long as they can (this provides the rush)—and then pull the ripcord to release a tiny parachute, hoping it will break their fall and a gust won't dash them into the mountainside.

▲**Trümmelbach Falls**—If all the waterfalls have you intrigued, sneak a behind-the-scenes look at the valley's most powerful, Trümmelbach Falls (10 SF, daily July–Aug 8:30–18:00, June 9:00–17:30, Easter–May and Sept–mid-Nov 9:00–17:00, closed mid-Nov–Easter, on Lauterbrunnen-Stechelberg road, take post bus from Lauterbrunnen TI or Stechelberg gondola station, tel. 033-855-3232). You'll ride an elevator up through the mountain and climb through several caves (wet, with lots of stairs, and—for some—claustrophobic) to see the melt from the Eiger, Mönch, and Jungfrau grinding like God's bandsaw through the mountain at the rate of up to 5,200 gallons a second (that's 20,000 liters—nearly double the beer consumption at Oktoberfest). The upper area is the best; if your legs ache, skip the lower falls and ride down on the elevator.

Lauterbrunnen Folk Museum (Heimatmuseum)—This humble collection, in Lauterbrunnen, shows off the local folk culture and two centuries of mountaineering. You'll see lots of lace, exhibits on cheese and woodworking, and classic old photos (free if you're staying in the region, 3 SF otherwise, mid-June–mid-Oct Tue, Thu, and Sat–Sun 14:00–17:00, closed off-season, just over bridge and below church at the far end of town, tel. 033-855-3586 or 033-855-1388).

Mürren Activities—This low-key Alpine resort town offers a variety of rainy-day options, from its shops to its slick Sportzentrum (sports center) with pools, steam baths, squash, and a fitness center (details on page 135). On Wednesday nights at 20:30 from June through August, Mürren's Sportzentrum hosts a lively free cultural night with alpenhorns, folk music, and local wine.

Interlaken Activities—For more bad-weather ideas, see "Sights and Activities—Near Interlaken," page 119.

SLEEPING AND EATING

In addition to my listings in Interlaken, Gimmelwald, Mürren, and Lauterbrunnen, consider these nearby places.

Sleeping in Wengen
(4,180 feet, 1.30 SF = about $1, country code: 41)
Wengen—a bigger, fancier Mürren on the other side of the valley—has plenty of grand hotels, many shops, tennis courts, mini-golf, and terrific views. This traffic-free resort is an easy train ride above Lauterbrunnen and halfway up to Kleine Scheidegg and Männlichen, and offers more activities for those needing distraction from the scenery. Hiking is better from Mürren and Gimmelwald. The **TI** is one block from the station; go up to the main drag, turn left, and look ahead on the left (June–Sept and Dec–mid-April daily 9:00–18:00; mid-April–May and Oct–Nov Mon–Fri 9:00–18:00, closed Sat–Sun; Internet access; tel. 033-855-1414, www.wengen-muerren.ch).

Sleeping Above the Train Station
$$$ Hotel Berghaus, in a quiet area a five-minute walk from the main street, offers 19 rooms above a fine restaurant specializing in fish (Sb-82–117 SF, Db-164–234 SF, 5 percent cheaper with this book and cash through 2005, elevator, guests can use pool at Park Hotel for free; call on phone at station hotel board for free pickup, or walk up street across from Bernerhof Hotel, bear right and then left at fork, 200 yards more past church on the left; tel. 033-855-2151, fax 033-855-3820, www.wengen.com/hotel/berghaus, berghaus @wengen.com, Fontana family).

$$$ Hotel Schönegg is a centrally located splurge, right on Wengen's main drag (Sb-100–110 SF, Db-200–220 SF; higher July–Aug: Sb-115–125 SF, Db-230–250 SF; non-smoking rooms, all rooms have balconies and great views, cozy family room with fireplace, Internet access, good restaurant with big terrace, look for big yellow hotel on main drag near TI, tel. 033-855-3422, fax 033-855-4233, www.hotel-schoenegg.ch, schoenegg@tcnet.ch, Herr und Frau Berthod).

Sleeping Below the Train Station
The first two listings are bright, cheery, family-friendly, and five minutes below the station: Leave the station toward the Co-op store, turn right and go under the rail bridge, bear right (paved path) at the fork, and follow the road down and around.

$$ Bären Hotel, run by friendly Therese and Willy Brunner, offers 14 tidy rooms with perky, bright-orange bathrooms (Sb-80 SF, Db-150 SF, Tb-210 SF, dinner-20 SF more, family rooms, tel. 033-855-1419, fax 033-855-1525, www.baeren-wengen.ch, info @baeren-wengen.ch).

$$ Familienhotel Edelweiss has 25 bright rooms, lots of fun public spaces, a Christian emphasis, and a jittery Chihuahua named Speedy (Sb-65–75 SF, Db-130–150 SF, non-smoking, great family rooms, elevator, TV lounge, game room, meeting room, kids' play-room, tel. 033-855-2388, fax 033-855-4288, www.vch.ch/edelweiss, edelweiss@vch.ch, Bärtschi family).

$$ Clare and Andy's Chalet (Trogihalten) offers three rustic, low-ceilinged rooms (1-room studio: Sb-52 SF, Db-80 SF; 2-room suite: Sb/Db-98 SF, Tb-131 SF, Qb-172 SF; 4-room flat: Tb-147 SF, Qb-176 SF; breakfast-15 SF, dinner by request-30 SF, 4-night minimum preferred, prices higher for shorter stays, no CC, all rooms with balconies, leave station to the left and follow paved path next to Bernerhof Hotel downhill, steep 5-min hike, tel. & fax 033-855-1712, mobile 079-423-7813, www.chaletwengen.ch, info@chaletwengen.ch, Clare's English, Andy's Swiss).

$ Backpackers' Wengen Lodge is an old former schoolhouse offering cheap beds a steep 10-minute hike below the station (25 SF per bed with sheets in a 10-bed, often empty dorm; S-30 SF, D-60 SF, no breakfast, kitchens, follow the signs from the station, tel. 033-855-1573, www.wengenlodge.ch, info@wengenlodge.ch, Angela).

Sleeping and Eating at Kleine Scheidegg
(6,762 feet, 1.30 SF = about $1, country code: 41)
Confirm price and availability before ascending. Both places serve meals.

$$ Bahnhof Buffet invites you to sleep face-to-face with the Eiger (dorm bed-50 SF with breakfast, 68 SF with dinner too, D-167 SF with breakfast and dinner, in the train station building, tel. 033-828-7828, fax 033-828-7830, www.bahnhof-scheidegg.ch).

$ Restaurant Grindelwaldblick, a 10-minute hike from the train station, really gets you up into the mountains (38 SF per bed in 12-bed room, includes sheets, closed Nov and May, tel. 033-855-1374, fax 033-855-4205, www.grindelwaldblick.ch).

Sleeping in Stechelberg
(3,025 feet, 1.30 SF = about $1, country code: 41)
Stechelberg is the hamlet at the end of Lauterbrunnen Valley, at the base of the lift to Gimmelwald, Mürren, and the Schilthorn.

$$ Hotel Stechelberg, at road's end, is surrounded by water-falls and vertical rock, with a garden terrace and 20 quiet rooms—half in a creaky old building, half in a concrete, no-character new building (D-86–104 SF, Db-130, Db with balcony-158 SF, T-147 SF, Tb-186 SF, Q-168 SF, Qb-234 SF, post bus stops here, tel. 033-855-2921, fax 033-855-4438, www.stechelberg.ch, hotel @stechelberg.ch).

$ **Nelli Beer,** renting three rooms in a quiet, scenic, and folksy setting, is your best Stechelberg option (S-35 SF, D-60 SF, 2-night min, no CC, over river behind Stechelberg post office at big *Zimmer* sign, get off post bus at post office, tel. 033-855-3930, some English spoken).

$ **Naturfreundehaus Alpenhof** is a homey, cozy Alpine lodge for hikers. New owners Marc (English) and Diane (Australian) have made it a quiet and peaceful place to relax (60 beds, 2–8 people per co-ed room, 22 SF per bed, D-44 SF, breakfast-9 SF extra, laundry-10 SF, no CC, tel. 033-855-1202, alpenhof@naturfreunde.ch). Behind Hotel Stechelberg (post bus stop), take the path to the right across the river.

Sleeping in Obersteinberg
(5,900 feet, 1.30 SF = about $1, country code: 41)
$ Here's a wild idea: **Mountain Hotel Obersteinberg** is a working Alpine farm with cheese, cows, a mule shuttling up food once a day, and an American (Vickie) who fell in love with a mountain man. It's a 2.5-hour hike from either Stechelberg or Gimmelwald. They rent 12 primitive rooms and a bunch of loft beds. There's no shower, no hot water, and only meager solar-panel electricity. Candles light up the night, and you can take a hot-water bottle to bed if necessary (S-81 SF, D-162 SF, includes linen, sheetless dorm beds-64 SF, these prices include breakfast and dinner, without meals S-37 SF, D-73 SF, dorm beds-20 SF, closed Oct–May, tel. 033-855-2033). The place is filled with locals and Germans on weekends, but it's all yours on weekdays. Why not hike there from Gimmelwald and leave the Alps a day later?

Sleeping in Isenfluh
(3,560 feet, 1.30 SF = about $1, country code: 41)
The tiny hamlet of Isenfluh is even smaller than Gimmelwald and offers better views.

$$ **Pension Waldrand** has a decent restaurant (including great fresh salads) and four reasonable rooms (Db-120–130 SF, Tb-150 SF, includes breakfast, hrly bus from Lauterbrunnen, 4/day from Interlaken, tel. 033-855-1227, fax 033-855-1392, www.waldrand.com, booking@waldrand.com).

ZERMATT
and the MATTERHORN

There's just something about that Matterhorn—the most recognizable mountain on the planet. Anyone who says, "You've seen one mountain, you've seen them all," hasn't laid eyes on this pointy, craggy peak. The Matterhorn seems to have a nearly mystical draw for people—it's the Stonehenge of Switzerland.

Oh, and there's a town, too. Zermatt, a little burg of 5,500 people, might well be the most touristy resort in Switzerland. While there are pockets of traditional charm, virtually every building in town has something to do with the tourist trade, and everyone you meet earns a living one way or another from those who flock here for a peek of the peak. Aside from the stone quarries you'll pass on the way, tourism is Zermatt's only industry.

But be warned: This is a one-mountain town. Many visitors find it touristy and overrated, especially considering its inconvenient

location (at the end of a long, dead-end valley in the southwest corner of the country). And if you make the long trek and find only cloudy weather, there's little else to do...other than wish for a T-shirt that reads, "I went all the way to Zermatt and didn't even see the lousy Matterhorn."

Planning Your Time
On a two-week trip in Switzerland, I'd suggest two nights and the better part of two days in Zermatt if the weather's good. (To check the weather, call the Zermatt TI at tel. 027-966-8100, www.zermatt.ch.)

Zermatt

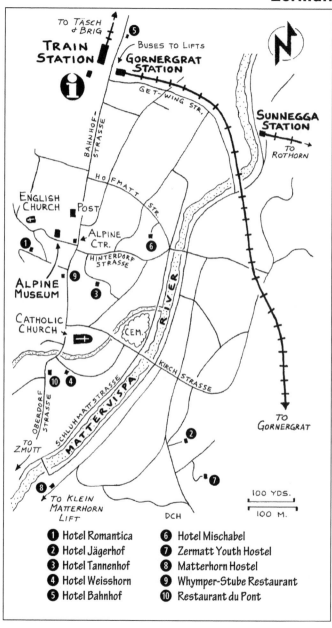

TO TÄSCH & BRIG

TRAIN STATION

⑤ BUSES TO LIFTS

GORNERGRAT STATION

GET-WING STR.

SUNNEGGA STATION

TO ROTHORN

BAHNHOF-STRASSE

HOFMATT STR.

ENGLISH CHURCH

POST

ALPINE CTR.

⑥

HINTERDORF STRASSE

① ⑨

ALPINE MUSEUM

③

CATHOLIC CHURCH

CEM.

RIVER

MATTERVISPA

SCHLUHMATT STRASSE

KIRCH STRASSE

⑩ ④

OBERDORF STRASSE

TO ZMUTT

②

TO GORNERGRAT

⑧

TO KLEIN MATTERHORN LIFT

⑦

DCH

100 YDS.

100 M.

❶ Hotel Romantica
❷ Hotel Jägerhof
❸ Hotel Tannenhof
❹ Hotel Weisshorn
❺ Hotel Bahnhof
❻ Hotel Mischabel
❼ Zermatt Youth Hostel
❽ Matterhorn Hostel
❾ Whymper-Stube Restaurant
❿ Restaurant du Pont

Zermatt vs. the Berner Oberland

I've said for years that the Berner Oberland offers far more high-mountain travel thrills than the Zermatt area (see Gimmelwald and the Berner Oberland chapter). And I still stand by that—if you're going to only one Alpine hideaway in Switzerland, the Berner Oberland is tops. If you're trying to make up your mind, here are a few comparisons:

The Berner Oberland is relatively easy to reach, thanks to its more central location in the country and its good rail connections to Bern and Luzern. Zermatt is farther off the beaten track, at the end of a dead-end valley near the Italian border—and the final approach by train (from Brig) is run by a private company, not covered by your Eurailpass.

Zermatt is essentially one town focused on a single mountain. The Berner Oberland is an entire Alpine region, with many towns and villages to visit—from the bustling administrative center of Interlaken to the tiny, traditional village of Gimmelwald. In Zermatt, most accommodations options are in the town itself. But in the Berner Oberland, you have your choice of the kind of place you want to stay—resort town or humble village; in the valley or

Arrive or leave on the Glacier Express; it's an all-day, cross-country scenic train ride to Chur, with good connections to Zürich and elsewhere in northeast Switzerland (see Scenic Rail Journeys chapter).

ORIENTATION

Zermatt (elevation 5,265 feet) lies at the end of the Nikolaital Valley, along the Mattervispa River in the shadow of the mighty Matterhorn (14,690 feet, "Cervino" in Italian).

The train station is at the bottom of town, a few steps from the main drag, Bahnhofstrasse. As you stand in front of the station with the tracks at your back, the heart of the village is to your right. Funiculars and cable cars to thrilling Matterhorn viewpoints leave from near the train station: The funicular up to Gornergrat is across the street and to your left; the station for the underground train/cable car to Rothorn is a few blocks ahead and to the left, along the river; and the gondola/cable car station up to Klein Matterhorn is through the village to your right, across the river (about three-quarters of a mile away). Details on all of these are listed below.

Zermatt brags that its streets are traffic-free. Well, not quite. Electric cars (big golf carts) buzz around the streets like four-wheeled Vespas, some with surprisingly aggressive drivers. Watch your step.

on a ledge overlooking the mountains.

As for sightseeing, the best part of the Berner Oberland is the Lauterbrunnen Valley, with great high-altitude attractions on both sides (the Jungfraujoch on one side, the Schilthorn on the other), plus other enjoyable lifts, towns, and hikes. Zermatt doesn't have nearly the same diversity. Budget travelers appreciate the Berner Oberland's cheaper accommodations and the discount given on mountain lifts to Eurailpass holders (unlike in Zermatt).

The Berner Oberland offers a wider variety of activities than Zermatt. On a rainy day, you can poke around one of the traditional villages (like Gimmelwald) or the bigger town of Interlaken, or walk through the thundering Trümmelbach Falls. Both areas are touristy, but there are more traditional tidbits of the authentic Swiss countryside in the Berner Oberland than in Zermatt.

You can tell where my heart lies. Still, if you've seen the Berner Oberland already, or if you want to sample two different mountain areas of Switzerland, Zermatt is worth a visit. And the Matterhorn is really something else—it's the reason this place is known around the world.

Addresses are generally not used in this small town. To find your hotel, use the map in this chapter, follow the free map from the TI, look for signs, or ask a local.

Tourist Information

Zermatt's **TI** is right at the train station (July–mid-Sept and mid-Dec–April Mon–Sat 8:30–12:00 & 14:00–18:00, Sun 9:30–12:00 & 16:00–18:00; off-season Mon–Fri 8:30–12:00 & 14:00–18:00, Sat 9:30–12:00 & 14:00–17:00, closed Sun; tel. 027-966-8100, www.zermatt.ch). They offer a variety of handy, free resources: an extremely detailed map, which labels every building in town; a magazine with hotels and lift schedules and prices; an events brochure; and a thick, directory-type information booklet. You can also buy hiking maps here, including a basic overview map of the region (2 SF, helpful for orientation to the region even if you're not hiking), the more detailed map for serious hikers (25.90 SF), and the good *Discovering Zermatt on Foot* hiking guide (29.50 SF, comes with the same basic map the TI sells separately for 2 SF).

Once weekly, there's a free one-hour village **tour** in English. This is a good rainy-day option; ask for the schedule at the TI.

Internet Access: You'll see coin-op Internet stations all over town. The going rate is 12 SF per hour.

Arrival in Zermatt

Zermatt's small train station is conveniently located in the middle of town; the TI is immediately to the right as you leave the tracks, and you'll also stumble on to a stand of Elektro-taxis right out front (see below).

Cars are not allowed in Zermatt. Drivers park in the huge lot at Täsch, a few miles before Zermatt (7.50 SF/day), then take the shuttle train into town (7.80 SF one-way, runs every 20 min until 23:00).

Getting Around Zermatt

Even though Zermatt is "traffic-free," there are ways to get around town faster than on foot. Two different electric **bus** lines depart across from the train station: to the lift station for Klein Matterhorn (2.50 SF, or free with lift ticket, about every 10 min), or to the cliff-hanging neighborhood above that station, called Winkelmatten (3.20 SF, about every 20 min). The buses are marked with their destination and make a few stops along the way before heading back to the station (when they're marked "Bahnhof").

You can also hire your own **Elektro-taxi** (10 SF for anywhere in the heart of town, extra charge for luggage and rides at night, taxi stand in front of train station, or call Bolero at tel. 027-967-6060, Imboden at tel. 027-967-7777, or Schaller at tel. 027-967-1212).

SIGHTS

In Zermatt

The town itself is short on attractions. On rainy days, the TI can only shrug, tell you optimistically about the Alpine Museum, and suggest that you go swimming in one of the big hotel pools.

Wander the Town—Zermatt is charming enough, despite its single-mindedness about catching the tourist dollar. The streets are lined with chalet after chalet. Just off the main drag, you'll spot small

stands of traditional shacks set on stone stilts to keep out mice (called *mazots*; look for them around Hotel Romantic, or near the river in the Hinterdorf area). You'll also spot a handful of churches, including the big landmark Catholic Church (can't miss it on Bahnhof-strasse) or the smaller English Church (built for the many British mountaineers who have flocked to this region; above and behind the Alpine Museum).

▲**Alpine Museum (Alpines Museum)**—This cute little museum, squeezed into two floors of a creaky old building, is worth a visit on a rainy day. Pick up the free English flier and twist your way around

Zermatt Area Hikes

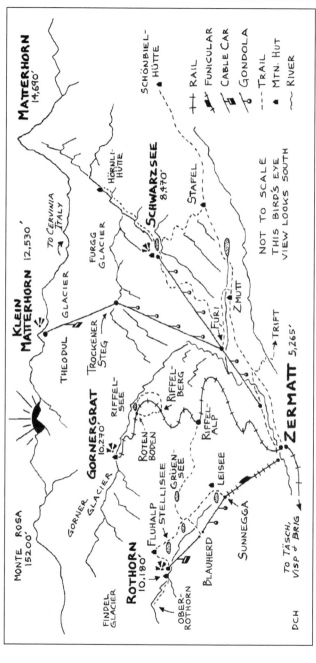

MATTERHORN
14,690'

KLEIN MATTERHORN 12,530'

MONTE ROSA 15,200'

TO CERVINIA, ITALY

THEODUL GLACIER

FURGG GLACIER

TROCKENER STEG

SCHÖNBIEL-HÜTTE

HÖRNLI-HÜTTE

SCHWARZSEE 8,470'

STAFEL

ZMUTT

FURI

TRIFT

GORNERGRAT 10,270'

RIFFEL-SEE

RIFFEL-BERG

ROTEN-BODEN

RIFFEL-ALP

GORNER GLACIER

GRÜEN-SEE

STELLISEE

FLUHALP

BLAUHERD

LEISEE

SUNNEGGA

ZERMATT 5,265'

ROTHORN 10,180'

OBER-ROTHORN

FINDEL GLACIER

TO TÄSCH, VISP & BRIG

NOT TO SCALE

THIS BIRD'S EYE VIEW LOOKS SOUTH

Legend:

- ┼┼ RAIL
- FUNICULAR
- CABLE CAR
- GONDOLA
- --- TRAIL
- ▲ MTN. HUT
- ∿ RIVER

DCH

the stuffed Alpine fauna, exploring the history of Zermatt and the Matterhorn. You'll find out why Teddy Roosevelt climbed the famous peak before he was president. The reliefs of the mountain (and surrounding region) offer a helpful topographic perspective. There's a morbid room displaying artifacts found after deadly accidents, and a room dedicated to July 14, 1865—the day the Matterhorn was finally conquered by a team of seven climbers. Tragically, four of them died on the descent. Upstairs are a couple of reproductions of rugged mountain-hut interiors, along with exhibits on glaciology, axes, and skiing (8 SF, June–Sept daily 10:00–12:00 & 16:00–18:00, Oct Mon–Sat 16:00–18:00, closed Sun, mid-Dec–May Mon–Sat 16:30–18:30, closed Sun, closed Nov-mid-Dec, well-signed off Bahnhofstrasse near the big Catholic Church, tel. 027-967-4100, www.alpinesmuseum.ch). This fun but expensive museum is cramped in its current quarters; for years, they've been trying to move it to a bigger home, but so far, they lack the funding.

High-Mountain Excursions from Zermatt

You have four options for lifts up and out of Zermatt:

1. A cable-car ride to the highest lift station in Europe, **Klein Matterhorn** (not the "real" Matterhorn).

2. A side spur off the Klein Matterhorn line leading to **Schwarzsee**, with some of the closest views you'll get of the Matterhorn.

3. An underground train, then gondola, then cable car to **Rothorn**, with classic Matterhorn views.

4. A funicular up to **Gornergrat**, for good views down on a glacier.

The first trip leads to a snowy wonderland, year-round skiing slopes, and a cave carved into the ice. The other three will take you to pristine pastures with Alpine lakes and Matterhorn vistas.

If the weather's clear and your pockets are deep, consider springing for a **Peak Pass**, which gives you unlimited access to all of these lifts; unfortunately, the minimum length of the pass is three days, so it's bad value for a one- or two-day visit (3 days-154 SF, 4 days-178 SF, 5 days-200 SF). The two-day **Panoramic Pass,** available only in summer, is a better deal—including Klein Matterhorn, Schwarzsee, and Rothorn (but not Gornergrat) for 119 SF. You can purchase passes at the TI or lift stations.

If you go after 14:30, you'll save about 20 percent on individual fares to Klein Matterhorn, Schwarzsee, or Rothorn—always ask (valid mid-June–late Sept). Buy individual tickets directly at the lift stations.

Eurailpass holders do not get a discount on Zermatt lifts, but Swiss Pass holders get 25 percent off.

Note that these descriptions and lift schedules are for the

summer season. If you're a skier, ask the Zermatt TI about specifics for your visit.

▲▲**Klein Matterhorn (12,530 feet) and Schwarzsee (8,470 feet)**—To really get your high-altitude high, zip up to the highest cable-car station in Europe, at Klein ("Little") Matterhorn. From way up here, the Matterhorn is just one of many cut-glass peaks; this is your best chance for a bird's-eye panorama of the Alps without hiking. But note that some visitors are disappointed by this particular view—since it's not the classic Matterhorn profile on all the post-card racks (for that, head to Rothorn—see below).

You'll reach Klein Matterhorn in three parts. First, you'll take a small, six-seat gondola on a six-minute ride over pretty glacier-carved foothills to the Furi station. (From Furi, you can take a different gondola to Schwarzsee—see below.) Then you'll take a larger cable car up to Trockener Steg. Finally, you'll board the last cable car up to Klein Matterhorn; on the left are great views down on glaciers and across to the Gornergrat funicular station. All the way up, you'll see plenty of ski lifts and picturesque little chalets. The area around Klein Matterhorn stays snow-covered all year long, making it a popular place for summer skiers.

Once up top, non-skiers have two sightseeing options: the observation deck and the Glacier Palace. As you leave the lift, follow the hall branching to the left, and take the elevator to the **observation deck** (12,200 feet). Exit the elevator and walk another 100 steps up to stunning panoramas. On a clear day, you can see Italy and France (including Mont Blanc, Europe's highest peak).

If you follow the hall from the lift all the way to the end, you'll reach the Panorama Bar and the exit. Go outside and walk a few steps downhill to the low-profile entrance of the **Glacier Palace,** marked Gletschergrotte (free, daily 9:00–15:00). This place brags that it's the "highest glacial grotto in the world"—a proud claim that makes other high-altitude glacial grottos seethe with envy. The "Palace" is basically a big hole dug into the glacier, allowing you to walk deep inside. As you wander, you'll see ice sculptures (including the Matterhorn and some  flowers encased in ice) and some lackluster exhibits about glaciers, local wines, and "glacier fleas" (a.k.a. "springtails," little bugs that live up here). You can also wriggle into an actual crevasse.

Rather than going all the way to Klein Matterhorn, you could take the gondola from Furi to the Alpine lake **Schwarzsee.** While a much lower elevation (8,470 feet), this area is the closest you can get to the Matterhorn (though it lacks the big-picture Alpine panorama that the other lift excursions offer). You can also do this on your way back down from Klein Matterhorn (when you reach Furi, follow signs to Schwarzsee instead of Zermatt, 26 SF round-trip for just this segment from Furi to Schwarzee and back to Furi, 18 SF one-way). Several popular hiking trails lead from here back down to the valley (see below).

Hikes: There are no hikes from the very top of Klein Matterhorn, since it's covered with snow year-round. The best hike on this series of lifts is actually at Schwarzsee. From the Schwarzee lift station, the hike directly down to Furi is quite steep; a longer but easier and more enjoyable route is to hike down to Stafel, then on to Furi, where you can catch the gondola back to Zermatt (or continue to Zermatt on foot). Plan on the better part of a day for this excursion; easier hikes are described below.

Cost, Hours, Location: Zermatt to Klein Matterhorn costs 78 SF round-trip (52 SF one-way); Zermatt to Schwarzsee is 39 SF round-trip (26 SF one-way). If you plan to do both, you'll save money by getting the Matterhorn Pass, which includes both Klein Matterhorn and Schwarzsee for 78 SF. The Matterhorn Pass, sold at the lift station, is a good deal if this combo-trip is the only one you plan to do in the area; the Peak and Panoramic Passes mentioned earlier cover this combo-trip and more.

The trip up to Klein Matterhorn is open daily year-round (generally Sept–June 8:30–16:05, July–Aug 7:00–16:20). The gondola from Furi to Schwarzsee is only open from mid-June through September (8:40–16:30, from 8:00 July–Aug). If the weather's iffy, confirm that the entire route (all the way to Klein Matterhorn) is open before you ascend—upper segments can close if it's too windy. The elevator to the Klein Matterhorn station is about three-quarters of a mile upriver from the train station (simply follow the river, or catch an electric bus marked "Klein Matterhorn" or "Schwarzsee" in front of the Gornergrat funicular station, across from the main train station).

▲▲**Rothorn (10,180 feet)**—While actually farther away from the famous peak than the other lifts described, Rothorn offers *the* classic Matterhorn view. When Matt Lauer wanted the best shot of the Matterhorn to broadcast on the *Today* show, he came here (and brought along some alphorn players). The passage up to Rothorn has three parts: first, an underground train to Sunnegga; then a gondola to Blauherd; and finally, a cable car to Rothorn. All along the way are typical glacial lakes, offering a picturesque foreground for your Matterhorn photos.

Hikes: You have plenty of easy options for walking around the lakes up here. Perhaps the best is the mostly level hike from the Blauherd station, around the Rothorn peak, past the Stellisee, to the restaurant at Fluhalp, then back again. Get details at the TI before you ascend.

Cost, Hours, Location: 54 SF round-trip, 36 SF one-way. In summer, you can get to Rothorn (or Blauherd) only from mid-June through September (8:00–16:40); the lower segment, to Sunnegga, is open longer (June–late April). The whole shebang is open and ready for skiers in winter. The station for the underground train from Zermatt is across the river from the train station, just downstream from the Gornergrat funicular tracks.

▲▲**Gornergrat (10,270 feet)**—This is somewhere between Klein Matterhorn and Rothorn—both geographically and in terms of your experience. A funicular train takes you from Zermatt up to Gornergrat in about 45 minutes, with stops at other stations along the way (Findelnbach, Riffelalp, Riffelberg, and Rotenboden). On the way up, sit on the right-hand side for good Matterhorn vistas. At Gornergrat, you'll enjoy a sweeping Alpine panorama with great views of the Matterhorn (though, again, it's not the perfect profile that you see from Rothorn). What's distinctive about Gornergrat is that it offers the best views of the Gorner Glacier that runs  between it and Klein Matterhorn. It also gets you up close and personal with the *other* big mountain in the neighborhood—actually taller than the Matterhorn—the Monte Rosa. This towering behemoth is the highest point in Switzerland (15,200 feet).

Hikes: The best option is to take the train from Gornergrat back to the Rotenboden station, where you can enjoy the pretty Riffelsee lake. Then walk down to the Riffelberg station and take the train back into Zermatt.

Cost, Hours, Location: 67 SF round-trip, 34 SF one-way. Two or three trains leave hourly mid-June–Sept, starting around 8:00 and ending 18:00 (fewer trains and shorter hours off-season). The funicular station is right across the street from Zermatt's train station.

Other Mountain Activities—Aside from hiking and views, more adventurous travelers have even more opportunities for Alpine thrills near Zermatt. **Parasailing** is an expensive but unforgettable experience, best at Rothorn (around 120 SF, Air Taxi Zermatt, tel. 027-967-6744). The hills above Zermatt are laced with great **mountain-bike** paths as well (get specifics from TI).

SLEEPING

Little Zermatt has over a hundred hotels—and all of them are expensive. This is a resort town, plain and simple, where even the budget bunks cost big bucks. I've scrutinized the options and presented you with the best deals I could find.

Sleep Code

(1.30 SF = about $1, country code: 41)
S = Single, **D** = Double/Twin, **T** = Triple, **Q** = Quad,
b = bathroom, **s** = shower only, **no CC** = Credit Cards not
accepted, **SE** = Speaks English, **NSE** = No English. Unless otherwise noted, credit cards are accepted, English is spoken, and
breakfast is included.

    To help you sort easily through these listings, I've divided
the rooms into three categories, based on the price for a standard
double room with bath:

    $$$ **Higher Priced**—Most rooms 150 SF or more.
    $$ **Moderately Priced**—Most rooms between 110–150 SF.
    $ **Lower Priced**—Most rooms 110 SF or less.

I've listed peak summer rates (generally highest July–Aug).
You'll pay less at most places in shoulder season, like June and
October, and more during ski season (Dec–mid-Jan). When there's
a range, higher prices are for busy times, and lower prices are when
it's slow (unless otherwise noted).

Many hotels close in the shoulder season. Some begin to close
as early as mid-April. They reopen beginning in early May, and
some stay on vacation until late June. Of course, several hotels are
open year-round.

$$$ Hotel Romantica, a few scenic steps up from the main
street, offers 15 rooms in a flower-dappled chalet surrounded by old-
fashioned huts. If you like all those huts, consider sleeping in one—
this hotel has converted two of them into accommodations, which cost
about the same as a standard double room. Both have tiny interiors
with two stories: sitting room and modern bathroom downstairs, loft
bedroom upstairs. Choose between the very low-ceilinged and rustic
hut (cozy and romantic) or the hut with more modern finishes (Sb-
78–85 SF, Db-140–180 SF, prices depend on demand and length of
stay, tel. 027-966-2650, fax 027-966-2655, www.reconline.ch
/romantica, romantica.zermatt@reconline.ch, Cremonini family).

$$$ Hotel Jägerhof has 48 homey rooms with new bathrooms
and lots of charm. It's a little farther from the center, across the river
towards the Klein Matterhorn lift station (Sb-82 SF, Db-164 SF,
most doubles have balconies, elevator, Internet access, tel. 027-966-
3800, fax 027-966-3808, www.hoteljaegerhofzermatt.ch, jaegerhof
@zermatt.ch, Perren family).

$$ Hotel Tannenhof is a great value hiding a few steps off
the main drag. Its 23 rooms are small, tight, and woody, without
much character, but the location is good and the place is well-run
(S-50 SF, Sb-80 SF, D-100 SF, Db-120–130 SF, T-120 SF,

tel. 027-967-3188, fax 027-967-3173, www.tannenhof.zermatt.info, tannenhof @zermatt.info, Schaller family).

$$ Hotel Weisshorn offers 17 basic but comfortable rooms over a restaurant, right in the heart of town. The rooms are nothing special, but the rates are reasonable (S-60 SF, Sb-76 SF, D-104 SF, Db-132–138 SF, T-147 SF, Am Bach 6, tel. 027-967-1112, fax 027-967-3839, hotel.weisshorn@bluewin.ch).

$ Hotel Bahnhof, with 17 slightly worn but tidy rooms (and three dorm rooms), could be Zermatt's best value. The basement features a relaxing lounge, dining room, and guests' kitchen. It's professionally run and conveniently located across the street from the train station (dorm bed-30 SF, S-60 SF, Sb-71 SF, D-88 SF, Db-99 SF, Qb-176 SF, no breakfast, laundry facilities, lockers, tel. 027-967-2406, fax 027-967-7216, www.hotelbahnhof.com, welcome@hotelbahnhof.com).

$ Hotel Mischabel is a traditional old place with 28 rooms a block off the main drag. In this ancient wooden chalet, everything creaks and squeaks—the floors, the doors, and the beds. This is the kind of rustic place you imagined staying at in Switzerland (S-52 SF, Sb-62 SF, D-104 SF, T-156 SF, tel. 027-967-1131, fax 027-967-6507, www.zermatt.ch/mischabel, mischabel.zermatt@reconline.ch).

$ Zermatt's official Youth Hostel is sparkling new, looking over town from a perch high above the river. It's slick and super-modern, with key cards and bathrooms inside most rooms. The hostel is an especially good deal, since the rates include dinner—a real plus in expensive Zermatt (prices per person: in 8-bed room without bathroom-56 SF, in 6-bed room with bathroom-58 SF, in 4-bed room without bathroom-62.50 SF, in 4-bed room with bathroom-66.50 SF, in twin D-75 SF, in D with 1 big bed-98 SF, in Db with 1 big bed-103 SF, all rates include sheets and are cheaper off-season, Internet access, no curfew, Staldenweg 5, tel. 027-967-2320, fax 027-967-5306, www.youthhostel.ch/zermatt, zermatt@youthhostel .ch). From the station, take the bus marked "Winkelmatten" to the Luchre stop; the hostel is a steep hike up from there (follow the International Hostel signs).

$ Matterhorn Hostel is a more low-key, easygoing place overlooking the river. Their mission is to provide cheap beds in an expensive town, and they deliver. The floor plan is claustrophobic, with not an inch of wasted space: 10 dorm rooms with graffiti decor are upstairs; the lounge and showers are in the basement; and a tiny Internet nook is tucked under the spiral staircase (bed in 6- to 8-bed dorm-29 SF, in 4-bed room-34 SF, in 2- or 3-bed room-39 SF, breakfast-7 SF, towel rental-2 SF, closed 10:00–16:00, or 11:00–16:00 in peak season, Schluhmattstrasse 32, tel. 027-968-1919, fax 027-968-1915, www.matterhornhostel.com, info@matterhornhostel.com). It's a 10-minute walk from the train station on the way to the Klein Matterhorn lift station, right on the river.

EATING

Zermatt's restaurants are as expensive as its hotels. If there's a cheap snack bar-type place here, I didn't find it (unless you count McDonald's). There are several handy bakeries and grocery stores for buying a picnic, and the streets are lined with restaurants featuring garish signs, interchangeable menus, and high prices. In a resort town like this, Back Door places just don't exist. Simply wander down the main drag (Bahnhofstrasse) and pick the place that looks best. I ate well without breaking the bank at the two places listed below. They're obvious and touristy (with Japanese signs outside), but the prices and food are acceptable—and I noticed several locals mixed in with the out-of-towners.

Whymper-Stube, named for the first brave soul to conquer the Matterhorn, specializes in cheese dishes—that means fondue (around 25 SF per person) and raclette (8 SF per serving, two servings is enough for most). While American and Japanese tourists photograph each other eating fondue, six barstools in the corner are warmed by local regulars (daily 12:00–14:00 & 18:00–22:00, on Bahnhofstrasse, on the right just before the big church, tel. 027-967-2296).

Restaurant du Pont claims to be the oldest restaurant in town. With low ceilings, Swiss folk sayings on the walls, and signs in a half-dozen languages, it's a touristy but cozy place to dine (fondue for two-44 SF, greasy *Rösti* for around 15 SF, open daily, on Bahnhofstrasse at end of square with big Catholic Church, tel. 027-967-4343).

TRANSPORTATION CONNECTIONS

Zermatt is at the end of the dead-end Nikolaital Valley, which you can only reach on a private rail line. This train, operated by the Matterhorn Gotthard Railway (www.mgbahn.ch), connects Zermatt to Brig hourly (90 min, second-class fares: 34 SF one-way, 67 SF round-trip, covered by Swiss Pass, Eurailpass not valid or discounted). Once in Brig, you can easily connect to destinations all over Switzerland (the Swiss Rail station is just across the street from the private Matterhorn Gotthard Railway station; online train schedules say you'll have to walk 7 min between them, but it's more like 1 min). Between Zermatt and Brig is Visp, which can be handier for connecting to some destinations (such as Lausanne).

From Brig by train to: Bern (hrly, 1.75 hrs), **Zürich** (hrly, 3 hrs, sometimes with transfer in Bern), **Lausanne** (hrly, 1.75 hrs; often faster to transfer in Visp), **Interlaken** (hrly, 1.5 hrs with transfer in Spiez), **Luzern** (nearly hrly, 3.5 hrs, transfer in Olten; see Luzern's "Transportation Connections," page 74, for a longer but more interesting route via the Glacier Express and William Tell Express), **Chur** or **St. Moritz** (see "Glacier Express," page 241).

APPENZELL

Welcome to cowbell country. In the moo-mellow and storybook-friendly Appenzell region, you'll find the warm, intimate side of the land of staggering, icy Alps. Savor Appenzell's cozy, small-town atmosphere.

Appenzell is Switzerland's most traditional region...and the butt of humor because of it. Entire villages meet in town squares to vote (an event featured on most postcard racks). Until 1989, the women of Appenzell couldn't vote on local issues. (But lately, the region has become more progressive. In 2000, its schools were the first to make English—rather than French—mandatory.)

A gentle beauty blankets the region of green rolling hills, overlooked by the 8,200-foot peak of Mount Säntis. As you travel, you'll enjoy an ever-changing parade of finely-carved chalets, traditional villages, and cows moaning, "Milk me." While farmers' bikini-clad daughters make hay, old ladies with scythes walk the steep roads, looking as if they just pushed the Grim Reaper down the hill. When locals are asked about Appenzell cheese, they clench their fists as they answer, "It's the best." (It is, without any doubt, the smelliest.)

If you're here in late August or early September, there's a good chance you'll get in on (or at least have your road blocked by) the ceremonial procession of flower-bedecked cows and whistling herders in formal, traditional costumes. The festive march down from the high pastures is a spontaneous move by the herding families, and when they finally do burst into town (a slow-motion Swiss Pamplona), locals young and old become children again, running joyously into the streets.

Appenzell Region

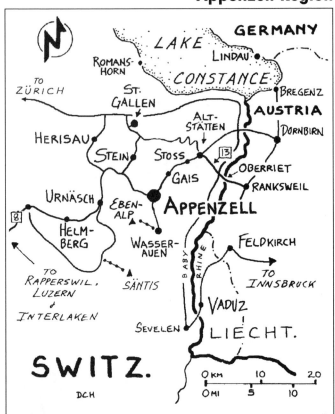

Planning Your Time

On a two-week trip through Switzerland, save a day for the Appenzell region. This pastoral area offers a good first look at Switzerland—but would be an anticlimax after the rugged Berner Oberland or Matterhorn. If you have only a week or less in Switzerland, skip the subtle charms of Appenzell and head instead for the high mountains.

In the Appenzell region, I prefer overnighting up on Ebenalp. But the accommodations are a little rustic for some travelers, who prefer the comfort of hotels and *Zimmer* in Appenzell Town.

Getting Around Appenzell

By car, Appenzell is a breeze. Using public transportation, you can easily get to Appenzell Town and Ebenalp, though connections are sparse otherwise.

The center of the region is Appenzell Town, connected by **train** with Wasserauen (near Ebenalp; hrly except 2/hr during rush hour, 20 min) and Herisau (same train, opposite direction, 40 min). From Herisau, bigger trains depart hourly for St. Gallen (20 min), Zürich (1.5 hrs), and Luzern (2 hrs). The Herisau train also stops at Urnäsch (20 min). Regional **buses** connect towns several times a day; for schedules, check with the TI or the post office.

Appenzell's shuttle service, **PubliCar**, takes passengers to locations—such as Stein—not serviced by buses (for Appenzell to Stein, figure about 9 SF). To reserve, inquire at the TI or call 0800-553-060.

Appenzell Town

In this traditional town, kids play "barn" instead of "house," while Mom and Dad watch yodeling on TV. The town center is a painfully cute pedestrian zone that delights tourists born to shop.

ORIENTATION

Tourist Information
The **TI** is on the main street at Hauptgasse 4 (May–mid-Oct Mon–Fri 9:00–12:00 & 13:30–18:00, Sat–Sun 10:00–12:00 & 14:00–17:00; mid-Oct-April Mon–Fri 9:00–12:00 & 14:00–17:00, Sat–Sun 14:00–17:00; tel. 071-788-9641).

The **Appenzell Card,** sold at the TI, covers trains, PubliCar rides, lifts, and some museums in the region (1 day-31 SF, 22 SF with Swiss Pass; 3 days-52 SF, 42 SF with Swiss Pass; 5 days-84 SF, 68 SF with Swiss Pass). This card can be a good deal if you're visiting the Appenzeller Folklore Museum and going round-trip to Ebenalp in a single day. Otherwise, it's not worth it.

Helpful Hints
Internet Access: Use the computers at the library on the church square (Tue–Wed 14:00–17:00, Thu 14:00–16:00, Fri 17:00–20:00, Sat 9:30–11:30, closed Sun–Mon).

Post Office: It's in front of the train station.

Bike Rental: Rent wheels at the train station (23 SF/half day, 30 SF/full day).

Launderette: Don't waste time looking for one.

SIGHTS

In Appenzell Town

▲**Folk Music**—Folk music concerts take place every Thursday (mid-June–mid-Oct) at 18:30 in the City Hall, and every Wednesday at 20:00 at Hotel Hof Weissbad. You can also sometimes find live music at local restaurants—ask at the TI.

▲**Appenzeller Folklore Museum (Appenzeller Volkskunde Museum)**—The folk museum next to the TI provides an excellent look at the local cow culture. Ride the elevator to the sixth floor and work your way down through traditional costumes, living rooms, art, and crafts (5 SF, covered by Swiss Museum Passport—see page 15, April–Oct daily 10:00–12:00 & 14:00–17:00, Nov–March Tue–Sun 14:00–17:00, closed Mon, ask to borrow English handbook).

Near Appenzell Town

Bike to the Rhine—To experience this area on two wheels, rent a bike at the train station and glide about two hours down into the Rhine Valley to the town of Alstätten. From there, take the single-car train back up the hill to Appenzell (details and bike map at TI).

▲**Stein**—The town of Stein has the **Appenzell Showcase Cheese Dairy** (Appenzell Schaukäserei, daily May–Oct 9:00–19:00, Nov–April 9:00–18:00, cheesemaking normally 9:00–14:00, tel. 071-368-5070). It's fast, free, smelly, and well-explained in a 15-minute English video and free English brochure (with cheese recipes). The lady at the cheese counter loves to cut samples. The dairy also sells yogurt and cheap boxes of cold iced tea. The restaurant serves powerful cheese specialties.

Stein's great **folk moo-seum** (Appenzeller Volkskunde Museum) is next door. With old-fashioned cheesemaking demonstrations, peasant houses, fascinating embroidering machinery, cow art, and folk-craft demonstrations, this museum is fun, but not worth the 7 SF if you've seen the similar museum in Appenzell Town (covered by Swiss Museum Passport—see page 15, Mon 13:30–17:00, Tue–Sat 10:00–12:00 & 13:30–17:00, Sun 10:00–17:00, Nov–March no demos but museum open, tel. 071-368-5056, www.appenzeller-museum-stein.ch).

Without a car, the only way to get to Stein is by PubliCar (see "Getting Around Appenzell," above).

▲**Urnäsch**—This appealing one-street town has Europe's cutest museum. The Appenzell Museum, on the town square, brings this region's folk customs to life. Warm and homey, it's a happy little honeycomb of Appenzeller culture. A 20-minute movie in English explains four of the major regional festivals (6 SF, covered by Swiss Museum Passport—see page 15, April–Oct daily 13:30–17:00,

Sleep Code

(1.30 SF = about $1, country code: 41)
S = Single, **D** = Double/Twin, **T** = Triple, **Q** = Quad,
b = bathroom, **s** = shower only, **no CC** = Credit Cards not
accepted, **SE** = Speaks English, **NSE** = No English. Unless otherwise noted, credit cards are accepted, English is spoken, and
breakfast is included.

    To help you sort easily through these listings, I've divided
the rooms into three categories, based on the price for a standard
double room with bath:

    $$$ **Higher Priced**—Most rooms 100 SF or more.
     $$ **Moderately Priced**—Most rooms between 50–100 SF.
      $ **Lower Priced**—Most rooms 50 SF or less.

Nov–March open only if you call ahead, winter entry fee-20 SF for
groups smaller than 10, guided tour-20 SF plus entry, good English
description brochure, tel. 071-364-2322).

SLEEPING

Sleep in touristy Appenzell Town if you want comfort—but for a
rustic, high-altitude thrill, I love the low-tech, no-shower dorms at
Ebenalp (see page 179). Appenzell Town is small, and the hotels are
central. The *Zimmer* are six blocks from the town center.

    $$$ Hotel Adler, above a delicious café/bakery (daily
7:30–19:30, closed Wed Nov–June), offers two kinds of rooms:
modern or traditional Appenzeller (with designer lamps imitating
traditional headwear of Appenzeller women). Helpful Franz Leu,
proud to be an Appenzeller, has turned the halls and traditional
rooms of his hotel into a museum of regional art and culture (Sb-
80–105 SF, Db-170–190 SF, suite-260–280 SF, elevator, between
TI and bridge on Adlerplatz, tel. 071-787-1389, fax 071-787-1365,
www.adlerhotel.ch).

    $$$ Restaurant Hotel Traube, two blocks from the TI, is
another cozy hotel, with seven tastefully decorated rooms above a
fine restaurant. The friendly Hunziker family has welcomed guests
here for three generations. Don't confuse Hotel Traube ("grape" in
German) with the similarly named Hotel Taube ("dove") nearby
(Sb-85–110 SF, Db-150–180 SF, Marktgasse 7, tel. 071-787-1407,
fax 071-787-2419, www.hotel-traube.ch, info@hotel-traube.ch).

    $$ Zimmer: To experience a pleasant Swiss suburban neighbor-
hood, consider the following: **Haus Lydia,** a six-room, Appenzell-
style home filled with tourist information and a woodsy folk
atmosphere, is on the edge of town and includes a garden and a

powerful mountain view. Its crisp, newly renovated rooms are a fine value if you have a car or don't mind a 20-minute walk from the town center (Sb-60 SF, Db-92 SF, great breakfast; east of town over bridge, past Mercedes-Esso station, take next right and go 600 yards, Eggerstandenstrasse 53, tel. 071-787-4233, fax 071-367-2170, www .hauslydia.ch, contact@hauslydia.ch, friendly Frau Mock-Inauen); Frau Mock-Inauen also rents a roomy apartment by the week (Db-82–86 SF, breakfast extra). **Gästezimmer Koller-Rempfler** is a family-friendly, five-room, traditional place several blocks before Haus Lydia, a little closer to the town center (Db-85–95 SF, Tb-115–120 SF, 5 SF less for 3-night stays, no CC, Eggerstandenstrasse 9, tel. 071-787-2117, niklauskoller@hotmail.com).

EATING

The Appenzeller beer is good, famous, and about the only thing cheap in the region. Ideally, eat an early dinner up on Ebenalp at **Berggasthaus Aescher,** even if you're staying in Appenzell Town (see page 175; last lift down at 19:00 July–Aug, 18:00 June and Sept, earlier off-season).

In Appenzell Town, many good restaurants cluster around Landsgemeindeplatz, where residents gather the last Sunday of each April to vote on local issues by show of hands. (The rest of the year, it's a parking lot.) The first four restaurants are within a block of this town square, just a few blocks up Hauptgasse from the TI (away from the bridge). All restaurants are open daily from about 8:00 to 24:00 unless otherwise noted.

Restaurant Hotel Traube offers pleasant dining indoors or out, with fresh ingredients and a wide selection of traditional Swiss and Appenzeller meals (20-SF plates, vegetarian options, Tue–Sun 9:00–24:00, closed Mon, see "Sleeping," above).

Hotel Appenzell serves fine salads and vegetarian dishes for around 22 SF (meat dishes also available; at corner of square closest to TI, tel. 071-788-1515).

Restaurant Marktplatz is filled with locals playing cards in a more traditional Appenzeller atmosphere (closed Thu, on small parking lot across from Landsgemeindeplatz fountain, walk around white building with horse head, tel. 071-787-1204).

Gasthaus Hof offers a huge variety of specials, including cheese dishes that give the place an unforgettable aroma (fondue-20–24 SF, healthy salad dishes, meat "vitamin corner" meals-15–33 SF, cold meals-15–22 SF, next to Hotel Appenzell, tel. 071-787-4030).

Gasthaus Freudenberg has reasonably priced meals and great views over Appenzell from outdoor tables. It's a 15-minute uphill walk from the town center (healthy *Fitnessteller*-20–35 SF, vegetarian dishes-12–17 SF, summer grill special-20–34 SF, closed Wed and Nov; go under train station, turn right, and follow yellow signs to Freudenberg; tel. 071-787-1240).

TRANSPORTATION CONNECTIONS

From Appenzell Town by train to: **Zürich** (2/hr, 1.75 hrs with change in Gossau, 2.25 hrs with change in St. Gallen), **Chur** (hrly, 2.5 hrs, transfer in St. Gallen), **Luzern** (hrly, 2.75 hrs, change in Herisau), **Bern** (hrly, 3.25 hrs, transfer in Gossau), **Interlaken** (hrly, 4.5 hrs, 2 transfers including Gossau or St. Gallen and Zürich or Bern), **Lausanne** (2/hr, 5 hrs, transfer in Gossau or St. Gallen), **Munich** (3/day, 4.5 hrs, transfer in St. Gallen).

Drivers: See "Route Tips for Drivers" at the end of this chapter.

Ebenalp

This cliff-hanging hut is a thin-air alternative to Appenzell Town. Ride the lift from Wasserauen, five miles south of Appenzell Town by road or rail line, to Ebenalp (5,380 feet). On the way up (left side), you'll get a sneak preview of Ebenalp's cave church and the cliffside board-walk that leads to the guest house. From the top, you'll enjoy a sweeping view all the way to Lake Constance (Bodensee).

ORIENTATION

Leaving the lift, take a 12-minute hike through a prehistoric cave (slippery and dimly lit—hold the railing, and you'll soon return to daylight), past a hermit's home (a tiny museum, always open) and the 400-year-old Wildkirchli cave church (hermit monks lived there 1658-1853), to a 170-year-old guest house built precariously into the cliff. Originally a hut housing farmers, goats, and cows, it evolved into a guest house for pilgrims coming to the monks for spiritual guidance. Today, Berggasthaus Aescher welcomes tourists, offering cheap dorm beds and hot, hearty plates of *Rösti* (see "Sleeping and Eating," below).

The region is a hit with hikers who make the circuit of mountain hotels. There are 24 hotels, each a day's hike apart. All origi-

nated as Alpine farms. Of these, Berggasthaus Aescher is the oldest and smallest.

From Ebenalp's sunny cliff-side perch, you can almost hear the cows munching on the far side of the valley. Only the para-sailors, like neon jellyfish, tag your world as 21st-century. In the distance, nestled below Säntis peak, is the isolated Seealpsee lake. The one-hour hike down to the lake is steep but pleasurable (take left at first fork below guest house).

Getting There: The Ebenalp lift runs at least twice hourly until 19:00 in July and August, 18:00 in June and September, and 17:30 in spring and fall (18 SF up, 24 SF round-trip, half price with Swiss Pass, free and reportedly safe parking at lift, free hiking brochure, closed for 2 weeks in both Nov and May for maintenance, tel. 071-799-1212, www.ebenalp.ch).

SLEEPING AND EATING

There's no reason to sleep in Appenzell Town. The Ebenalp lift, across from the tiny Wasserauen train station, is a few minutes' drive or a 10-minute train ride south.

$$$ Berggasthaus Ebenalp sits atop the mountains just above the lift. Its newly refurbished rooms are booked long in advance for Saturdays, but otherwise empty (4-, 6-, or 8-bed dorms with comforters-30 SF per person; D-104 SF, coin-op shower, tel. 071-799-1194, Sutter family).

$$ From Wasserauen, you can hike up the private road to **Berggasthaus Seealpsee,** on the idyllic Alpine lake Seealpsee (loft dorm beds with sheets-27 SF, S-50 SF, D-100 SF, showers-2 SF, tel. 071-799-1140, fax 071-799-1820, www.seealpsee .ch, berggasthaus@seealpsee .ch, Dörig family).

$ Berggasthaus Aescher (see photo on previous page) promises a memorable experience. The 170-year-old house has only rainwater and no shower. Friday and Saturday nights sometimes have great live music, but are often crowded and noisy, with up to 45 people, and parties going into the wee hours. Monday through Thursday, you'll normally get a small, woody dorm to yourself. The hut is actually built into the cliff; its back wall is the rock itself. From the toilet, you can study this Alpine architecture. Sip your

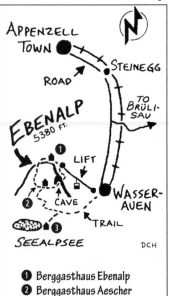

Ebenalp

- ❶ Berggasthaus Ebenalp
- ❷ Berggasthaus Aescher
- ❸ Berggasthaus Seealpsee

coffee on the deck, sheltered from drips by the gnarly overhang 100 feet above. The guest book goes back to 1940, there's a fun drawer filled with an Alpine percussion section, and the piano in the comfortable dining/living room was brought in by helicopter. Claudia can show you rock-climbing charts. For a strenuous 45-minute predinner hike, copy the goats: Take the high trail toward the lake, circle clockwise up toward the peak and the lift, then hike down the way you originally came (dorm bed-35 SF, comes with comforter, no towels or showers available, breakfast-14 SF, dinner-14–22 SF, no CC, closed Nov–April, 12 min by steep trail below top of lift, tel. 071-799-1142, www.aescher-ai.ch, reserve by phone, run by Claudia and Beny Knechtle-Wyss and their 5 children—Bernhardtage 20, Reto-19, Lukas-16, Lilian-15, and Dominik-13—plus 3 pigs, 5 goats, 3 donkeys, 20 rabbits, and 2 dogs).

TRANSPORTATION CONNECTIONS

Route Tips For Drivers

Appenzell to Interlaken/Gimmelwald (120 miles): It's a three-hour drive from Appenzell to Ballenberg (Swiss Open-Air Museum), and another hour from there to the Gimmelwald lift. Head out of Appenzell Town following signs to Herisau/Wattwil. A few scenic miles out of town, in Stein, Schaukäserei signs direct you to the Appenzell Showcase Cheese Dairy (see page 176). From there, head for Wattwil. Drive through Ricken into the town of Rapperswil. Once you're in Rapperswil, follow the green signs to Gotthard/Zürich over the long bridge, then continue south, following signs to Einsiedeln and Gotthard. You'll go through the town of Schwyz, the historic core of Switzerland that gave its name to the country.

From Brunnen, one of the busiest, most impressive, and expensive-to-build roads in Switzerland wings you along the Urnersee. It's dangerously scenic, so stop at the parking place after the first tunnel (on right, opposite Stoos turnoff), where you can enjoy the view and a rare Turkish toilet. Follow signs to Gotthard through Flüelen, then the autobahn for Luzern, vanishing into a long tunnel that should make you feel a little better about your 40-SF autobahn sticker. Exit at the Stans-Nord exit (signs to Interlaken). Go south along the Alpnachersee toward Sarnen. Continue past Sarnensee to Brienzwiler before Brienz. A sign at Brienzwiler will direct you to the Freilichtmuseum Ballenberg (Swiss Open-Air Museum)/Ballenberg Ost. You can park here, but I prefer the west entrance, a few minutes down the road near Brienz.

From Brienzwiler, take the autobahn to Interlaken along the south side of Lake Brienz. Cruise through the old resort town, down Interlaken's main street. From the Ost Bahnhof (East Train Station), drive past the cow pasture with a great Eiger-Jungfrau view on your left and grand old hotels, the TI, post office, and banks on your right, to the West Bahnhof (West Train Station) at the opposite end of town. If stopping in Interlaken, park there. Otherwise, follow signs to Lauterbrunnen. Gimmelwald is a 30-minute drive and a five-minute gondola ride away (see Gimmelwald chapter).

Side-Trip Through Liechtenstein: If you must see the tiny and touristy country of Liechtenstein, take this 30-minute detour: From Feldkirch, drive south on E77 (follow FL signs) and go through Schaan to Vaduz, the capital. Park near the City Hall, post office, and TI. Passports can be stamped (for 2 SF) in the TI (tel. from Switzerland 00423/232-1443). Liechtenstein's banks (open until 16:30) sell Swiss francs at uniform and acceptable rates. The prince looks down on his 4-by-12-mile country from his castle, a 20-minute hike above Vaduz (castle interior closed to visitors, but offers a fine view; catch trail from Café Berg). To leave Liechtenstein, cross the Rhine at Rotenboden, immediately enter the autobahn, drive north from Sevelen to the Oberriet exit, and check another country off your list.

LAKE GENEVA
and FRENCH SWITZERLAND

Lake Geneva, in the southwest corner of the country, is the Swiss Riviera. Separating France and Switzerland, the lake is surrounded by Alps and lined with a collage of castles, museums, spas, resort towns, and vineyards. Its crowds, therefore, are understandable. This area is so beautiful that Charlie Chaplin and Idi Amin both chose it as their second home.

French is the predominant language at Lake Geneva ("Lac Léman" in French, "Genfersee" in German). To establish a better connection with the locals, see the "French Survival Phrases" in the appendix, *s'il vous plaît*.

Skip the big, dull city of Geneva; instead, sleep in fun, breezy Lausanne. Explore the romantic Château de Chillon and stylishly syncopated Montreux. The French Swiss countryside offers up chocolates, vineyards, Gruyère cheese, and a fine folk museum.

Planning Your Time
On a quick trip, you can get a good overview of Lake Geneva's highlights in a day or less. Lausanne makes the best home base. If you're in a hurry, make a beeline for Château de Chillon. With more time, lazily float your way between Lausanne and Chillon on a scenic boat cruise, and get lost in Lausanne's old town and unique museums (the Olympics and Art Brut museums are best). If you have a car, explore some of the countryside options to the north (handiest if you're driving between here and Bern or Murten; see "French Swiss Countryside," page 199).

Getting Around Lake Geneva

Trains easily connect towns along Lake Geneva. Take the faster Direct trains if you're going between larger cities, such as Lausanne or Montreux, or the slower Régional or REV trains if you're heading for a smaller destination, such as Château de Chillon or Villeneuve (check the TV screens in the station for Direct, Régional, or REV to find the right train).

Boats carry visitors to all sights of importance. Daily boat trips (4/day in each direction May–Sept, fewer off-season) connect Lausanne with Vevey (60 min, 16 SF), Montreux (80 min, 20.60 SF), and Château de Chillon (90 min, 22 SF). First class costs about one third more and gets you passage on the deck up top, where you should scramble for the first-come, first-served chairs (Eurailpass holders sail free, but it uses up a flexi-day of the pass, tel. 021-614-6200, www.cgn.ch).

The short cruise between Montreux and Château de Chillon is fun. The pretty town of Vevey gives you the most scenic 60-minute boat ride from Lausanne and 30-minute ride from Chillon, and makes an enjoyable destination. Evian, immediately across from Lausanne, is the French spa town famous for its mineral water. Boats go hourly (30 min, passport required) filled with people ready to enjoy its spa and tour its mineral water facilities.

Lausanne

This is the most interesting city on the lake, proudly dubbing itself the "Olympic Capital" (it's been home to the International Olympic Committee since 1915). Amble the serene lakefront promenade, stroll through the three-tiered, colorful old town, explore the sculptures at Olympic Park, and visit the remarkable Collection de l'Art

Brut. Take a peek at the Gothic Cathedral and climb its tower for the view.

Lausanne was founded on the lakefront by Romans. But with the fall of Rome and the rise of the barbarians, the first Lausanners fled for the hills, establishing today's old town. The Roman site was abandoned (scant ruins today), but in the age of tourism, the waterfront—a district called Ouchy—thrived. So, the city has a design problem that goes back

Lausanne

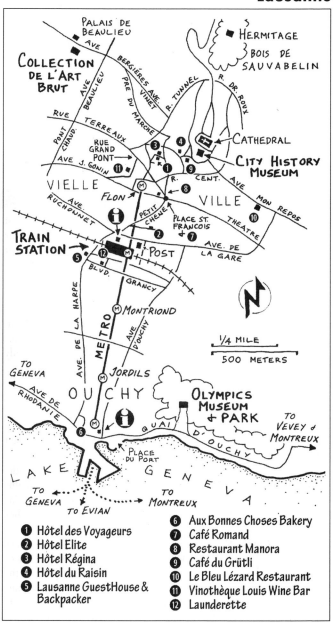

PALAIS DE BEAULIEU

HERMITAGE

BOIS DE SAUVABELIN

COLLECTION DE L'ART BRUT

AVE. BEAULIEU

BERGIÈRES AVE.

PRÉ DU MARCHÉ

AVE DU VINET

R. TUNNEL

R. DR. ROUX

RUE TERREAUX

PONT CHAUD.

RUE GRAND PONT

AVE. J. GONIN

CATHEDRAL

CITY HISTORY MUSEUM

VIELLE

FLON

R. CENT.

AVE. MON REPOS

VILLE

AVE. RUCHONNET

PETIT CHÊNE

PLACE ST. FRANCOIS

THEATRE

TRAIN STATION

BLVD. GRANCY

POST

AVE. DE LA GARE

AVE. DE LA HARPE

METRO

MONTRIOND

AVE. D'OUCHY

TO GENEVA

JORDILS

OUCHY

AVE. DE RHODANIE

OLYMPICS MUSEUM & PARK

TO VEVEY & MONTREUX

QUAI D'OUCHY

PLACE DU PORT

LAKE GENEVA

TO GENEVA

TO EVIAN

TO MONTREUX

¼ MILE

500 METERS

N

1. Hôtel des Voyageurs
2. Hôtel Elite
3. Hôtel Régina
4. Hôtel du Raisin
5. Lausanne GuestHouse & Backpacker
6. Aux Bonnes Choses Bakery
7. Café Romand
8. Restaurant Manora
9. Café du Grütli
10. Le Bleu Lézard Restaurant
11. Vinothèque Louis Wine Bar
12. Launderette

1,500 years—two charming zones separated by a nondescript residential/industrial urban mess. Thankfully, the waterfront and the old town are easily linked by a steep and handy Metro line.

Lausanne has the energy and cultural sophistication of a city larger than its 300,000 people. A progressive city government (with a mayor from the Green Party), which subsidizes art and culture, and a university with plenty of foreign students carbonate the place with a youthful spirit. That spirit shows itself in Lausanne's notoriety as a mecca for inline skating and skateboarding.

ORIENTATION

The tourist's Lausanne has two parts: 1) The lakefront Ouchy (oo-shee), with good restaurants and the Olympics Museum; and 2) the old town, or *vieille ville* (vee-yay veel), with creaky Old World charm and other fine museums, directly uphill from the lake. The train station is located between the two neighborhoods, and everything's connected by a funicular Metro.

Be careful to pronounce Lausanne correctly (loh-ZAHN), and don't confuse it with Luzern.

Tourist Information

Lausanne has two **TI**s, one in the train station (daily 9:00–19:00) and the other at the lakefront Ouchy Metro stop (daily April–Sept 9:00–20:00, Oct–March 9:00–18:00, tel. 021-613-7373 and 021-613-7321, www.lausanne-tourisme.ch).

At either TI, ask about **walking tours** in English (10 SF, free for students and seniors, 90-min tours offered May–Sept Mon–Sat usually at 10:00 and 15:00, in English only if there's a guide and demand, meet in front of City Hall at Place de la Palud, call 021-321-7766 to confirm time and language). Also, check if any free **concerts** are scheduled at the cathedral.

For a busy two-day visit, the **Lausanne Card** can be a good value. It covers city transit and offers 30 percent discounts on all recommended museums (15 SF/2 days, sold at TI, costs virtually the same as two 24-hour transit passes plus offering discounts).

Arrival in Lausanne

By Train: The **train station** is midway between the old town and the lakefront. This sounds inconvenient, but the simple Metro takes you either up to the old town or down to the lake in two minutes (departures every 7 min). The Metro station is across the street from the train station (next to McDonald's, two entrances—be sure to wait on the correct side...ask for help). For most recommended hotels, take the Metro up to Flon, where you ride an elevator up to an elevated bridge (follow the crowds over that, cross Rue Grand-Pont, and you're in the old town). It seems confusing only until you do it. A taxi from the train station to your hotel will run 15 SF.

By Car: Drivers headed for the old town exit the autoroute at Lausanne Centre, following signs to "Centre" and the "Riponne" underground parking garage. If you want the lakefront, take the freeway to Ouchy (where it ends), and you'll find a big pay lot. Coming from Montreux, the smaller road (follow blue signs) leads you along the lakeshore directly into Lausanne.

Getting Around Lausanne

Lausanne is steeper than it is big. A five-stop funicular Metro system connects the lakefront (stop called **Ouchy**, with boat landing) with the train station **(Gare-CFF)** and the upper part of Lausanne (*vieille ville* or *centre ville*, stop called **Flon**). Your ticket choices are 1.30 SF (1 stop, from train station to Flon), 1.50 SF (good for 3 bus stops or 2 Metro stops), 2.40 SF (good for 1 hr of buses and Metro), or 7.20 SF (24-hr pass for buses and Metro). Buy Metro tickets from the TI, ticket windows, or ticket machines; the machines, while modern-looking, don't give change (dropping in a big coin is a costly mistake). For buses, buy tickets before boarding from the white-and-yellow machine at the bus stop. Your Eurailpass is not good on public transportation in Lausanne (except lake boats—see above).

Taxis are pricey—figure 15 SF per short ride.

Helpful Hints

Launderette: Quick-Wash is well-run and handy to the train station (Wed–Mon 8:30–20:30, Sat–Sun from 9:00, closed Tue, self-service only, good English instructions, change machine, Boulevard de Grancy 44, at corner with Passage de Montriond, below train station, tel. 079-449-3761).

Internet: Get online at Quanta (daily 9:00–24:00, across street from train station and above McDonald's at Place de la Gare 4) or Cyberland (daily 9:00–24:00, in old town, just over pedestrian walkway at Rue du Grand-Pont 10).

Bike Rental: Rent bikes at the train station baggage office (23 SF/half day, 30 SF/full day, daily 6:40–19:40, reserve ahead on weekends, tel. 0512-24-2162; ask about leaving bike at another train station—costs 6 SF extra, limited to a few stations). In Ouchy, the bike rental shop next to the Metro station keeps unreliable hours (tel. 079-606-2761). Bikes cost 3 SF on the Metro and are not allowed on buses. Don't use bikes in town, but for exploring the lakeside and vineyards. It's a three-hour lakefront pedal, through vineyards and villages, to Montreux.

Late-Night Groceries: The train station has a grocery store open long hours (daily 6:00–24:00).

Market Days: On Wednesday and Saturday mornings, produce stands fill the pedestrian streets of the old town. Saturday is flea market day on Place de la Riponne.

Old Lausanne (Vieille Ville) Walk

There's no way to see this town without lots of climbing. Locals are used to it (enjoy the firm legs). This self-guided walk introduces you to Lausanne's charming old town. It's a big counterclockwise circle, taking you from the Church of St. Francis up to the cathedral (and castle just beyond), then more or less back to the starting point. While you can begin this walk at the Church of St. Francis (skip down to "Place St. Francois"), most visitors will arrive at the Flon Metro station.

Rue du Grand-Pont: From the Flon station—at the top of the Metro—ride an elevator to the high pedestrian bridge. This leads to the main thoroughfare through the city, Rue du Grand-Pont. Orient yourself from midway across the pedestrian bridge (Passerelle du Flon). Below you stretches Flon—until recently, a down-and-dirty industrial zone. Now, the old warehouses are renovated and throb at night with trendy bars, restaurants, theaters, and discos. The recommended Louis Vinotheque is immediately below (see page 196). The only reminder of the mills that once churned here is the name of the hottest dance club in town: Mad (stands for "Moulin A Danse," or "Dance at the Mill," Rue de Genève 23, tel. 021-340-6969). The huge construction site is a new Metro line—a super high-tech job that will zip from Flon to the top of town in 2008.

Walk to where the pedestrian bridge hits the busy arterial. Head for the green copper spire of the Church of St. Francis (to the right). As you walk along Rue du Grand-Pont, enjoy fine views of the cathedral on your left; you'll see the Metro construction below on your right.

Place St. Francois: The Church of St. Francis marks the town's center and transportation hub, with the grand post office and banks on the right. The church is Gothic, founded by Franciscans in the 13th century. But in 1536, it went Protestant—and was gutted of decorations. Later, a grand Baroque organ was installed. (Note that bus #2 goes from here to the Collection de l'Art Brut—see "Sights," page 191.)

Head uphill (passing to the left of the church) up Lausanne's pedestrianized "Fifth Avenue," Rue de Bourg—home to the finest shops. When the street ends, turn left, continuing uphill and over the bridge toward the cathedral. The railing on the bridge is psychologically designed to discourage suicidal people from leaping. While Switzerland seems to have it all, life here can be stressful—or even depressing. In fact, between Christmas and New Year's, social workers are stationed on this bridge with soup and coffee to counsel and comfort the distraught people who congregate here, contemplating ending it all.

Walking towards the cathedral, you'll notice that Lausanne's old town—filled with administration buildings, offices, schools, and apartments—is subdued compared to most other European old towns, which are lively with lots of eateries. Climb past the cathedral (we'll come back) and continue up the cobbled Rue Cité-Derriere to the summit of the old town, where you'll find the castle.

Castle: Lausanne's castle is closed to the public, but the views are free. The statue celebrates "Major Davel," a local William Tell–like hero. In 1536, the Bernese swept into this region (Canton Vaud) and took over, converting it to Protestantism and ruling it for two centuries. In 1723, Davel's heroic attempt to free his country ended in his decapitation. Only in 1798 was Napoleon able to free Vaud. In 1803, the region entered the Swiss Federation.

Walk downhill (towards the big, blocky cathedral tower). Halfway to the church on your right is the Cantonal High School (called "Gymnasium" here). One of two great buildings from the Bernese period, this was built as a school to train a new kind of Christian leader after the Reformation. This was the first French-speaking Protestant school (c. 1590)—predating similar schools in Geneva (which, under the leadership of John Calvin, was the center of the Swiss Reformation). Across the street, an evocative arch leads to La XIII ("The 13th Century"), a dance place popular with local students and young adults (more fun than trendy, gay on Sun, closed Mon–Tue, no sign, Rue Cité-Devant 10, tel. 021-312-4064).

Cathedral: This is the biggest church in Switzerland, at 100 yards long. Go inside (April–Sept Mon–Fri 7:00–19:00, Sat–Sun 8:00–19:00, Oct–March until 17:30; tower and welcome center open April–Sept Mon–Sat 8:30–11:30 & 13:30–17:30, Sun 14:00–17:30; Oct–March until 16:30).

This is an **Evangelical Reform Church**, meaning that it belongs to the tradition of early Protestant reformer John Calvin—and like its founder, it remains very strict (members aren't allowed to dance, or even to have buckles on their shoes). Iconoclasm, the removal of religious symbols, suited the Calvinists well (see page 91). The once ornate cathedral, originally dedicated to Mary, was cleared of all its statues and decorations. Its frescoes were plastered over, and its fine windows were trashed and  replaced by plain ones (the colored windows were added in the 20th century).

The **pipe organ** is American-made by Fisk, a Boston company that won the commission. Locals love their organ and figure its cost (4,000,000 SF) was money well spent. There are many free concerts here, generally held on Friday evenings. Look back at its 6,700 pipes—the "stiletto in Oz" design represents the wings of angels. (The old pipes now toot in a church in Gdańsk, Poland.)

The **rose window** in the south transept has the church's only surviving 13th-century glass. The rest of the glass dates from the early 20th century. The north transept has some dreamy blue Art Nouveau scenes. Below the rose window (and just left) is the Mary Chapel—once the most elaborate in the church. In 1536, it was scraped clean of anything fancy or hinting of the Virgin Mary. Look at the bits of surviving original paint, and imagine the church in its colorful glory six centuries ago.

The **Painted Portal** (on the right side of the nave, the church's main entrance in the Middle Ages) is remarkable for its painted Gothic statuary: Jesus overseeing the coronation of Mary. The panels below illustrate Mary's death and Assumption.

For a grand view of nearly the entire lake—and lots of Alps—climb the 225-step **tower** (2 SF, April–Sept Mon–Sat 8:30–11:30 & 13:30–17:30, Sun 14:00–17:30, Oct–March until 16:30).

As the city was made of wood in centuries past, it burned down several times. Since the Middle Ages, a **watchman** has lived in the church's tower. His job: to watch for fires and to call out the hours. The city is made of stone today—so there's little danger of fire—and people now sport watches of their own. Nevertheless, Lausanne's night watchman still calls out the hours. Each night on the hour, from 22:00 to 2:00 in the morning, he steps onto his balcony and hollers. His first announcement: "I am the watchman. I am the watchman. We just had 10 o'clock. We just had 10 o'clock."

Esplanade de la Cathedral: Belly up to the fine viewpoint immediately in front of the cathedral. On a clear day, look behind the spire of the Church of St. Francis to see the French Alps (Chamonix and Mont Blanc, over there somewhere, are just out of sight). Evian, the famous French spa town, is immediately opposite Lausanne. On the right, the soft, rolling Jura Mountains, which mark the border of France and Switzerland, stretch all the way from Lake Geneva to Germany.

Notice that the City History Museum is across the square from the cathedral (see "Sights," below). Now's a good time to visit. Then go from the cathedral to...

Place de la Palud and Place de la Riponne: A covered wooden staircase (Escaliers du Marche) leads down from the cathedral. You'll pass Le Barbare ("The Barbarian"), a pub famous for its fine hot chocolate, and the recommended Café du Grütli (see "Eating," page 195). Place de la Palud (pictured on page 184) is marked by its colorful Fountain of Justice (with the blindfolded figure of justice holding her sword and scales...commanding fairness as she stands triumphantly over kings and bishops). Imagine the neighborhood moms sending kids here to fetch water in the days before plumbing. The City Hall is the other fine Bernese building in town (1685, on right). Uphill from City Hall, Rue Madeleine leads to our last stop, the vast and modern Place Riponne. The Palais du Rumine (former university), overlooking the square, now houses a collection of museums (all of which you may skip).

SIGHTS

In the Old Town

▲▲**City History Museum**—Facing the cathedral, this museum traces life in Lausanne from Roman times to the present with many fascinating displays. You'll see exhibits on music (from the time of Bach), the Reformation and its roots, the cathedral before Calvin, the Bernese epoch (Protestant, 1536–1798), and the beginnings of the modern era.

The highlight for many is the 1:200-scale model of Lausanne in the 17th century (based on an engraving from 1638—see copy on wall). You're viewing the town from the perspective of the lakefront district of Ouchy. The Church of St. Francis is in the foreground. You can see river valleys that have since been obliterated by the modern city. The little water mills mark the birthplace of industrial Flon. While the city's walls are long gone, its vineyards survive. (When you enter the museum, request to hear the 18-minute recorded English commentary on the model, and they'll book you a time.) Adjacent rooms show the construction of the Grand-Pont and an interesting collection of historic photos (8 SF includes helpful audioguide, covered by Swiss Museum Passport—see page 15, Tue–Thu 11:00–18:00, Fri–Sun 11:00–17:00, closed Mon, Place de la Cathédrale 4, tel. 021-331-0353).

▲▲**Collection de l'Art Brut**—This well-displayed, thought-provoking collection shows art produced by untrained artists, many labeled (and even locked up) by society as "criminal" or "insane." Read thumbnail biographies of these outsiders (posted next to their works), and then enjoy their unbridled creativity.

In 1945, the artist Jean Dubuffet began collecting art he called "Brut"—untrained, ignoring rules, highly original, produced by people "free from artistic culture and free from fashion tendencies." In

the 1970s, he donated his huge collection to Lausanne, which now displays 30,000 works by 500 artists—loners, mavericks, fringe people, prisoners, and mental ward patients. Dubuffet said, "The art does not lie in beds ready-made for it. It runs away when its name is called. It wants to be incognito" (8 SF, covered by Swiss Museum Passport—see page 15, Tue–Sun 11:00–18:00, closed Mon except July–Aug; bus #3 from station, direction: Bellevaux, stop: Beaulieu; or bus #2, direction: Desert, stop: Jomini; each bus stops within 100 yards of museum, Avenue des Bergières 11, tel. 021-315-2570, www.artbrut.ch).

In Ouchy, Lausanne's Waterfront

The charm of Lausanne lies on its lakefront. The handy Metro connects Ouchy with the train station and the old town every seven minutes. Within 100 yards of the Ouchy Metro stop, you'll find everything (except shopping opportunities and a sandy beach): TI, bike rental, boat dock, the start of the lakeside promenade, and a park. The place is lively from Easter through October, and dead otherwise.

A big C-shaped **weathervane** stands on the breakwater. Identify which of the four winds is blowing by lining the "C" up with semicircle cutouts in the four granite pillars (crouch). By matching the "C" with the pillar that creates a perfect "O," you learn the prevailing wind. Nearby, notice the solar-powered **tour boats** (30-min tours, 7 SF)—they go quietly, smoothly, slowly, and green. Lausanne's current mayor, from the Green Party, is making environmentalism popular. Speaking of green, this city has more green space per inhabitant (300 square feet) than nearly any city in Europe.

▲▲**Olympic Park and Museum**—This beautiful park and high-tech museum celebrate the colorful history of the Olympic Games.

The expensive but excellent museum is great for Olympics buffs—or for those of us who just watch every two years. Given the great explanations and many thrilling video clips to see, plan on spending two hours here (14 SF, family-34 SF, covered by Swiss Museum Passport—see page 15, excellent English descriptions throughout, more in-depth English explanations with the 3-SF audioguide, May–Sept daily 9:00–18:00, Oct–April closed Mon; from Ouchy Metro stop, turn left and walk 5 min to Quai d'Ouchy 1, then ride the outdoor rolling staircase; tel. 021-621-6511, www.olympic.org).

The ground floor traces the history of the Games (including impressive ancient Greek artifacts) and displays a century's worth of ceremonial torches. As you enter, note the time of the next six-minute introductory video—it's good. The museum celebrates Pierre de Coubertin, who in 1894 founded the International Olympic Committee and restarted the games after a 1,500-year lapse. The Olympic spirit is one of peace. Coubertin acknowledged that to ask nations to love each other was naive, but to ask them to respect one another is a realistic and worthy goal.

Upstairs are medals and highlights from each Olympiad, and historic, well-described equipment used for various Olympic events (find Jesse Owens' spiky jumping shoe from 1936—a design that led to the first Adidas; Carl Lewis' shoes from L.A. in 1984; the Michael Jordan–signed basketball from the 1992 Barcelona "Dream Team"; and Cathy Freeman's shoes from the 2000 Sydney games). At the top of the museum, you'll find a lakeview terrace and swanky restaurant (healthy *plat du jour* for 18 SF).

In the basement is a great 3-D theater (Salle Nagano, note the posted movie times as you buy your ticket, and plan accordingly) and an extensive film archive of suspenseful moments in the history of the Games (roughly 5 minutes each, 450 to choose from). Your ticket includes two of these mini-documentaries—if addicted, you can buy three more for 5 SF.

Pauper athletes can enjoy much of the complex for free. Walk through the spiraling core of the complex for a sense of the action. Then enjoy the park's Olympic flame (in front of museum), athletic monuments, and lake views (take escalator to top, ask in museum for free brochure explaining sculptures, and wander back down to lake—avoid the café in the park).

Lakeside and Vineyard Excursions on Foot or Bike—A delightful promenade stretches in both directions from the Ouchy Metro. The best easy **walk** is east (left as you face the lake, 75 min to Lutry). From Lutry, you can catch the train back to Lausanne (hrly, 8 min). If you hike, bring the TI's *Discover the Terraces of Lavaux* flier (describes several hikes, including this one). The trail is marked with blue plaques explaining in English the flora, fauna, and culture you're enjoying.

Picturesque **vineyards** abound along the lake near Lausanne. My favorite plan: a 5- to 10-minute train ride to Chexbres or Grandvaux, then a walk through the villages toward Lutry for stunning views of Lake Geneva. From Lutry, hop the train back to Lausanne (hrly, 8 min).

The best **bike** path goes west (after sharing with cars for half a mile, the trail leaves the road and hugs the shoreline all the way to Morges). You'll pass Vidy (with its Roman ruins—just foundations, free), the headquarters of the International Olympic Committee (not open to the public), lots of sports facilities, and finally just peaceful lakefront parkland stretching to Morges (about 6 miles away, easy return by boat or train).

Sleep Code

(1.30 SF = about $1, country code: 41)
S = Single, **D** = Double/Twin, **T** = Triple, **Q** = Quad,
b = bathroom, **s** = shower only, **no CC** = Credit Cards not
accepted, **SE** = Speaks English, **NSE** = No English. Unless otherwise noted, credit cards are accepted, English is spoken, and
breakfast is included.

To help you sort easily through these listings, I've divided
the rooms into three categories, based on the price for a standard
double room with bath:

$$$ **Higher Priced**—Most rooms 170 SF or more.
$$ **Moderately Priced**—Most rooms between 110–170 SF.
$ **Lower Priced**—Most rooms 110 SF or less.

SLEEPING

Lausanne hotels are expensive. Price ranges depend on view, season,
and room location. The only inexpensive doubles are at the Lausanne
GuestHouse.

The Régina, Voyageurs, and Raisin hotels are in the old town
(take the Metro up to Flon, ride up the elevator, cross the pedestrian bridge, cross Rue du Grand-Pont, walk up Rue Pichard, and
take the first right); the rest are closer to the train station.

$$$ Hôtel des Voyageurs has 33 predictable rooms across the
street from Hôtel Régina (below). Part of the Comfort chain, it's a
lesser value, without the Régina's charm, but in an equally good loca-
tion (Sb-140 SF, Db-185 SF, Tb-205 SF, about 10 percent cheaper
July–Aug, non-smoking rooms, elevator, Rue Grand Saint-Jean 19,
tel. 021-319-9111, fax 021-319-9112, www.voyageurs.ch, info
@voyageurs.ch).

$$$ Hôtel Elite, run by the Zufferey family, is on a quiet, leafy,
residential street just above the train station. Its 33 rooms are pleas-
ant and modern (Sb-130 SF, Db-170–240 SF depending on size
and view, Tb-200–255 SF, non-smoking rooms, elevator; from station cross the street and go uphill around McDonald's, take first
right to Avenue Sainte-Luce 1; tel. 021-320-2361, fax 021-320-
3963, www.elite-lausanne.ch, info@elite-lausanne.ch).

$$ Hôtel Régina, on a steep pedestrian street immersed in old-
town charm, is a great find: 36 comfy, newly remodeled rooms, hos-
pitable hosts (Michel and Dora), and a great location (Sb-128 SF,
Db-168 SF, third person-40 SF, suites-165–325 SF depending on
number of people, 10 percent less Fri–Sun, cheaper in winter, non-
smoking rooms, free Internet access, Rue Grand Saint-Jean 18,

tel. 021-320-2441, fax 021-320-2529, www.hotel-regina.ch, info
@hotel-regina.ch).

$$ Hôtel du Raisin, an Old, Old, Old World dive with dingy,
faded furnishings, has 12 rooms in a great but noisy location on a
lively square in the old town (S-55 SF, Ss-70 SF, D-120 SF, Ds-
140 SF, attached restaurant with sidewalk café, Place de la Palud 19,
tel. & fax 021-312-2756, NSE).

$ Lausanne GuestHouse & Backpacker has got to be one of
Switzerland's best hostels. This elegant, century-old house, which
offers dorm beds and private rooms, turns its back on the train tracks.
All of its rooms overlook the lake on the quiet side (bed in 4-bed
dorm-35 SF, S-80 SF, Sb-90 SF, D-88 SF, Db-100 SF, no smoking,
no curfew, reception open 7:30–12:00 & 15:00–22:00, no breakfast,
Internet access, lockers, laundry, bike rental, kitchen, garden, parking;
5-min walk from train station: leave out the back by track 9, go down
the stairs and turn right to Epinettes 4, tel. 021-601-8000, www
.lausanne-guesthouse.ch, info@lausanne-guesthouse.ch).

EATING

In Ouchy

The lakeside Ouchy district is *the* place to relax. Immediately in
front of the Metro stop is a fun zone with fountains, parks, play-
grounds, promenades, and restaurants. The only good budget eating
option is a picnic with the local office gang on any of the many invit-
ing benches or scenic lakeside perches. **Aux Bonnes Choses** is a
small bakery with a heart for picnickers, offering good sandwiches,
salads, pastries, and drinks to go (daily 6:30–19:00, left as you exit
Metro, Place de la Navigation 2, tel. 021-617-8857). This is infi-
nitely better then the lousy kiosk options in the waterfront park.

In the Old Town

Café Romand is a classic Swiss brasserie—plain, smoky, and filled
with locals under old-time photos enjoying hearty French/Swiss
home cooking. Students, pensioners, and businessmen eat in this
characteristic yet simple place like they own it (20- to 25-SF plates,
Swiss white wines by the glass and carafe—see listing of what bottles
are open behind bar, daily specials, closed Sun, hiding behind the
Pizza Hut at Place St. Francois 2, tel. 021-312-6375).

Restaurant Manora is part of a modern, self-service chain
offering a quick and healthy series of buffet lines where you grab
what looks good—hot meals, salads (4-SF, 7-SF, and 9-SF plates),
fancy fruit juices, desserts, and so on (daily 6:45–22:30, where Rue
du Grand-Pont hits Place St. Francois).

Café du Grütli (named for the birthplace of Switzerland) offers
typical French Swiss cuisine near Place de la Palud. Choose from

three tempting areas to eat: outside on a cozy cobbled lane; ground-floor, circa-1850, Parisian-bistro style; or upstairs, with antlers and the ambience of a 13th-century castle. As the owner's family is into hunting, you'll find game on the menu (20–30-SF plates, Mon–Fri 11:30–14:30 & 18:00–23:00, Sat until 18:00, closed Sun, Rue de la Mercerie 4, tel. 021-312-9493).

Le Bleu Lézard has great French cuisine, a typical French atmosphere, and a trendy clientele that appreciates its candlelit, bohemian interior and fun outdoor porch (20-SF salads, good veggie options, daily 7:00–24:00, open later on weekends, smoky interior, jazz bar downstairs, Rue Enning 10, tel. 021-321-3830).

Vinothèque Louis is primarily a wine bar, where you can choose from 40 different wines available by the glass (and many more by the bottle). To order appetizers, see their short "tapas" menu. To make your wine choice easier, take advantage of their clever color code, classifying wines by their character. Browse among the many bottles (take-away prices and drink-in prices marked), and take your favorite into the bistro. The ground floor has the *vinothèque* and bistro, with tasty and beautifully presented Mediterranean dishes (25- to 35-SF plates, strong on vegetables). Locals sip their wine and hang out on the big modern sun terrace (daily 11:30–23:00, below the pedestrian bridge, down the elevator, across from Flon Metro stop at Place de l'Europe 9, tel. 021-213-0300). The top floor has the expensive Restaurant Gastronomique (60- to 100-SF *menus*).

TRANSPORTATION CONNECTIONS

From Lausanne by train to: Montreux (2/hr, 20 min on Direct train), **Château de Chillon** (hrly, 35 min on REV train), **Geneva** (3/hr, 40 min), **Bern** (2/hr, 70 min), **Murten** (hrly, 90 min, change in Fribourg, Neuchâtel, or Payerne), **Basel** (hrly, 2 hrs, change in Bern or Biel), **Interlaken** (hrly, 2.25 hrs, transfer in Bern; or go via Golden Pass scenic route, with transfers in Montreux and Zweisimmen—see Scenic Rail Journeys chapter), **Luzern** (every 2 hrs, 2.75 hrs direct; more with transfer in Olten; or go via Golden Pass route—see Scenic Rail Journeys chapter), **Zürich** (2/hr, 2.5 hrs), **Lyon** (almost hrly, 2.75–3.25 hrs, transfer in Geneva), **Chamonix** (every 2 hrs, 2.5 hrs, change in Martigny and Le Châtelard-Frontière), **Paris** (6/day, 4 hrs), **Milan** (6/day, 3.25–4 hrs). Train info: toll tel. 0900-300-3004.

Château de Chillon

This medieval castle, set wistfully at the edge of Lake Geneva, is a ▲▲▲ joy. Remarkably well preserved, it has never been damaged or destroyed—always inhabited, always maintained. The Savoy family (their seal is the skinny red cross on the towers) enlarged it to its current state in the 13th century, when this was a prime location—at a crossroads of a major trade route from England and France to Rome.

Château de Chillon (shee-yon) was the Savoys' fortress and residence, with four big halls (a major status symbol) and impractically large lakeview windows (because their powerful navy could defend against possible attack from the water). Later on, though, when the Bernese invaded in 1536, the castle was conquered in just two days, and the new governor made Château de Chillon his residence (and a Counter-Reformation prison). With the help of Napoleon, the French-speaking people on Lake Geneva finally kicked out their German-speaking Bernese oppressors in 1798. The castle became—and remains—the property of the Canton of Vaud. It's been used as an armory, a warehouse, a prison, a hospital, and a tourist attraction. Rousseau's writings first drew attention to the castle, inspiring visits by Romantics such as Lord Byron and Victor Hugo, plus other notables, including Dickens, Goethe, and Hemingway.

ORIENTATION

Follow the free English brochure from one fascinating room to the next. Enjoy the castle's tingly views, dank prison, battle-scarred weapons, simple Swiss-style mobile furniture, and 700-year-old toilets (rooms #15 and #22). Bonivard's Prison (#7) is named for a renegade Savoy who was tortured here for five years (lashed to the fifth column from the entrance). When the Romantic poet Lord Byron came to visit, Bonivard's story inspired him to write *The Prisoner of Chillon*, which vividly recounts a prisoner's dark and solitary life ("And mine has been the fate of those / To whom the goodly earth and air / Are bann'd, and barr'd—forbidden fare"; full text available in the gift shop). You can still see where Byron scratched his name in a column (third from entrance, covered by glass). The chapel (#18) uses projectors to simulate the original frescoes. Models in room #24 explain the construction of the castle.

Remember the grand views from the lakeside windows? Notice the small slits facing the road on the landside (courtyard, #25)—more practical for defense. The 130-step climb to the top of the keep (#32) isn't worth the time or sweat. Stroll the patrol ramparts, then curl up on a windowsill to enjoy the lake.

Cost, Hours, Information: 9 SF, April–Sept daily 9:00–18:00, shorter hours off-season, easy parking, tel. 021-966-8910, www .chillon.ch. Guided tours will likely be available for individuals in English at 11:30 and 15:00 for an extra 6 SF (mid-June–mid-Sept).

Getting to Château de Chillon: The castle sits at the eastern tip of Lake Geneva, about 20 miles east of Lausanne (and about a mile east of Montreux).

From Lausanne, you can connect to the castle using a combination of various methods: train, bus, boat, and hike.

The hourly **REV train** (direction: Villeneuve, 35 min, 10.40 SF) takes you directly to the station at Veytaux-Chillon, a few minutes' walk along the lake (ideal for picnicking) from the castle.

The faster and more frequent **Direct train** whisks you to Montreux (2/hr, 20 min, 9.80 SF), where you transfer to a bus. From the Montreux station, cross Avenue des Alpes and go down the stairs. Cross the street and find the blue bus stop on your right, where you can hop **bus** #1 to Château de Chillon (2.80 SF, direction: Villeneuve, stop: Chillon; buy tickets at bus stop or from machine on board). You can also **hike** the one mile from Montreux to Château de Chillon.

To return to Lausanne, simply reverse the directions (catch the train from the Veytaux-Chillon station back to Lausanne—trains leave hrly at :07—or bus from Château de Chillon to Montreux-2.80 SF, direction Vevey, stop Escaliers de la Gare, climb up to the station and catch the train the rest of the way to Lausanne).

A slower but more scenic route is by **boat** between Château de Chillon and Montreux or Vevey, connecting to Lausanne with trains. For a longer trip, sail all the way between Château de Chillon and Lausanne, one-way (90 min) or, for true *See*farers, round-trip (see "Getting Around Lake Geneva," page 184).

Montreux

This expensive resort has a famous jazz festival each July. The lakeside promenade takes you along parks, palm trees, *crêperies,* ice-cream stands, and modern sculptures. In the center, meet the statue of Freddie Mercury, who had strong bonds with Montreux. His band, Queen, bought the local Mountain Recording Studios in 1978.

The Montreux **TI** (Mon–Fri 9:00–18:00, Sat–Sun 10:00–17:00, tel. 021-962-8484) has a list of moderate rooms in the center.

Ask about the Chocolate Train to Broc (see page 200).

If you're driving from Montreux to Lausanne, consider visiting the **Corniche de Lavaux.** This rugged, sometimes frightening Swiss Wine Road swerves through picturesque towns and the stingy vineyards that produce Lake Geneva's tasty but expensive wine. From Montreux, go west along the lake through Vevey, following blue signs to Lausanne along the waterfront and taking the Moudon/Chexbres exit. Be sure to explore some of the smaller roads. **Hikers** can take the boat to Cully and explore on foot from there.

SLEEPING

In Montreux, consider **$$ Hôtel-Restaurant du Pont**, which has a restaurant that serves good pasta (Sb-70 SF, Db-130 SF, Rue du Pont 12, tel. 021-963-2249, hoteldupont@hotmail.com, NSE). The **$ hostel** is on the lake, a 10-minute stroll north of Château de Chillon (dorm bed-30 SF, D-80 SF, nonmembers pay extra, Passage de l'Auberge 8, tel. 021-963-4934, fax 021-963-2729, montreux @youthhostel.ch).

Cheap beds in nearby Vevey can be found at the **Backpackers Riviera Lodge** (dorm bed-26 SF, D-80 SF, 3 min from station in 19th-century townhouse next to lakeshore, lots of handy facilities, Place du Marche 5, tel. 021-923-8040, www.rivieralodge.ch, info @rivieralodge.ch).

French Swiss Countryside

The sublime French Swiss countryside is sprinkled with crystal-clear lakes, tasty chocolates, smelly cheese, and sleepy cows. If you're traveling between Murten, Lausanne, and Interlaken (see map on page 200), take time for a few of the countryside's sights, tastes, and smells.

Cross-country buses use Fribourg and Bulle as hubs—**Bulle–Gruyères** (2/day, 15 min), **Fribourg-Bulle** (hrly, 30 min). The train is definitely the best bet between Bulle and Gruyères (hrly, 7 min).

Bulle

Musée Gruèrien
Somehow the unassuming little town of Bulle built a refreshing, cheery folk museum (rated ▲▲) that manages to teach you all about life in these parts and leave you feeling very good (5 SF, covered by

French Switzerland

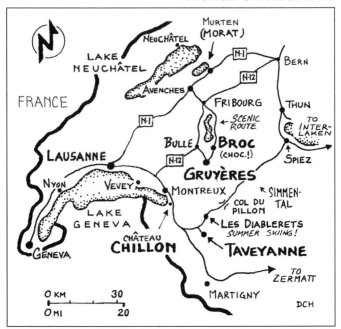

Swiss Museum Passport—see page 15, free English guidebook, Tue–Sat 10:00–12:00 & 14:00–17:00, Sun 14:00–17:00, closed Mon, tel. 026-912-7260). When it's over, the guide reminds you, "The Golden Book of Visitors awaits your signature and comments. Don't you think this museum deserves another visit? Thank you!"

Bulle has a **TI** (tel. 026-912-8022) and a fun folk market on summer Tuesdays.

Broc

Caillers Chocolate Factory

The Caillers factory, churning out chocolate in the town of Broc, welcomes visitors with a hygienic peek through a window, a 15-minute movie, and free samples (4 SF, April–Oct Mon 13:30–16:00, Tue–Fri 9:00–11:00 & 13:30–16:00, closed Sat–Sun and Nov–March, follow signs to Nestlé and Broc Fabrique, groups of 4 or more should call a day in advance to reserve, tel. 026-921-5151).

The sleepy, sweet-smelling town of Broc has a small, very typical hotel, **Auberge des Montagnards** (D-70 SF, great view of Gruyeres, elegant dining room, tel. 026-921-1526, fax 026-921-1576). Broc is connected by tram to Bulle (hrly, 10 min) and

Montreux (Chocolate Train, June–Oct 1–2 wkly, usually Wed and Mon, €50, €18 with railpass, includes Broc and Gruyeres factory tours—see route on page 222).

Gruyères

This ultratouristy town, famous for its cheese and worth ▲, fills its fortified hilltop like a bouquet. Its ramparts are a park, and the ancient buildings serve tourists. The castle is mediocre, but do make

a short stop for the setting. Minimize your walk by driving up to the second parking lot. Hotels here are expensive.

For a spooky, offbeat contrast to idyllic Gruyères, consider the town's **H.R. Giger Museum,** dedicated to the Swiss artist who designed the monsters in the *Alien* movies. The museum, not for the faint of heart, shares those movies' dark aesthetic (10 SF, covered by Swiss Museum Passport—see page 15, daily 10:00–18:00, tel. 026-921-2200).

Gruyère Fromageries: There are two very different cheese-making exhibits to choose from in and near Gruyères—one new and handy, the other old and up in the hills, and both worth ▲▲.

Ye Olde Cheesemaker: Five miles above Gruyères, a dark and smoky 17th-century farmhouse in Moléson gives a fun look at the traditional, smelly craft (3 SF, mid-May–mid-Oct daily 9:30–18:00, closed off-season, cheese actually being made at 10:00 and 14:30, TI tel. 026-921-1044, www.fromagerie.fr.st).

New Cheese Factory: Closer and modern, the cheese-production center at the foot of Gruyères town (follow *Fromagerie* signs) opens its doors to tourists with a continuous English audiovisual presentation (5 SF, daily 9:00–19:00, tel. 026-921-8400, www.lamaisondugruyere.ch). The cute cheese shop in the modern center has lunches and picnic goodies.

Glacier des Diablerets

For a grand Alpine trip to the tip of a 10,000-foot peak, take the three-part lift from Reusch or Col du Pillon. The trip takes about 90 minutes and costs 50 SF. Stay for lunch. From the top, you can see the Matterhorn and a bit of Mont Blanc, the Alps' highest peak. This is a good chance to do some summer skiing (normally expensive and a major headache). A lift ticket and rental skis, poles, boots, and coat cost about 65 SF. The slopes close at 14:00 during the summer, and at 17:00 from October through April.

The base of the lift is a two-hour drive from Murten or Gimmelwald. Your best public-transportation bet is to catch an early train to Diablerets with a transfer in Aigle. Then bus to Col du Pillon (7/day) and take the cable car to the top (last departure at 16:00). For more ski information, call 024-492-0923 or check www.glacier3000.ch.

Taveyanne

This remote hamlet—worth ▲▲—is a huddle of log cabins used by cowherds in the summer. The hamlet's old bar is a restaurant, serving a tiny community of vacationers and hikers. Taveyanne is two miles off the main road between Col de la Croix and Villars. A small sign points down a tiny road to a jumble of huts and snoozing cows stranded at 5,000 feet.

The inn is **Refuge de Taveyanne** (from 1882), where the Seibenthal family serves meals in a rustic setting with no electricity, low ceilings, and a huge, charred fireplace. Consider sleeping in their primitive loft (12 SF, no CC, 5 mattresses, access by a ladder outside, bathroom outside, closed Tue except July–Aug, closed Nov–April, tel. 024-498-1947). It's a fine opportunity to really get to know prize-winning cows.

LUGANO

The town of Lugano—Switzerland with an Italian accent—sprawls luxuriously along the shores of Lake Lugano. The town's charm is its southern feel. The short, scenic train ride over the Alps completely changes the dressing on your Alpine salad. This splashy, zesty, Mediterranean ambience attracts vacationers from the rainy north for its sunshine, lush vegetation, inviting lake, and shopping. While many come here for the fancy boutiques, those on a budget make this an affordable base for hiking, cruising the lake, and passing lazy afternoons in the many gardens.

Planning Your Time

Lugano lies conveniently at the intersection of the William Tell Express and the Bernina Express—two of Switzerland's most scenic train rides. Taking the William Tell Express from Luzern, you can choose whether you want to stay in Lugano or Locarno, a touristy lakeside resort. I prefer Lugano, which feels more authentic. Blitz sightseers arrive on the William Tell one day and take off on the Bernina Express the next. If relaxing is on your itinerary, spend two nights and a full day here, departing and leaving on the scenic trains.

ORIENTATION

The old town is on Lake Lugano, which is bordered by promenades and parks. A funicular connects the old town with the train station above. Funiculars also lift visitors from downtown to commanding views on nearby mountains.

Note that most people in Lugano speak Italian (you're surrounded on three sides by Italy; see "Italian Survival Phrases" in the appendix). In this corner of Switzerland, *Strasse*s become *Via*s, and *Platz*es become *Piazza*s.

Lugano

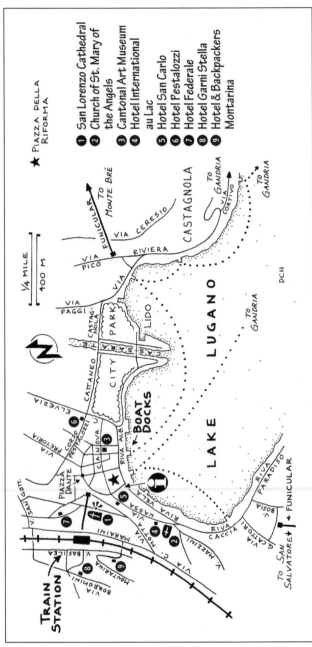

1. San Lorenzo Cathedral
2. Church of St. Mary of the Angels
3. Cantonal Art Museum
4. Hotel International au Lac
5. Hotel San Carlo
6. Hotel Pestalozzi
7. Hotel Federale
8. Hotel Garni Stella
9. Hotel & Backpackers Montarina

★ PIAZZA DELLA RIFORMA

Tourist Information

The Lugano TI is in the Town Hall; enter from the lakeside (Mon–Fri 9:00–19:00, Sat 9:00–17:00, Sun 10:00–15:00, Palazzo Civico, Riva Albertolli, tel. 091-913-3232, fax 091-922-7653, www.lugano-tourism.ch).

Internet Access: The Manora supermarket has several terminals on the third floor in the customer section (Mon–Fri 8:15–18:30, Sat 8:15–16:00, closed Sun, Piazza Dante Alighieri). At Burger King, any meal is a happy meal for those with e-mail concerns—as it comes with 30 minutes of free Internet access (lakefront, on Piazza R. Rezzonico).

Arrival in Lugano

The train station has handy baggage storage, ATMs, an information center, and a convenient grocery, Shop Aperto di Lugano (daily 6:00–22:00). The easiest way to get to the town below is by funicular (1.10 SF, free with Swiss Pass, daily 5:20–23:50, every 5 min).

SIGHTS

Churches and Museums

San Lorenzo Cathedral (Cattedrale San Lorenzo)—The exuberantly decorated interior of this cathedral—dark, mysterious, and Byzantine-feeling—hides behind its austere granite early-Renaissance facade. Frescoes on the pilasters date from the 14th to 16th centuries. Behind the altar, 3-D frescoes give the impression that the architecture continues beyond the actual walls. Enjoy the commanding city and lake views from the church's terrace.

Church of St. Mary of the Angels (Chiesa Santa Maria degli Angioli)—The city's best frescoes are in this unpretentious little lakefront church. Bernardino Luini painted the *Passion and Crucifixion of Christ* and the *Last Supper* in 1529. While clearly inspired by Leonardo da Vinci's *Last Supper* in nearby Milan, Luini gives his work a very personal interpretation. The church, with its grandiose interior, often hosts classical concerts (Piazza B. Luini).

Cantonal Art Museum (Museo Cantonale d'Arte)—This museum offers a humble collection of art from the region (7 SF, Tue 14:00–17:00, Wed–Sun 10:00–17:00, closed Mon, Via Canova 10, tel. 091-910-4780, www.museo-cantonale-arte.ch).

Exploring the Mountaintops near Lugano

Lugano has two hometown mountains. Both are about 3,000 feet above sea level, both are served by funiculars from downtown (20 SF each, every 30 min, 12-min ride), and both offer fine views of Lake Lugano and surrounding mountains. San Salvatore offers slightly better views, while Monte Brè has modern art and sculptures.

San Salvatore—While there is no village here, the viewpoint offers a self-serve and gourmet restaurant, free picnic area, playgrounds, and a little city history museum. The funicular runs daily except in winter (June–Aug 8:30–23:00, April–May and Sept 8:30–18:30, mid-March and Oct–mid-Nov 8:30–17:00, closed mid-Nov–mid-March, www.montesansalvatore.ch).

Monte Brè—A restaurant is adjacent to the funicular, and the village of Brè offers further lunch options and an outdoor museum of modern art. The Lugano TI's brochure explains the exhibited sculpture. The funicular runs daily (9:15–11:45 & 13:15–18:15, www.monte-bre.ch).

Exploring Lake Lugano by Boat and on Foot

Along with pedal boats and simple cruises from village to village, there are fancier excursions (a lunch trip, a grand tour, a shopping excursion into Italy, and an evening dinner cruise). For details, ask at the TI.

The best basic trip is from Lugano to Gandria and back (75 min, 20 SF). This can be combined with a great little lakeside hike: Start your walk in Lugano. The lakefront promenade leads you to

the city park, the Lido beach, and along the main street. The path then leads through the town of Castagnola to the fishing village of Gandria, with its narrow streets and cute houses. After the hour-long walk, you can have lunch in Gandria and hop the next boat back to Lugano. As most of the villages along this cruise can only be reached by foot or by boat, they have a special charm. The first stop after Gandria is Museo Doganale, a customs museum on the other side of the lake (free, April–Oct daily 13:30–17:30, closed Nov–March). From here, you can catch the next boat or follow the yellow path (to the right) along the lake. When you've had enough walking, catch a boat back to Lugano (from Cantine di Gandria, Grotto dei Pescatori, Caprino, or S. Rocco).

SLEEPING

In Lugano's Old Town

$$$ Hotel International au Lac is a classic old hotel with 80 rooms and views on Lake Lugano. It's conveniently and scenically located where pedestrian-only Via Nassa hits the lake. Four generations of Schmids have maintained the turn-of-the-20th-century ambience since 1906, with old photos, inviting lounges, and antique furniture (Sb-110–185 SF, Db-200–298 SF, Tb-270 SF, top prices come

Sleep Code

(1.30 SF = about $1, country code: 41)
S = Single, **D** = Double/Twin, **T** = Triple, **Q** = Quad,
b = bathroom, **s** = shower only, **no CC** = Credit Cards not
accepted, **SE** = Speaks English, **NSE** = No English. Unless otherwise noted, credit cards are accepted, English is spoken, and
breakfast is included.

To help you sort easily through these listings, I've divided
the rooms into three categories, based on the price for a standard
double room with bath:

$$$ **Higher Priced**—Most rooms 180 SF or more.
$$ **Moderately Priced**—Most rooms between 130–180 SF.
$ **Lower Priced**—Most rooms 130 SF or less.

with lake views, elevators, free Internet access, swimming pool, terrace restaurant, parking-18 SF/day, family-friendly, Via Nassa 68,
tel. 091-922-7541, fax 091-022-7544, www.hotel-international.ch,
info@hotel-international.ch).

$$ Hotel San Carlo, also on the pedestrian-only shopping street,
but closer to the center, rents 22 small but modern and cheerful
rooms. This welcoming place is run by Anna Martina and Beppe (S-
95 SF, Sb-120 SF, D-140 SF, Db-160 SF, cheaper off-season, non-
smoking rooms, elevator, Via Nassa 28, tel. 091-922-7107, fax
091-922-8022, www.hotels-suisse.ch/san-carlo, sancarlo@ticino.com).

$$ Hotel Pestalozzi is close to the city park, with some lake
views, offering bright, fresh, modern rooms with a woody Nordic
touch. A stylish belle époque restaurant downstairs serves reasonably
priced meals (S-62 SF, Sb-98 SF, D-104 SF, Db-168 SF, elevator,
Piazza Indipendenza 9, tel. 091-921-4646, fax 091-922-2045,
www.attuale.com/pestalozzi.html, pestalo@bluewin.ch).

Near the Train Station

$$$ Hotel Federale, a family-run place with a grand feel and taste-
fully furnished rooms, is located just below the train station and above
the old town (Sb-145–160 SF, Db-195–240 SF, superior Db-
240–260 SF, junior suite-260–280 SF, some rooms with lake views,
Internet access, fitness center, sauna, Via Paolo Regazzoni 8, tel. 091-
910-0808, fax 091-910-0800, www.hotel-federale.ch, info@hotel
-federale.ch).

$$ Hotel Garni Stella, a surprising little oasis, is just behind
the train station and between the slick modern office buildings.
Owner Antoinette Burkhard's love of modern art is evident, with
statues on the patio and fun paintings throughout (Sb-100–110 SF,
Db-140–160 SF, 5 percent off in 2005 with this book, some rooms

with terraces, free Internet, swimming pool, exit the station at rear, go uphill to Via F.Borromini 5, tel. 091-966-3370, fax 091-966-6755, www.hotel-stella.ch, info@hotel-stella.ch).

$ **Hotel & Backpackers Montarina,** situated in a palm garden overlooking the lake, offers a hotel with private rooms as well as dorm beds (dorm bed in 6- to 16-bed room with sheets-30 SF, S-70 SF, Sb-80 SF, D-100 SF, Db-120 SF, breakfast buffet-12 SF, Internet, small kitchen, swimming pool, reception open 7:30–23:00, Via Montarina 1, tel. 091-966-7272, fax 091-966-0017, www.montarina .ch, info@montarina.ch). As you exit the train station at the rear, you'll see the pink buildings and the big sign on your left.

EATING

These restaurants are all in Lugano's old town.

Manora is an easy and healthy self-service restaurant with indoor and outdoor seating, in the Manor supermarket on Piazza Dante Alighieri (Mon–Sat 7:30–22:00, Sun 10:00–22:00).

La Tinera, beloved by locals, serves affordable, traditional Ticinese cuisine. It's tucked away in an old wine cellar, with heavy wooden furniture and a display of wine bottles and antique copper cookware (smaller dishes 13 SF, meat dishes 20–30 SF, Mon–Sat 8:30–15:00 & 17:30–23:00, closed Sun, Via dei Gorini, behind Piazza Riforma, tel. 091-923-5219).

Around Piazza Riforma: Several restaurants offer decent food and great people-watching from outdoor tables on the square: **Sass Café** (classy wine bar with 18-SF daily specials and 30-SF à la carte items), **Olympia** (19-SF pastas, 30-SF main dishes), **Pizzeria Tango** (across the square, with similar prices in a less elegant setting), and **Vanini Cafe** (tops for desserts and coffee).

TRANSPORTATION CONNECTIONS

Lugano is a long detour from virtually anywhere else in Switzerland. It's best connected to other Swiss destinations by scenic trains: the William Tell Express (to Luzern) or the Bernina Express (to Chur in east Switzerland). For more details on these, see the Scenic Rail Journeys chapter on page 221.

From Lugano by train to: Luzern (hrly, 2.75–3 hrs direct), **Zürich** (hrly, 2.75–3.25 hrs direct), **Interlaken** (hrly, 5.5–6 hrs, transfer in Luzern or Zürich), **Bern** (hrly, 4–4.25 hrs, transfer in Zürich or Olten).

PONTRESINA, SAMEDAN, and ST. MORITZ

High in the mountains of the canton called Graubünden, in the southeast corner of Switzerland, two valleys meet, carving out a picturesque region called the Upper Engadine ("Oberengadin" in German). This area is rich with rugged mountain scenery and colorful folk traditions, and is a handy stopover for tourists taking the scenic Bernina Express. The most famous town here is the glitzy ski resort of St. Moritz, but for a more authentic Back Door experience, head for Pontresina or Samedan—where workaday Swiss people go to find some high-altitude fun.

Planning Your Time

The three towns in this chapter—Pontresina, Samedan, and St. Moritz—form a convenient little triangle, each about 10 minutes apart by train. With a full day here, you can sample all three, and maybe throw in a hike to boot. This area isn't worth a long detour to get to, but it's right on the way if you're linking scenic rail trips (see Scenic Rail Journeys chapter). The Bernina Express passes through Pontresina and St. Moritz, and the Glacier Express begins in St. Moritz before heading through Chur on the way to Zermatt. Hop off the train, set up a home base in one of these towns (Pontresina is best), explore, spend a night or two—then continue on your way.

This remote region has two distinct tourist seasons: summer (June–Oct) and winter (Jan–March). Outside of these seasons, many places are closed and the area can feel dead.

Pontresina

Pontresina—a popular winter and summer mountain resort with about 2,000 residents—makes a good home base for visiting the

Pontresina, Samedan, and St. Moritz Area

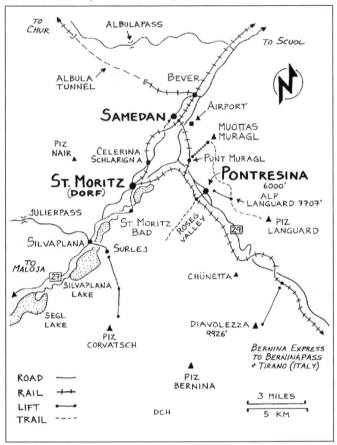

region. At 6,000 feet above sea level on a wind-protected terrace overlooking the Bernina Valley, Pontresina faces southwest and enjoys plenty of sunshine. Popular trails through its larch forests offer spectacular views of the 13,000-foot Piz Bernina peak and the immense Morteratsch glacier.

Pontresina's first tourists, mostly German and British, arrived in the 1850s. For a while, it was a summer-only destination. But by the early 1900s, the Muottas Muragl railway was inaugurated, the first grand hotels were built, and tourists began showing up in winter, too.

Graubünden

Switzerland's biggest canton, isolated by high mountain ranges, is also one of its most conservative. The name Graubünden goes back to 1395, when a group of farmers wearing gray clothes organized themselves in the "Grey League" to fight for their autonomy. This fiercely independent region didn't join the Swiss Confederation until 1803.

People in Graubünden love their beautiful countryside and cherish their customs—predictably voting against EU membership and other issues that might compromise Swiss neutrality and self-determination. Graubünden has three official languages: German, Italian, and Romansh (an ancient dialect that comes directly from Latin). You'll overhear conversations where one person speaks Italian, the other replies in German, a third butts in with Romansh...and everybody understands each other. On the trains, the announcements are in German and Romansh.

Graubünden cuisine is hearty. Try *Pizokel*, a *Spätzle*-like creation of cheesy flour dumplings. In fall, you might find *Pizokel* made from chestnut flour and served with wild mushroom stew. The Graubünden's air-dried beef, *Bündnerfleisch*, very expensive and sliced paper-thin, is popular throughout Switzerland. *Capuns* are cabbage leaves stuffed with a mix of dough, leeks, bacon, onion, and air-dried beef. *Bündner Gerstensuppe* is a creamy barley and vegetable soup. For a Graubünden dessert, it's got to be *Nusstorte*, a rich walnut cake.

ORIENTATION

Pontresina sits on a terrace between two rivers overlooking its valley. Most of the hotels, shops, banks, and the swimming pool line Via Maistra.

Tourist Information: The TI is in the heart of town in the slick new Rondo Culture and Congress Center (July–Aug Mon–Sat 8:30–12:00 & 14:00–18:00, Sun 16:00–18:00, shorter hours off-season, tel. 081-838-8300, fax 081-838-8310, www.pontresina.com).

Arrival in Pontresina

The train station lies at the foot of the town. You can either walk uphill to the center, following the white signs to Pontresina (10 min); or take bus #1 or #2 to Pontresina Post (may be a long wait, 2.60 SF, free with Swiss Pass, buy ticket at counter inside train station). Walking from Pontresina back down to the train station on Via da Mulin offers spectacular gorge views along the way.

Helpful Hints

Groceries: The Co-op grocery store (Mon–Sat 8:00–12:15 & 14:00–18:30, closed Sun) is between the train station and the town center on Via da Mulin.

Internet Access: You'll find public Internet terminals at Hotel Post (8 SF/30 min, daily 8:00–21:00, closed in May, Via Maistra) and Hotel Saratz (5 SF/30 min, daily 24 hours, closed Oct–May, Via Maistra).

SIGHTS AND ACTIVITIES

Church of St. Mary—Above town, next to the five-sided, 13th-century Spaniola Tower, stands this remarkable little church. Faded 13th-century, Byzantine-inspired frescoes survive on the west wall. The other walls and ceiling were richly decorated by an Italian workshop (1497). The bright colors are original; it's never been repainted. The frescoes depict the legend of Mary Magdalene and (above) the story of Lazarus' resurrection. Imagine this church packed with illiterate villagers five centuries ago (attendance back then was compulsory).

Alpine Museum—This little museum is worth a quick visit. Situated in an old Engadine town house, it offers exhibits on the development of Alpine mountain climbing, the regional mining industry, hunting, and local animals (133 of the 250 different bird species found in the Upper Engadine are shown here; you can listen to their recorded songs). The 20-minute slideshow, while in German, is interesting for its images of "the mountain experience" (5 SF, June–Oct Mon–Sat 16:00–18:00, closed Sun, Via Maistra).

Biking—Several sports stores rent bicycles, inline skates, tennis rackets, and other gear. Fähndrich Sport rents good mountain bikes with various suspensions (20–25 SF/half day, 30–40 SF/day, helmets-7 SF/half day, 10 SF/day, Mon–Sat 8:00–12:00 & 14:00–18:30, closed Sun except July–Aug, at Hotel Allegra on Via Maistra, tel. 081-832-7155, www.faehndrich-sport.ch). The Pontresina train station also rents mountain bikes (23 SF/half day, 30 SF/full day, includes helmets, daily 8:00–18:30, bikes can be returned until 21:00, reservations recommended, tel. 081-842-6337).

Music—Free summer classical music concerts are offered in the Tais Forest across the river, and (on rainy days) in the Grand Hotel Kronenhof (daily at 11:00, mid-June–mid-Sept, confirm and get details at TI).

Swimming—The covered public pool (7 SF, Mon–Fri 10:00–21:00, Sat–Sun 10:00–19:00, on Via Maistra) also has a sauna (mixed daily except Thu, when it's women-only; 14 SF, includes pool entrance).

Shopping—Many sports and souvenir shops line Via Maistra. A typical product from the Upper Engadine is a wood carving made from Arven pine, unique to this region. The wood starts out light, darkens with time, and has spots where the branches used to be. Look for the tree's characteristic three-needle clusters when hiking.

Hiking

Pontresina is a hiker's paradise. The town boasts Switzerland's largest mountaineering school and has a good reputation for adventure sports. Shops lining Via Maistra rent all kinds of sports gear.

Upper Engadine trails come with high altitudes. Hikers should bring the appropriate gear (solid shoes, sun protection, windbreaker, hat, and water). Even in summer, with cold winds blowing down from the snow-capped mountains, it can get cold—especially on chairlifts. The sun is strong and the air is thin, so use sunscreen. Hiking trails are marked according to their difficulty. Yellow signs indicate easy hikes and walks. White-and-red signs indicate more demanding hikes, where real hiking boots are in order. Blue signs indicate Alpine routes that require serious gear (these dangerous trails include rock climbing and glacier crossings).

The flowers in the Alps are protected; pick one, and you may be fined. Some meadows are also protected for haymaking. Signs ask you to stick to the trails, as trampled grass is hard to cut.

The TI sells a great brochure with a panoramic map listing the region's many hikes (2.50 SF). Of the 80 hikes it lists and describes, consider this one first...

Pontresina to Alp Languard to Muottas Muragl—One of the most attractive hikes is right above Pontresina. From Pontresina (6,000 feet), take the chairlift up to Alp Languard (7,710 feet; 13 SF one-way, 19 SF round-trip, 25-SF combo-ticket also includes Muottas Muragl funicular back down—see below, daily 8:30–17:30). Then hike to Muottas Muragl (3 hrs); each year, a different theme is displayed along this trail, such as the effects of global warming on the Alps. From Muottas Muragl, you can hike back to Pontresina, or catch the funicular down to the valley. From the base of the lift, bus #1 or #2 takes you to Pontresina (2.60 SF, every 20 min). For details on Muotta Muragl, see page 217.

Other Hiking Options—A fun way to explore the nearby Roseg Valley and marvel at its glacier is to hike two hours up the valley and take the horse-drawn "omnibus" back to Pontresina (reservations required, June–Oct departures at fixed hours, 16 SF one-way, 26 SF round-trip, Luigi Costa, tel. 081-842-6057). You can also rent a private carriage (100 SF one-way, 150 SF round-trip).

Consider taking the train up to the Bernina Pass (7,000 feet), hike around for a couple of hours, then take the train back—or, to get even higher, ride the cable car from the Bernina Pass up to Diavolezza (9,930 feet, 20 SF one-way, 28 SF round-trip, free with Swiss Pass, daily 8:30–17:00, every 30 min).

The TI offers various guided hikes with themes (such as "Experiencing Wilderness with Marmots and Ibex," 10 SF, reservations required). While the hikes are guided in German, some mountaineers speak English and can be hired privately through the TI.

SLEEPING

$$$ Hotel Müller, centrally located at the upper part of the village, is a homey place with a garden, terrace, cozy sitting room, restaurant, and bar (Sb-85–130 SF, Db-150–240 SF, extra bed-70 SF, prices vary with size of room and view, elevator, Via Maistra, tel. 081-839-3000, fax 081-839-3030, www.hotel-mueller.ch, info@hotel-mueller.ch). The Müller family, who have run the place for over a century, offer all guests named Müller (or Miller) a 5 percent discount.

$$$ Chesa Mulin Hotel Garni, below the main street, is a friendly place offering modern, bright, and comfortable rooms, each with a painting depicting a local legend. An inviting sitting area with open fireplace and library makes bad weather tolerable. The friendly Isepponi-Schmid family offers no discount to folks with their last name...but they still take good care of their guests (Sb-114 SF, Db-198 SF, 5 SF cheaper May–June and mid-Sept–Oct, Internet access, sauna, sundeck, Via da Mulin 107, tel. 081-838-8200, fax 081-838-8230, www.chesa-mulin.ch, info@chesa-mulin.ch).

$$ Hotel Engadinerhof, while less cozy, can be a good value. Its 75 rooms are scattered through several buildings. The cheaper

Sleep Code

(1.30 SF = about $1, country code: 41)
S = Single, **D** = Double/Twin, **T** = Triple, **Q** = Quad, **b** = bathroom, **s** = shower only, **no CC** = Credit Cards not accepted, **SE** = Speaks English, **NSE** = No English. Unless otherwise noted, credit cards are accepted, English is spoken, and breakfast is included.

To help you sort easily through these listings, I've divided the rooms into three categories, based on the price for a standard double room with bath:

$$$ **Higher Priced**—Most rooms 180 SF or more.
$$ **Moderately Priced**—Most rooms between 130–180 SF.
$ **Lower Priced**—Most rooms 130 SF or less.

Most hotels in this region have a severe cancellation policy (30 days with no penalty, but thereafter, you'll generally have to pay for the entire period you reserved).

sink-only rooms ("Category A") are clean and have well-preserved furniture from the 1930s (S-60 SF, D-110 SF). "Category B" offers the same old-fashioned rooms, plus antique bathrooms (Sb-80 SF, Db-150 SF). "Category C" gets you modern rooms (Sb-90 SF, Db-170 SF, Internet access, Via Maistra, tel. 081-839-3100, fax 081-839-3200, www.engadinerhof.com, info@engadinerhof.com).

$ **Youth Hostel Tolais** rents 130 beds at the train station. There's no curfew, and guests have 24-hour access (though check-in is limited to 16:00–18:30 & 19:30–22:00, checkout is 7:30–10:00; prices per person: D-75 SF, Q-60 SF, and 6-bed-room-50 SF; prices include dinner and breakfast, 7 SF less for breakfast only, members pay 6 SF less per day, self-serve restaurant, game and TV room, tel. 081-842-7224, fax 081-842-7031, www.youthhostel.ch/pontresina, pontresina@youthhostel.ch)

EATING

Apart from a few bakeries that serve reasonably priced meals, virtually all restaurants in Pontresina are part of a hotel.

Café Puntschella is the local favorite for good, healthy, reasonably priced, local-style dishes. It offers indoor and outdoor seating with great views and the most entertaining menu in town (Engadine specialties-15 SF, pasta-14 SF, salads-11–15 SF, healthy *Fitnessteller*-20 SF, daily 7:30–21:30, shorter hours off-season, Via da Mulin, tel. 081-838-8030, www.cafe-puntschella.ch).

Cozy **Colani Stübli** serves regional and seasonal specialties (17 SF for local dishes such as *Krautpizokel* and *Capuns*, daily lunch special-20 SF, entrées-30–40 SF, daily 11:30–14:00 & 18:00–21:00, smaller dishes after 21:00, at Hotel Steinbock on Via Maistra, tel. 081-839-3626).

Bündnerstübli serves hearty, traditional meals with fish and game in a woody, Old World setting (fish and game-35 SF, vegetarian dishes-16–20 SF, *Fitnessteller*-28 SF, daily 18:00–23:00, at Hotel Rosatsch, Via Maistra 71, tel. 081-838-9800).

Stüva-Bella Restaurant is expensive and exclusive, with a flair for serving inventive and light regional and international cuisine (soups-16 SF, warm salad-25 SF, entrées-40–50 SF, June–Sept and Jan–March daily 12:00–14:00 & 19:00–21:00, closed April–May and Oct–Dec, in Hotel Walther on Via Maistra, tel. 081-839-3636).

Eating above Pontresina: **Alp Languard Chalet,** at the top of the lift (7,710 feet up—see "Hiking," page 213), serves affordable meals with unbeatable views (raclette-15 SF, daily special-18 SF, June–Oct daily 8:30–16:00, tel. 079-682-1511).

TRANSPORTATION CONNECTIONS

From Pontresina by train to: St. Moritz (hrly, 10 min, 4.60 SF), **Samedan** (hrly, 7 min, 4.60 SF), **Chur** (hrly, 2 hrs, transfer in Samedan), **Tirano** (hrly, 2–2.25 hrs), **Zürich** (hrly, 3.75 hrs, transfer in Samedan and Chur).

By bus: Bus #2 connects Pontresina with Punt Muragl and Samedan (2/hr, 2.60 SF).

Samedan

Little Samedan offers just about the best possible peek at Upper Engadine culture and architecture. In the town center, fine old houses on every corner come with traditional Engadine elements: characteristic fortress-like windows, slate shingles, carved doors, thick walls, and *sgraffito* ornamentation. To make *sgraffito*, facades are covered with a layer of dark paint, which is then covered with white plaster. Decorations—which are much more durable than painted facades—are scratched through the white layer, so that the dark background appears.

Tourist Information: Samedan's **TI** is on Via Plazzet (Mon-Fri 8:00–12:00 & 14:00–18:00, Sat 9:00–12:00 & 15:00–17:30, no lunch break July–Aug, always closed Sun, tel. 081-851-0060, fax 081-851-0066, www.samedan.ch).

Samedan Town Stroll

There's little to do in Samedan other than relax and hike.

For a short **hike** from the town center, walk uphill on Surtuor, following the white sign for "Kath. Kirch" ("Catholic Church," neo-Romanesque from 1910, with a bell dating back to 1505). Continue uphill, passing the ski lift, and pause at the yellow benches for the gorgeous view. Samedan lies at the point where the two valleys of the Inn and Flaz rivers merge. From here, the Inn River continues through Innsbruck before joining the Danube.

Huff and puff the thin air (you're at 6,000 feet) to the dramatically situated Protestant **Church of St. Peter**. The Romanesque bell tower (c. 1100) predates today's late Gothic church (c. 1480; to enter, ask for key at TI).

Benches line the cemetery walls and offer sunny, wind-protected picnic spots. Beneath you stretches the highest-altitude **airport** in Europe, a favorite among gliders (launched by a yellow truck with a huge winch, rather than an airplane).

Muottas Muragl

This impressive Alpine perch overlooking Samedan (8,105 feet) is accessible by foot (from Pontresina, described above) or funicular (from Punt Muragl, a request-only stop on the train between Samedan and Pontresina—press the green button, or it won't stop). The funicular (2/hr, 18 SF one-way, 26 SF round-trip, runs daily 8:00–23:00, cheaper after 18:00) takes you up top, where you can hike, lounge around

on deck chairs (10 SF), have a meal (self-service or pricey but good restaurant), or even spend the night.

SLEEPING

$$ Berghotel Muottas Muragl offers a secluded overnight, high in the Alps. When the lift takes the last tourist down, it's just you, the ibex, and the marmots—peaceful as the Alps can be. Rooms are clean and simple (open June–Oct only, S-78 SF, S with view-88 SF, D-136 SF, D with view-156 SF, Q-232 SF, tel. 081-842-8232, fax 081-842-8290, www.muottasmuragl.ch, mmb.rest@cbbag.ch).

TRANSPORTATION CONNECTIONS

From Samedan by train to: St. Moritz (hrly, 8 min), **Pontresina** (hrly, 7 min), **Chur** (hrly, 2 hrs), **Tirano** (hrly, 2.5 hrs, usually with transfer in Pontresina), **Zürich** (hrly, 3.5 hrs, transfer in Chur).

St. Moritz

The oldest—and perhaps best-known—winter resort in the world, St. Moritz has long been the winter haunt of Europe's rich and famous. It's said that in 1864, St. Moritz hotel pioneer Johannes Badrutt offered British summer guests free accommodations if they'd also spend their winter vacations here. They did, had a great time, and

brought their friends along the next year.

Winter is prime time in St. Moritz. Summer is quiet and prices are more reasonable. While celebrity-spotting drops way, way off in the summer, it's a great time for hiking and adventure sports. Visitors enjoy inline skating, polo, golf, paragliding, horseback riding, and evening concerts. Cable cars zip you to some great mountaintops.

St. Moritz itself is little more than luxury hotels and designer boutiques, though it offers livelier nightlife than surrounding towns.

ORIENTATION

St. Moritz has two centers: the town (Dorf) and the spa (Bad). The Dorf is on a steep slope. The train station, at the foot of St. Moritz Dorf, is a downhill hike from the town center. St. Moritz Bad sprawls on a level plain along the lake. Along with the spa, you'll find all the sport facilities at St. Moritz Bad (covered pool, tennis courts, ice-skating hall, horseback riding facilities, and so on). Bus #3 connects Dorf, Bad, and the train station (4/hr, 2.60 SF).

Tourist Information: The **TI** is in the center of St. Moritz Dorf (July–Aug Mon–Fri 9:00–18:30, Sat–Sun 9:00–12:00 & 16:00–18:00; off-season Mon–Fri 9:00–12:00 & 14:00–18:00, Sat–Sun 9:00–12:00; Plazza Mauritius, tel. 081-837-3333, fax 081-837-3366, www.stmoritz.ch).

Arrival in St. Moritz

St. Moritz's train station is near the lake, just below the Dorf. Pick up a free map at the train information counter (lockers but no TI or bike rental at station). The train station café is a good budget eatery (9–17 SF, daily 7:00–21:00). To avoid the steep uphill hike from the train station to Dorf, hop on bus #3 (4/hr, 2.60 SF).

Helpful Hints

Altitude Alert: Don't forget that St. Moritz is at a high elevation (6,090 feet); you might feel dizzy and tired, and your body needs to adapt. Top athletes from all over the world come here for altitude training before the Olympics.

Shopping: The Co-op grocery and department stores are on Plaza da Scoula and Via dal Bagn (Mon–Thu 8:00–18:30, Fri 8:00–22:00, Sat 8:00–17:00, closed Sun).

SIGHTS

Segantini Museum—This place is dedicated to the ultimate painter of Alpine life. Giovanni Segantini captured the bright, sharp, crystal-clear mountain light like no other. Painting in the open air with bold brushstrokes, he created works reminiscent of the French Impressionists. The tiny museum, which looks like a neo-Byzantine church, is actually based on Sargantini's design of the Swiss Pavilion for the 1900 World's Fair in Paris—but made of local stone, rather than the originally intended steel. Segantini died in 1899, and money ran out before this grandiose building could be built. Segantini's masterpiece, the *Alpine Triptych*, was painted for the World's Fair, but also never completed (10 SF, June–Oct and Dec–April Tue–Sun 10:00–12:00 & 15:00–18:00, closed Mon, March–May, and Nov, take bus #2 to Via Somplaz 30, tel. 081-833-4454, www.segantini-museum.ch).

Engadiner Museum—The historic, domestic, and social cultures of the Engadine region are displayed in this museum. The building (from 1905) houses interiors from throughout the Engadine (such as a patrician living room, a smoky farm kitchen, and a four-poster bed), as well as an exhibit on the discovery of the spa water that put St. Moritz on the vacation map (5 SF, June–April Mon–Fri 9:30–12:00 & 14:00–17:00, Sun 10:00–12:00, closed Sat and May, Via dal Bagn 39, take bus #3 to Via Aruons, tel. 081-833-4333).

SLEEPING

$$$ Hotel Soldanella is a cozy, homey place with a central location and gorgeous views. The lounge is furnished with old sport shoes, helmets, antique bobsleds, and lots of games for bad weather. Its terrace deck chairs come with the best views in town. The century-old hotel is run by the Degiacomi family, with friendly Frau Baumann at the reception desk (Sb-110–140 SF, Db-180–250 SF, prices vary with view, elevator, Internet access, sauna, Turkish bath, Via Somplaz 17, tel. 081-830-8500, fax 081-830-8505, www.hotel-soldanella.ch, info@hotel-soldanella.ch).

$ Youth Hostel Still is at the boring, residential eastern end of St. Moritz Bad (prices per person: D-65 SF, Db-76 SF, Q-51 SF, prices include breakfast and 3-course dinner, members pay 6 SF less, reception open 7:00–10:00 & 16:00–22:00, 10-min walk from bus stop on Via Sela, Via Surpunt 60, tel. 081-833-3969, fax 081-833-8046, www.youthhostel.ch/st.moritz, st.moritz@youthhostel.ch).

EATING

As in Pontresina, most of St. Moritz's restaurants are in hotels. An exception is **Restaurant Engiadino**, famous for its fondues (35 SF, lunch specials around 19 SF, Mon–Sat 11:30–14:00 & 18:15–21:30, closed Sun, in center of St. Moritz Dorf at Plaza da Scuola). The **Veltlinerkeller**, decorated with a huge stuffed moose head, serves a variety of grilled meats and Italian specialties (lunch special-18 SF, entrées-26–30 SF, daily 9:00–14:00 & 17:00–23:00, in St. Moritz Bad at Via dal Bagn 11, tel. 081-833-4009).

TRANSPORTATION CONNECTIONS

From St. Moritz by train to: Pontresina (hrly, 10 min), **Samedan** (hrly, 8 min, direction Zuoz or Chur), **Chur** (hrly, 2 hrs), **Tirano** (hrly, 2.5 hrs), **Zürich** (hrly, 3.75 hrs, transfer in Chur).

SCENIC RAIL JOURNEYS

Switzerland has one of the world's best rail networks—and many of its tracks run through some of the world's best scenery. While just about any train ride in Switzerland is photogenic, four stand out as spectacular: the Golden Pass, William Tell Express, Bernina Express, and Glacier Express. These are aggressively marketed to a tourist audience looking for stunning high-altitude vistas along with their transportation.

This chapter provides you with all the logistical, nuts-and-bolts information you'll need to splice each of these journeys into your itinerary. I've provided commentary on each route to explain some insights about what you'll be seeing. For obvious reasons, I've described these routes in the direction that most travelers go. But the train rides can be reversed, too. In these cases, the same information still applies— just hold the book upside down.

I've also included some information about Chur, a town that's not really worth a visit, except that it lies at the intersection of the Bernina Express and Glacier Express routes. Chur makes for a handy pit stop or overnight if connecting these trips.

Tickets
Schedules: Timetables for most of these trains appear on the Swiss Rail Web site: www.rail.ch. (Also try the German Rail site,

Scenic Swiss Rail Journeys

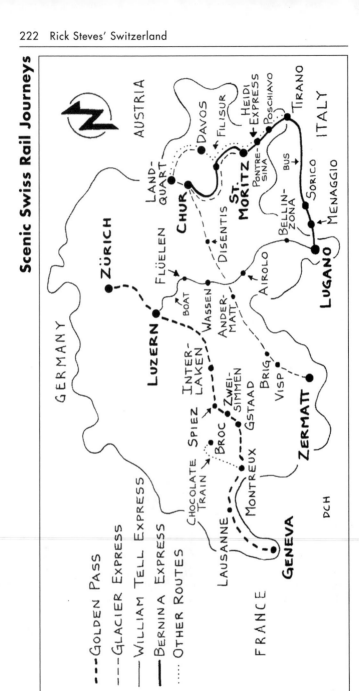

http://bahn.hafas.de/bin/query.exe/en.) Any train station in Switzerland can provide you with schedules. Each scenic rail line also operates its own Web site, with even more details (listed in each section, below).

The specific times I've listed in this chapter are for 2004. They may change in 2005; it's always smart to confirm before you travel.

Buying Tickets: Tickets and reservations for all of these scenic rail lines can be purchased at any train station in Switzerland, even for those run by private rail companies. In the United States, you'll pay more (about $20 per order) to get tickets and reservations through your travel agent or at www.raileurope.com.

Reservations: You can book these journeys as early as two months ahead, or as late as the day before. The Glacier Express, Bernina Express, and William Tell Express (full route with boat cruise) all require reservations. Reservations are recommended for the Golden Pass if you want a front-row VIP seat, or if you're departing on a summer midmorning; otherwise, you don't need to book ahead for the standard, non-panoramic cars. Reserve at any Swiss train station, or contact the companies directly (listed below per journey).

Eurailpass and Swiss Pass: There are two major types of rail-passes that can be useful in Switzerland: A Eurailpass (or Eurail Selectpass), or a Swiss Pass. (For details on all of the options, see page 19 in the Introduction.) Aside from the reservation fees, these railpasses cover most of your travel on these rail journeys. But there are a few exceptions. Even if you have a Eurailpass or Swiss Pass, you'll pay 47 SF (which includes the reservation and a lunch) for the boat trip segment of the William Tell Express (though doing the same trip by train is fully covered). And there's one segment of the Glacier Express that is covered by the Swiss Pass, but not by a Eurailpass: the journey between Disentis and Zermatt (free with Swiss Pass, 77 SF extra with Eurailpass).

If you have a railpass, present it when you're booking your ticket or buying reservations in person (or mention it if booking by phone). Make sure the ticket agent understands what type of pass it is (for example, Swiss Pass vs. Eurailpass) and exactly what trip you're taking. Make sure you've got all the reservations and other tickets you need to complete your trip. While rail agents generally know what railpasses cover, sometimes they don't—leading to frustrating run-ins with conductors insisting that you've only paid for part of your trip.

Train Types

Various types of trains, with various types of cars, run these routes. Here are some key distinctions to look for:

Classes: Most trains have first- and second-class cars (denoted with a big "1" or "2" by the door; first-class cars also have a yellow stripe above the windows). In bigger train stations, a digital panel on the tracks indicates departure time, destination, and the composition of the train (in which sector of the train station the first- and the second-class coaches will be).

Panoramic vs. Standard Cars: All of the routes in this chapter offer special panoramic cars. On some trains (like Golden Pass and Bernina Express), all of the cars are panoramic (no need to splurge for first class); on others (like Glacier Express and William Tell Express), you can choose between more expensive panoramic (first-class) and cheaper standard (second-class) cars.

Panoramic cars have huge wraparound windows, allowing you to see through part of the ceiling. The Alpine panoramas hit you

right in the face, no matter where you're sitting. The Golden Pass goes one better: The driver sits in a little bubble upstairs, leaving the very front of the train open for windshield VIP seating with completely unobstructed views of what's coming up. The windows in the panoramic cars generally can't open, meaning that photographs often come with a glare, and the interior can heat up in sunshine (though they're air-conditioned, which helps).

Standard cars are typical train cars, featuring regular windows. With a smaller field of vision than the panoramic cars, these require a little more bobbing and weaving to enjoy the views. Aside from being cheaper, the chief advantage of the standard cars is that the windows generally can be opened, for cool air and unobstructed views. Note that if you're in a panoramic car, you're free to walk to the standard cars to open a window and snap a photo.

Standard vs. Tourist Trains: In many cases, standard trains operated by Swiss Rail run these same routes—usually more frequently, and sometimes less expensively (you'll sacrifice things like fancy dining cars and souvenir keychains). In these cases (such as the Bernina Express), the standard trains are used by local commuters, and may stop at more stations along the route than the designed-for-tourists panoramic trains. Some travelers enjoy the flexibility of following the scenic route on standard trains, enabling them to hop off and explore a village, then hop on the next standard train that comes through—without any need for making reservations.

Golden Pass

The exceptionally picturesque Golden Pass train route cuts a swath diagonally across the pristine center of Switzerland, connecting Zürich with Lake Geneva. Of all the rail journeys in this chapter, its central location—lacing together many of Switzerland's top sights—makes the Golden Pass the one you're most likely to take.

ORIENTATION

The Route

The Golden Pass officially runs between the cities of Zürich and Geneva (nearly 8 hrs total), but most travelers focus on the segment between Luzern and Lake Geneva's Montreux. Better yet, hone in even more tightly—on the very best stretch, from Interlaken to Montreux.

Special panoramic cars are used for the most scenic part between Luzern and Montreux. Because the tracks change from narrow to standard gauge to narrow again, two train changes are required (at Interlaken Ost and Zweisimmen).

Route Breakdown: The entire Golden Pass route (almost 8 hrs) is run by various companies and involves several train changes. Here's the breakdown.

Zürich to Luzern: Standard trains run by Swiss Rail (2/hr, 1 hr).

Luzern to Interlaken Ost: Narrow-gauge panoramic trains run by Brünig Railway (5/day, 2 hrs); also standard trains by Swiss Rail (hrly, 2 hrs).

Interlaken Ost to Zweisimmen: Direct panoramic trains run by Golden Pass (2/day, 1 hr); also standard trains run by Swiss Rail (at least hrly, 1.25 hrs, requires change in Spiez).

Zweisimmen to Montreux: Direct, narrow-gauge panoramic trains run by Golden Pass (5/day, 2 hrs); also standard trains run by Swiss Rail (9/day, 2 hrs).

Montreux to Geneva: Standard trains run by Swiss Rail (hrly, 1 hr).

Though you can mix and match these trains depending on your schedule, note that two departures each day are designed to connect all of the panoramic cars along the best Luzern-to-Montreux stretch (2004 schedule: going north to south, departs Luzern at 7:34 and 9:34, Interlaken Ost at 9:35 and 13:35; going south to north, departs Montreux at 10:26 and 14:26, Interlaken at 15:30 and 17:30; in both directions, the earlier departure comes with a longer layover in Interlaken).

Planning Your Time: Because it connects so many knockout Swiss destinations (Zürich, Luzern, Interlaken, and Lake Geneva)—

and because it goes in both directions—the Golden Pass can be spliced into your itinerary in many different ways. I'd focus on the best stretch, using it to connect Interlaken and Lake Geneva (3 hrs total, including the lovely 2-hr segment from Zweisimmen to Montreux).

Cost and Schedule

The trip from Luzern to Montreux costs 67 SF second class; just the "best of" segment from Interlaken on to Montreux is 50 SF. The entire ride is covered by a Eurailpass or Swiss Pass. Reservations, while not required, are recommended for summer midmorning departures and the super-scenic front seats (15 SF for the front-row VIP seats; 7 SF for other seats in panoramic cars).

Standard trans run from Spiez to Montreux every hour (2-hr trip, change trains in Zweisimmen). These regular regional trains show you the same scenery without the big windows. Special panoramic carriages—some with front-row VIP seating—depart several times each day.

Information: Most of the route is part of the Swiss Rail network. Special panoramic trains on the Luzern–Interlaken route are run by Brünig Railway (www.bruenig.ch). Panoramic trains on the section between Zweisimmen and Montreux are operated by MOB (not the Mafia—it stands for Montreux-Oberland Bernois; tel. 021-989-8190, www.mob.ch). For more on the full route, see www.goldenpass .ch. An English-language guidebook describing the route is sold on the train (8 SF).

Seating: There are both standard and panoramic trains on the entire Luzern-to-Montreux route.

The best stretch, from Zweisimmen to Montreux, is covered by standard trains (9/day); trains with panoramic cars (2/day); and some special "Grande Vue" trains with both typical panoramic cars and special VIP seats (3/day May–Nov, 1/day Dec–April). On these "Grande Vue" cars, the conductor drives the train from a little domed area upstairs—leaving both the front and back of the train open for passengers. The  most sought-after seats are in the very front row, where you have a full view of the pristine Alpine scenery coming right at you. The first two rows, offering VIP seats with full-frontal Alps, require a supple-ment of 15 SF (reserve in advance, or just grab one if available and pay the conductor on the spot). The non-supplement seats just behind the supplement seats give you a bit of the grand front view (and cheapskates have been know to grab a few free minutes up front). The non-smoking panoramic cars have first- and second-class seating (with panoramic ceilings in both—no need to spring for first class, unless you want VIP seats). Cars have standard seating mixed with lounge areas with sofas, tables, and a bar.

Note that on the Luzern–Interlaken section, you'll need to choose between panoramic (first class only) and non-panoramic (second class) cars.

THE JOURNEY BEGINS

I've described only the best and most scenic portion, the three-hour stretch from Interlaken to Lake Geneva, focusing on the *crème de la crème*—the two hours between Zweisimmen and Montreux (described from north to south).

As you pull out of Interlaken, the train cruises along the south bank of **Lake Thun** (Thunersee). "Interlaken" literally means "between the lakes"—it's situated between the big lakes of Thun and Brienz. Before long, at the town of Spiez, you'll split off and head southwest to Zweisimmen.

Leaving Zweisimmen, you'll roll through **Simmental** valley, famous among American farmers for its top-end cows. Big farmhouses lie scattered in the lush meadows—an indication that the farmland is good here. The large wooden buildings are typical of Bernese farm architecture: housing the barn, sheltering the crops, and storing agricultural machines, all under one huge roof. Farming is heavily subsidized in Switzerland, and farmers form the strongest economical lobby. Trying to increase their modest income, many farmers have switched to exotic crops (like melons) or animals. These days, ostriches, yaks, bison, and highland cattle have become a common sight in the Swiss Alps.

Between Saanenmoser and Schonried, the train reaches its highest point (about 4,000 feet) and stops at the famous resort town of **Gstaad**. Although known as a favorite hangout for the jet set ("backpackers" like Monaco's Princess Caroline, Liz Taylor, Roger Moore, and Michael Jackson), the town does not offer many exciting sights. In winter, the modest ski slopes are almost empty, as most of the skiers are more into *après*-ski activities. Sipping their cocktails, they eye each other and discuss the latest trends in ski gear fashion. In summer, Gstaad hosts the Swiss Open tennis, polo, and golf tournaments, as well as music festivals. Violin virtuoso Yehudi Menuhin founded the Menuhin Festival here. While it started as an opportunity for young classical musicians to show their talent, today it's known for high-quality classical concerts.

Just south of Gstaad, you say *Auf Wiedersehen* to the German-speaking part of Switzerland and *Bonjour* to **French Switzerland**. *Merde*, those mountains are jagged. In fact, many are called *dents*, the French word for "teeth." With the change in language, you'll also see a change in culture and architecture. French-style gray stone houses are replacing half-timbered, woody, German-style chalets. The mountain airstrips—generally made for the Swiss Air Force during World War II—are used today for sightseeing flights around the Alps. The cute village of Rougemont, with its traditional chalets, is famous among the Swiss as place where the wealthy send their girls to boarding school.

Happy **cows** spend their summers on the Alps, wandering freely and munching the fragrant herbs of these lush Alpine meadows. The resulting milk is the secret ingredient for tasty Gruyère cheese. On steep hillsides here, the grass is still cut by hand. It dries in the summer sun, then is collected and stored in the barns to serve as cow salads through the winter (see "Swiss Cow Culture" sidebar in Gimmelwald chapter, page 130).

You might consider interrupting your journey in **Château d'Oex,** known for its Hot Air Ballooning Week (last week of January). Bertrand Piccard and Brian Jones took off from here on March 1, 1999, and sailed their balloon all the way around the world. Below the train station, Le Chalet restaurant gives insight on Gruyère cheese production.

South of Château d'Oex, the valley narrows to a deep gorge. Up on the hillsides, the damage of the devastating 1999 winter storm **"Lothar"** can still be seen. Entire forests were leveled, aggravating the already precarious avalanche situation. The trees on the steep slopes stop the snow from sliding down and burying the villages. Once the trees are gone, they don't grow back. Artificial avalanche barriers need to be erected. Landslides and floods have been relatively common in recent years—an unfortunate consequence of uncontrolled deforestation and construction of vacation homes in areas that traditionally served as pastures and forestlands.

The small **lake** is dammed and used for hydroelectric power. Switzerland makes good use of its Alps for production of electricity. Although it has some nuclear power plants, 60 percent of Switzerland's energy is hydroelectric. The country exports its electricity to France and Italy.

Montbovon is the place to change trains if you're going to Bulle or Gruyères (see "French Swiss Countryside," page 199). After the first tunnel, an inscription on the barn to the right welcomes the traveler in the Gruyère region: *La Gruyère vous salue.*

The train winds its way uphill with more curves and tunnels than before. Passing through the **Jaman Tunnel**, you're engulfed in nearly two miles of darkness, then you emerge in another world—leaving the feudal Middle Ages and entering the 19th-century belle époque. At the village of Les Avants, one of Switzerland's oldest winter resorts, you catch the first glimpses of Lake Geneva sprawling deep underneath you and begin a steep descent. A series of sharp bends in tunnels takes you out of the mountains and down to lake level.

The architecture has even more of a French flair now that you've entered the Swiss Riviera. Palm trees, vines, and many sanatoriums indicate this is a warmer climate. You're surrounded by the vineyards of the Lavaux region, famous for its white wine. The view broadens to include the French Alps of Savoy across the lake, the lakeshore of the Swiss Riviera to the west, and the broad Rhône Valley to the east. As you approach Montreux—with its grand hotels—the train meanders its way intimately through private gardens (grab a carrot).

Montreux has the only train station in Europe with three different rail gauges: regular, narrow (which you're on), and very skinny (for the Rochers de Naye train, taking sightseers to a nearby peak with views less exciting than those you've just enjoyed).

From here, it's an easy train trip to Lausanne, or a quick bus ride or scenic hike to Château de Chillon (see Lake Geneva chapter).

TRANSPORTATION CONNECTIONS

From Luzern by train to: Zürich (2/hr, 1 hr), **Zürich Airport** (2/hr, 1.25 hrs), **Bern** (every 2 hrs direct, 1.5 hrs; or 2/hr with transfer in Olten, 1.5–2 hrs), **Lugano** (hrly, 3 hrs), **Chur** (hrly, 2.25 hrs, change in Thalwil).

From Interlaken by train to: Lauterbrunnen (hrly, 30 min, 9 SF each way) **Spiez** (2/hr, 20 min), **Brienz** (hrly, 30 min), **Bern** (hrly, 50 min), **Zürich** and **Zürich Airport** (hrly, 2.25 hrs, most direct, but some with transfer in Bern).

From Montreux by train to: Lausanne (2/hr, 20 min), **Bern** (2/hr, 1.75 hrs, transfer in Lausanne), **Geneva** (hrly, 1 hr).

William Tell Express

The William Tell Express figured it deserves the most famous name in Switzerland (that's "Wilhelm Tell" in German). Tell exists only in legend, but his story—being forced to shoot an apple off his son's head because he refused to bow to the Hapsburg hat—helped inspire the Swiss to rebel against their Hapsburg rulers. The train route crosses the place where the first Swiss cantons pledged "all for one and one for all," the birthplace of the Confederation Helvetia. The scenic trip is half by boat and half by train from Luzern to Lugano, in the Italian-speaking region of Ticino. While the boat ride is nothing special, the train ride comes with some especially impressive Swiss rail engineering.

The William Tell Express is probably the least exciting of these four scenic rail journeys. Don't go out of your way to do it. But if you're going between Lugano and Luzern, you're certain to follow this same route, and can still make use of the self-guided commentary.

ORIENTATION

The Route

The William Tell Express begins with a slow, scenic boat trip on Lake Luzern from the city of Luzern to Flüelen (3.5 hrs). Then a train cuts down into the Italian-speaking canton of Ticino, ending at the town of Lugano (2 hrs). This is the one scenic rail journey that cannot officially be reversed (no package deal is available going from south to north; however, the panoramic train comes back up to Luzern each afternoon, leaving Lugano at 16:57). Standard (non-panoramic) trains make the trip hourly in each direction.

Planning Your Time: The value of riding the official William Tell Express train is debatable. The only thing that comes "extra" if you do the official package is a mediocre lunch on the boat; big windows in the panoramic cars; and a souvenir Swiss Army knife keychain at the end.

The boat trip to Flüelen is pleasant, but a little too long—you can get a flavor for the lake by doing a shorter round-trip cruise during your time in Luzern. Then take the train to Flüelen (1 hr from Luzern, as opposed to 3.5 hrs by boat); you'll see essentially the same scenery as the William Tell "Express" boat, but three times faster.

Whether you ride the boat or train from Luzern, in Flüelen you can join the William Tell Express panoramic train (departs Flüelen 15:16). The other option is to skip Flüelen entirely; standard (non-panoramic) trains head hourly from Luzern straight to Lugano without changing along the same route (3 hrs total).

Cost and Schedule

The cost for the full William Tell Express route is 163 SF first class, 135 SF second class (pay only a 47 SF reservation fee—including the cost of lunch—if you have a Eurailpass or Swiss Pass). If you do the trip with a standard train (see above), there's no reservation fee.

There is one official William Tell Express departure daily (May–Oct only; boat leaves Luzern at 11:20, arrives Flüelen at 14:57; panoramic train leaves Flüelen at 15:16, arrives Lugano at 17:23). Remember to confirm all times.

Information: The official William Tell Express departure is operated by the Lake Luzern Navigation Company (tel. 041-367-6767, www.lakelucerne.ch). The official trip comes with an informational booklet.

Helpful Hints

Boat Ride: If you're doing the full William Tell Express route, board the boat across from the Luzern train station. Present your ticket and pick up your package deal, including a lunch voucher and information flyers (boat departs from pier 1 at 11:20).

During the 3.5-hour ride, the boat stops at several nondescript, modern-feeling villages where hikers can ride lifts to the high country to kick off various hikes: Kehrsiten for the lift to Bürgenstock; Weggis and Vitznau for the lift to Rigi (described in Luzern chapter, page 77); Beckenried for the lift to Klewenalp; and Treib for Seelisberg. Rather than leaving this boat for a hike, you'll do better using Luzern as a home base for enjoying the walks on Pilatus or Rigi (see page 79).

Lunch: The official William Tell Express boat trip also comes with a lunch. The set-menu meal is included (drinks extra), but you can pay an exorbitant 30 SF extra to choose what you want from a menu.

Train Trip: On the official William Tell Express train from Flüelen, you'll find first class and the panoramic car way out on the platform in sector C. Yellow slips mark which seats are reserved. If you have no reservation, take any seat without a yellow marker.

THE JOURNEY BEGINS

Here's what you'll see if you're doing the entire William Tell Express package. If you're just doing the train, skip down to that section (next page).

Boat Trip

The boat trip crisscrosses **Vierwaldstättersee** (literally, the "Lake of Four Forest Cantons"—or simply "Lake Luzern" in English). The trip is popular with the older generation of locals, who eat and drink their way through the lazy route. On a sunny day, you can sit on the deck enjoying the mountain views.

After two hours, you enter the **Canton of Uri** and the landscape gets rougher, the slopes steeper, and the villages fewer and more rustic. This is William Tell country. The legendary Swiss national hero represents the essence of the country's spirit, still felt today: the desire for independence from foreign rule. William Tell has been a popular muse: Schiller wrote a play about him

based on ancient Swiss chronicles, and Rossini set the legend to music in an 1829 opera.

Swiss patriots get excited as the boat approaches **Rütli**. The meadow above is the birthplace of the Swiss Confederation. In 1291, three representatives of the founding cantons met here and swore allegiance to each other, against their oppressive Hapsburg neighbors. Over 700 years later, Switzerland is still a confederation—but now it's up to 26 cantons.

Some hikers choose to disembark at Rütli and head for the mystical meadow marked by a big Swiss flag. Then they follow the **Weg der Schweiz** ("Path of Switzerland"), a trail leading around the lake. Along the way, they contemplate stone signs representing each of the 26 cantons in the order they joined the union. The canton markers are spaced according to each canton's population (the 20-mile-long trail is designed to have exactly 5 millimeters for each Swiss citizen).

Later, the boat stops at **Tellskapelle**. This 16th-century frescoed chapel marks another legendary spot—where William Tell jumped ship on the way to prison and swam to freedom.

At about 15:00, you'll jump ship in Flüelen, where the panoramic train awaits. The boat staff will escort you to the correct track.

Train Trip

The train departs Flüelen at 15:16. On this leg of your journey, you'll climb from 1,540 feet up to 3,600 feet, at the Gotthard tunnel—the primary north-south transportation route through the Alps. You enter a classic Alpine world of snowcapped mountains towering above wild valleys, with narrow gorges carved by eons of angry white water. Wooden chalets, pine forests, and lush meadows dotted with munching cows complete this image of picture-perfect Central Switzerland.

The train tracks are protected from avalanches, landslides, and waterfalls by concrete galleries. Gazing out the window, you'll see some of the greatest accomplishments of Swiss road and railroad engineering. **Wassen**—marked by its striking chapel—is every trainspotter's Mecca—with more trains passing per minute than just about anywhere else. First, the chapel is on your right. Then the train loops around the tiny town, and the chapel is on your left. Your train disappears into a tunnel, and when you emerge, the same chapel is still there. (The train actually spirals up the slopes. Check out the map you got in your travel package.)

Göschenen (where you can transfer to Andermatt, and on to the Glacier Express—see below) is the last stop before the 9.5-mile-long **Gotthard tunnel.** After 10 minutes of darkness, you emerge in a whole different world—a different canton (Ticino, rather than Uri) and language (Italian, rather than German). Since the 13th century—long before this tunnel was built—the Gotthard Pass has been *the* major trade route over this part of the Alps, connecting northern and southern Europe. The trade continues to rumble under rather than over the pass. These days, heavy truck traffic brings pollution and traffic jams—but little money—to Switzerland. An ambitious project is underway to get the heavy trucks off the roads and transport the merchandise on the train. The new high-speed train tunnel should open in 2012.

Welcome to **Ticino**, Switzerland's botanical garden. While the weather around Lake Luzern is often iffy, Ticino feels Mediterranean—warm and southern—making it a favorite weekend destination for the Swiss. Rather than cuckoo-clock-like chalets, the houses are now plain, square, and made of stone. Instead of conifers, the forests are full of chestnut trees. You'll see vineyards, oleander, and even palm trees. And the upcoming train stops are announced in Italian now: "*Prossima fermata....*"

While life seemed almost too good in the pristine and touristic Lake Luzern region, here in the valley of **Leventina**, the economy is tougher. Unemployment rates are high, young folks have to commute into the cities further south for a job, houses and roads aren't as well maintained, and window boxes no longer come with so many flowers. Around the town of Biasca, you'll see industrial buildings and factories.

As you leave **Biasca**, notice a modern square building with pebble walls on your left-hand side. This is the information center for the new Gotthard tunnel, which will be the longest train tunnel in the world (Tue–Sun 9:00–18:00, closed Mon, tel. 091-873-0550, www.infocentro.ch).

After **Bellinzona**, the train continues past the northern tip of Lake Maggiore and along a quiet, lush valley lined with picturesque villages and chestnut trees to **Lugano**. Enjoy your time in Italian Switzerland!

TRANSPORTATION CONNECTIONS

From Luzern by train to: Zürich (2/hr, 1 hr), **Zürich Airport** (2/hr, 1.25 hrs), **Bern** (every 2 hrs direct, 1.5 hrs; or 2/hr with transfer in Olten, 1.5–2 hrs), **Interlaken** (hrly, 2 hrs direct to Ost station), **Lausanne** (every 2 hrs direct, 2.75; more with transfer in Olten), **Chur** (hrly, 2.25 hrs, change in Thalwil).

From Lugano by train to: Zürich (hrly, 2.75–3.25 hrs direct), **Interlaken** (hrly, 5.5–6 hrs, transfer in Luzern or Zürich), **Bern** (hrly, 4–4.25 hrs, transfer in Zürich or Olten). From Lugano, you can continue on to the **Bernina Express** (below).

Bernina Express

The Bernina Express is one of the most tremendous train rides through the Swiss Alps. For some travelers, it's the best one of all, thanks to its diversity: It runs from the sunny palm-tree climate in Lugano, to a taste of Italy along beautiful Lake Como, and twisting like a corkscrew up and over the Bernina Pass, before arriving in the mountain towns of Pontresina, Samedan, St. Moritz, and Chur. The little red train with panoramic cars spirals up to 7,380 feet, passing steep mountains and cliffs, glaciers, waterfalls, and a wild, rugged landscape.

ORIENTATION

The Route
The Bernina Express combines a bus trip through Italy with a train ride up into the mountains. The bus begins in Lugano and runs along the west side of Italy's Lake Como, eventually arriving at Tirano. From Tirano, the train crosses back into Switzerland and spirals up the steep mountainside north, mastering a 70 percent grade on regular tracks (no cogwheels) en route to the most spectacular stretch: over the Bernina Pass. Then the train winds back down the other side, stops in mountain towns (such as Pontresina), and finally deposits you in Chur. The route can be reversed (Chur to Tirano by train, then bus to Lugano). In fact, this way arguably provides an even better experience: Approaching Pontresina from the north is breathtaking, and it gets even better when the train gets to the Bernina Pass.

Planning Your Time: The trip is spectacular but long, and the seats aren't the most comfortable. It helps to break the journey with an overnight or two in the Pontresina area (see Pontresina, Samedan, and St. Moritz chapter). The Bernina Express is especially enjoyable in July and August, when you can take one of the open-top yellow coaches.

If you have more time, consider taking a standard regional train along this route (rather than the official panoramic Bernina Express train). That way, you can get off as you like for hiking and exploring (see "Local Train Alternative," next page).

Cost and Schedule
The one-way trip from Lugano to Chur costs 76 SF second class, 114 SF first class. If you're only going as far as Pontresina, it's cheaper (49 SF second class, 64 SF first class). The entire trip (including the bus) is covered by a Eurailpass or a Swiss Pass—but you still have to buy reservations.

If you do the official Bernina Express trip, **seat reservations** are required for both the bus and the panoramic train (7 SF for train, 12 SF for bus). Remember, you can do the same stretch on a regular train without reservations (optional reservation charge-5 SF; no such option for bus).

The Bernina Express runs daily from mid-May through mid-October. In winter, only the train segment (Tirano to Chur) runs—the bus is out of commission. In July and August, you can make the trip in cheerful yellow open-air cars from Tirano to St. Moritz.

The bus leaves daily in summer from outside Lugano's train station at 10:30 and heads for Tirano (facing the lake with the station at your back, walk about 100 yards to the left; bus stop has yellow sign for "St. Moritz" and "Tirano"). You'll arrive in Tirano at 13:15, then hop on the train up and over the mountains (departs Tirano 14:50, arrives Chur 18:49). If you're doing it the other way around, here are some options: train leaves Chur 8:48, arrives Tirano 12:46; train leaves St. Moritz 9:40, arrives Tirano 11:59. The bus from Tirano leaves at 14:15 and arrives in Lugano 17:15. Remember to confirm all times.

Information: The Bernina Express is operated by Rhaetian Railway (tel. 081-288-6104, fax 081-288-6105, www.rhb.ch). You can buy an English guidebook about the Bernina Express on the train or at gift shops along the way (12 SF). A recorded English commentary plays on the train's loudspeaker.

Helpful Hints

Bus Trip: The Lugano-to-Tirano leg of the Bernina trip (through Italy) is on a bus. Make yourself comfortable—the seats recline, and the footrests, armrests, and individual fans give you more comfort that on a standard postal bus. There are no WCs or food on the bus, so buy your snacks and drinks before boarding (a convenient spot is the Apero shop at Lugano's train station, daily 6:00–22:00). The bus will stop for a WC and snack break in Italy (accepts Swiss francs). Bags can be put under the bus.

The bus trip is almost entirely through Italy. Keep your passport accessible; you'll need to produce it when you transfer to the train in Tirano. Since your one rest stop in Italy is at a place that accepts Swiss francs, you don't need to get euros.

Train Trip: Once you reach Tirano, you'll switch to a panoramic train. The train has five cars: one is first-class only, with panoramic windows that don't open and uncomfortable black leather seats that don't recline. The other four are regular cars (with non-panoramic windows that open); two have first- and second-class seating, two are second-class only. If it's too sunny, lower the shutters on the windows.

Local Train Alternative: The train segment of the Bernina Express can be done on a standard (non-panoramic) local train. These trains stop at all stations, allowing you to hop off and walk around in the beautiful scenery, while the Bernina Express only stops after passing the Bernina Pass. Get off at the Bernina Pass for hiking, or at Diavolezza to do a cable-car trip. Alp Grüm and Ospizio Bernina are starting points for several great hikes. Train connections are easy and quick if you're just passing through.

Heidi Express: The Bernina Express covers the route from Tirano over the Bernina Pass to Pontresina/St. Moritz and on to Chur; meanwhile, the Heidi Express takes you from Tirano over the Bernina pass to Davos and on to Landquart (mid-May–mid-Oct only, almost hrly, no reservations). These two rail lines follow the same route from Tirano up until Filisur, north of St. Moritz. Both of them go over the Bernina Pass. If you're taking the Heidi Express, the self-guided commentary works through Filisur.

If you plan carefully, you can hop back and forth between these two scenic lines to maximize sightseeing (see "Optional Side-Trip to Poschiavo," below).

THE JOURNEY BEGINS

Bus Trip

The bus is more scenic than relaxing. It takes you around Lake Lugano on narrow, windy roads, frequently honking its horn to warn oncoming traffic at tight passages.

As you leave Lugano, you'll pass the town of Gandria (fun to visit from Lugano by boat—see page 206 of Lugano chapter). Shortly after Gandria, you cross the border into **Italy** (it's a non-event—bus doesn't stop, no need to show passports—but look for the big I-for-Italy on the bumper stickers). You may notice a change in architecture: While the Swiss love meticulously manicured gardens and painstakingly renovated houses, the Italians take things a bit easier. Many houses could use a makeover.

Once the bus leaves Lake Lugano, the road broadens and takes you through modern Italian villages before hitting picturesque **Lake Como** (Lago di Como). Above the town of Menaggio are your first views of the lake. The picturesque village is the *real* Bellagio (not the Las Vegas casino). At the nearby village of Dongo, the Italian fascist dictator Mussolini was captured at the end of World War II. Tunnels occasionally disrupt your views, but you can catch glimpses of the lush lakefront. In Gravedona, the street gets narrow enough to touch the houses on both sides. Posh private villas and gardens line the street; look for the 12th-century Romanesque Church of Santa Maria del Tiglio. From here, the trip takes you to the tiny harbor town of Domaso. This area is touristy—notice the signs in several languages pointing to campgrounds, hotels, and swimming pools.

Shortly before noon, the bus stops for 10 minutes in **Sorico,** at the northern tip of Lake Como. You'll have a chance to use the WC and buy a snack or drink at Bar Pace (Swiss francs accepted). Check out the big photograph behind the bar—George Clooney posing with the bar's proud owner on a 2002 visit. Clooney owns a grandiose villa on Lake Como.

The bus then crosses the **"Pian di Spagna"**—famous for a tense standoff between Spanish and Swiss troops during the religious wars of the Counter-Reformation. The trip continues up the fertile **Valtellina Valley**, where some of northern Italy's white wine is produced. The sunny slopes on the left side are reserved for vineyards, the right lower slopes are for woodland, and the bottom of the valley is occupied by apple plantations. This region belonged for centuries (from 1512 until Napoleon in 1797) to Switzerland's largest canton, Graubünden. Today, this region is Italian, but many Swiss still think of the local Veltlin wine as their own.

Tirano is our next stop. In the old town, the bus passes an impressive Renaissance church (Madonna di Tirano, on the left) before arriving at the train station at 13:20. You have time for lunch and some sightseeing before hopping on the Bernina Express train (departing at 14:50). Or, to cram in more sightseeing, take the Heidi Express (leaving at 14:02) for an optional side-trip to Poschiavo, and meet up with the Bernina Express later (see below).

To get to the train tracks, you'll have to go through Italian customs, so have your passport ready.

Optional Side-Trip to Poschiavo

Your reservation to Chur will probably be for the 14:50 train. But to maximize sightseeing fun, consider this alternate plan: If you find free seats on the 14:02 Heidi Express, hop on and take it to the charming little town of **Poschiavo** (arriving at 14:44; remember, it follows the same route as the Bernina Express for this stretch, so the self-guided commentary, below, still works). You can explore Poschiavo before claiming your reserved seats on the Bernina Express (leaves Poschiavo at 15:35). This works only when the Heidi Express is running (mid-May–mid-Oct).

In Poschiavo, walk to the main street and turn left, following the signs to *Centro* and the **TI.** Cross the river over the pedestrian bridge and continue left, then right, then left, following the "Information" signs. The main square, **Piazza Comunale**, is lined with neoclassical and neo-Gothic buildings, including an impressive

Catholic church (Chiesa di San Vittore Mauro). A church stood here as early as 703, but the building has been rebuilt and renovated several times: The bell tower dates from 1202, and the Baroque front door was carved in the 1700s. Don't miss the little yellow building just before the church, with the intricate wrought-iron grills. Have a peek inside, and don't be startled by the skulls lining the walls—you're standing in front of the local ossuary.

The **TI** is located in the old Town Hall, below the 12th-century church tower. Pick up a map and the English translation for a short orientation walk: Go from the main square a block north and find the **Church of St. Ignazio**. It's ironic that this Protestant church's namesake, St. Ignatius of Loyola, was the founder of the militant Jesuit order—whose main purpose was to fight "heretic" Protestants. Notice the inscription above the central pulpit, which is fervently Protestant: *Chiesa cristiana vangelica riformata da gli errori e superstizioni umane* ("Christian evangelical church, reformed from human errors and superstitions").

But...you've got a train to catch!

Bernina Express Train Trip, Part One: From Tirano to Pontresina

The ride is more comfortable than the bus, and English announcements explain the sights along the way.

From Tirano, the train becomes a streetcar, slowly crossing the center of town before starting the climb up to **Brusio**. Here the train takes the famous circular viaduct, the only one in the world—an ingenious construction allowing the train to reach higher altitudes without the help of a cogwheel mechanism. As the train twists up, you can see the front and back cars curving in front of and behind you, riding over the viaduct.

Lay back and enjoy the most scenic part of the trip. Dark old pine forests with needle-and-moss-covered boulders remind you of the fairy tales from your childhood. Wildflowers along the track include bright orange lilies and mountain azaleas. The train slaloms up the steep mountain and offers more and more views of waterfalls, steep cliffs, and views to the Poschiavo valley and lake far below you.

After leaving Poschiavo, and before you reach the Bernina Pass, you'll spot the first glacier, **Palü Gletscher** (behind the little lake of Palüsee on the left). It lies nestled between the peak Piz Varuna (11,330 feet) on the left and the eastern summit of Piz Palü on the right (12,790 feet).

Ospizio Bernina—at the **Bernina Pass**—is the highest point of this trip (7,380 feet). You'll see the White Lake (Lago Bianco), whose color comes from the melting water, also called "glacier milk." A watershed mark next to the lake explains that this is a European continental divide: From here, rivers flow either north (towards the Inn, Danube, and finally to the Black Sea) or south (to the Adriatic Sea via the Adda and Po rivers).

Behind the White Lake, you can see the glaciers of **Sassal Masone** and **Piz Cambrena**. This mountain pass not only separates European drainage basins, but also cultures. In winter, the remote Italian-speaking valley of Poschiavo was often cut off from Switzerland, and turned itself towards its southern neighbor, the valley of Veltlin (where you were just riding the bus).

The train crosses the barren landscape and starts its descent to the **Engadine** valley (Pontresina, St. Moritz, and Samedan). This part of Switzerland was discovered by tourists and convalescents at the end of the 19th century. After the railroad opened this secluded valley to the world, the first hotels and sanatoriums were built (the air and sunshine supposedly helped fight various diseases). Poets found their muse in the wild, romantic landscape, while painters flocked in, attracted by the quality of the light. Keep an eye out for typical Engadine architecture—small windows set in thick walls, etched *sgraffito* decorations, and carved wooden doors.

The **Montebello curve** offers you the best views over the Morteratsch glacier on the left, with the impressive peaks in the background; from left to right: the Bellavista Range (12,770 feet), Crest Agüzza (12,690 feet), and the highest peak in the canton, Mount Bernina (13,280 feet). Mount Bernina was first climbed in 1850 by a team led by rangers from the village of Schanf. Their gear consisted only of thick woolen pants; a shirt and jacket; hobnailed shoes; and a hat with a black veil to shade them from the strong sunshine.

As you continue, the tracks are lined by more and more larch trees, and several hiking paths cross the blueberry bushes in the forests. Larch trees turn bright yellow in fall and lose their needles, growing new bright green ones the next spring.

The milky-white waters from Lago Bianco and the Morteratsch glacier run wild in a broad riverbed alongside the tracks, as satisfied cows chew away on the meadows and waterfalls tumble down the cliffs.

Next stop: **Pontresina**. This town is a good place to break the journey (see Pontresina, Samedan, and St. Moritz chapter). Consider spending a night or two in Pontresina, exploring the quaint village of Samedan, visiting the glitzy resort of St. Moritz, and maybe doing some hiking before continuing on your way.

Bernina Express Train Trip, Part Two:
From Pontresina to Chur

Although you're leaving the glaciers behind, your trip will still lead you through magnificent mountain scenery, with steep cliffs and deep gorges.

First, you'll slide through the broad and mellow valley around Samedan, following the shortest river in Switzerland, Flazbach. On the right, look for the funicular heading up to **Muottas Muragl**, a viewpoint overlooking the valleys that come together in Samedan (for details, see page 217). This is also home to Europe's highest airport. It serves glider enthusiasts and the rich and famous who come to vacation in St. Moritz.

After Samedan, in **Bever**, the train leaves the valley and climbs to another highly spectacular leg of its journey. The section between Bever and Bergün boasts amazing engineering work. Technicians from all over the world come here to admire the diversity of spiral tunnels, looping viaducts, galleries, and bridges that span the Albula Gorge.

The train works its way up along a cheerfully splashing mountain creek, between the Arven pine and larch trees and some isolated farmhouses. The **Albula tunnel,** the highest subterranean Alpine crossing in Europe, takes you up to 5,970 feet. This pass serves as another barrier between cultures and climate—the weather is often different on either side of the tunnel. Hikers can follow the tracks and read the information panels about the construction of the train line. The street along the tracks is closed in winter and considered paradise for sledders. Every winter, 100,000 sled enthusiasts are attracted by this closed, windy road, giving them the ride of their life on a three-mile, downhill, car-free stretch.

From **Preda**, the train loops down through five spiral tunnels and two straight tunnels, crossing nine viaducts and going under two galleries—considered the most ingenious railway line ever built. It covers nearly eight miles and descends over 1,365 feet in altitude. The village of **Bergün** will be visible three separate times as you loop around the valley. Bergün greets you with a modern public open-air swimming pool and an onion-shaped "Roman tower." As the train continues winding down the pretty valley, you'll often be able to see other parts of the track below or next to you—try to trace where you've been and where you're going next.

Next stop is **Filisur**, where travelers to Davos (on the Heidi Express) will change trains. After Filisur, the Bernina Express enters a tunnel, and an announcement reminds you to ready your camera and position yourself on the left side. Just after the tunnel, you'll cross the famous **Landwasser viaduct.** A masterpiece of engineering, its pillars were built without scaffolding. Iron towers formed the center of each pillar, and brick was laid around. Each tower was topped with a crane that lifted building materials. The

425-foot-long viaduct curves elegantly in a radius of 330 feet. Below, the wild Albula River carves the dramatic gorge; above, the panoramic windows allow you to see the steep and rugged cliffs looming over the tracks (the most scenic stretch is right after Solis).

Thusis is the commercial hub of the broad and lush Domleschg valley. The trip takes you down along the Lower Rhine River. Notice the many fortresses, castles, towers, and ruins along the river, a reminder that taxes were levied on the traders traveling this major route between northern and southern Europe. One of Switzerland's most popular mineral waters originates in Rhäzüns. The 13th-century castle above the town now belongs to a local chemical company.

Reichenau marks the spot of confluence of the Upper and Lower Rhine. This town became wealthy from the taxes it got from the passing merchants. The 17th-century Reichenau Castle on the Lower Rhine was once used as a school, but is now privately owned.

The train follows the Rhine at the foot of Calanda Mountain to our final stop, Chur. You can overnight in Chur (see page 245) and continue the next day on the Glacier Express (see below).

TRANSPORTATION CONNECTIONS

From Lugano by train to: Luzern (hrly, 2.75–3 hrs direct), **Zürich** (hrly, 2.75–3.25 hrs direct), **Interlaken** (hrly, 5.5–6 hrs, transfer in Luzern or Zürich), **Bern** (hrly, 4–4.25 hrs, transfer in Zürich or Olten).

From Pontresina by train to: St. Moritz (hrly, 10 min), **Samedan** (hrly, 7 min), **Zürich** (hrly, 3.75 hrs, transfer in Samedan and Chur).

From Chur by train to: Zürich (hrly, 1.5 hrs), **Luzern** (hrly, 2.25 hrs, transfer in Thalwil). Chur is also a smart launch pad for the Glacier Express.

Glacier Express

This most promoted of the Swiss scenic rail routes travels between Zermatt in the southwest of Switzerland and St. Moritz or Davos (via Chur) in the east. If you stay on for the whole ride, you'll spend 7.5 hours crossing 291 bridges, going through 91 tunnels, and reaching an altitude of 6,670 feet.

While it's an impressive and famous journey, the Glacier Express is not necessarily the be-all and end-all of Swiss rail trips. Much of the journey is down in valleys (as opposed to along the sides of cliffs), meaning that high-altitude views are a little lacking. But the stark landscape, carved by the glaciers that gave the train its name, is striking. The trip largely lives up to the hype, and offers an extremely scenic way to connect the Chur area with tucked-away-in-the-mountains Zermatt (see Zermatt and the Matterhorn chapter).

ORIENTATION

The Route

The Glacier Express is a misnomer—it's hardly an "express." Not only does it take its time (7.5 hours for full trip), but it also makes several stops along the way. The route cuts along the southern part of Switzerland, between St. Moritz or Davos (in the east) and Zermatt (in the west). For simplicity, I'll focus on Chur as the eastern endpoint (as that's where the St. Moritz and Davos lines come together). You can ride in either direction.

Planning Your Time: The most distinctive stretch of the trip is the high-mountain pass between Disentis and Brig. If you don't want to commit to the whole 7.5 hours, you can try to connect a trip with this segment only (about 3 hrs). Remember that you can join or leave the trip whenever you like (for example, Chur in the east and Brig in the west link conveniently into Swiss rail lines to other major destinations).

Cost and Schedule

You'll pay 131 SF for second class and 218 SF for first class between St. Moritz and Zermatt. Prices are slightly lower from Davos. Note that there are some first-class, but non-panoramic, cars. Paying for this is a waste of money—it's like second class with more legroom.

The entire trip is covered by the Swiss Pass (except the reservation fee, see below). But a Eurailpass covers only part of the journey; the high-altitude segment between Disentis and Zermatt is privately run, so you'll have to buy a supplement for that part (Disentis-Brig 43 SF second-class, Brig-Zermatt 34 SF).

In addition to your train ticket, you'll have to buy a **reservation**. In peak season (daily mid-June–mid-Aug, Sat–Sun mid-Aug–Sept), it actually costs less to reserve the entire route (St. Mortiz/Davos-Zermatt, 12 SF peak season, 9 SF off-season) than to book a segment of the route (same price no matter what segment: 17 SF peak season, 9 SF off-season).

The trip goes at least once in each direction every day of the year. You can also join or leave the trip at any of the stations along the way. Chur makes sense as a starting/ending point in the east, as it allows for easy connections to the Bernina Express (see above).

From mid-May through mid-October, there are four trains daily each way (2004 schedule: going west to east starting from Chur at 8:57, from Davos at 9:02, and from St. Moritz at 9:25 and 10:02; going west to east starting from Zermatt at 8:10, 8:50, 9:30, and 10:10). Off-season, frequency drops to one per day in each direction (leaving St. Moritz at 9:02 and Zermatt at 10:10).

Note that in peak season, when four trains per day go in each direction, your choice of class might be determined by the departure time you choose. One train per day each way has only panoramic cars (no second class), and two don't have panoramic cars at all. If you're paying for first class anyway, you might as well be sure to get on a panoramic car.

Information: The Glacier Express is operated by Matterhorn Gotthard Bahn, based in Brig (Nordstrasse 20, tel. 027-921-4111, fax 027-921-4119, www.glacierexpress.ch or www.mgbahn.ch). There's a little recorded commentary on the train about what you're seeing, but for more insight, pick up a guidebook before you board the train (I like the official one, by Photoglob, for 12 SF).

Helpful Hints

Picking the Best Seat: It's obviously more enjoyable to sit facing front (though be aware that the car changes directions in Brig). For most of the trip—including the most dramatic stretch, between Disentis and Brig—it's also slightly preferable to sit on the left-hand side of the train coming from St. Moritz/Chur (generally seat numbers ending in 1, 2, 3, and 8), which is the right-hand side if you're coming from Zermatt/Brig (same seat numbers).

Luggage: You'll keep your luggage with you (they don't check it through). In second class, there are luggage racks above your seat. In panoramic class, people tend to leave it in the storage area at the head of each car, or slip it between the backs of the seats.

No-Show Bridges: Most promotional materials show the Glacier Express train venturing across ancient aqueducts and old stone bridges. It makes for pretty scenic publicity. But realize that you won't see these bridges from the train itself...because you're on them.

Do-It-Yourself Altitude Gauge: I like to buy a drink in a plastic bottle before boarding these high-altitude trips. Not only is it cheaper than buying a drink on the train; it's also fun to watch the bottle pucker and swell with the ups and downs.

Eating on the Glacier Express: The train has a fancy restaurant car that offers lunch—handy if you're in for the full 7.5 hours. For 36 SF, you get a salad (summer) or soup (winter), a main dish, and a dessert; 25 SF buys you just the main dish (drinks cost extra). Their trademark gizmo: a tilted wine glass. Since lunch is generally served when the train is going up a steep incline (11:00–13:30), these gimmicky glasses always get a laugh. Reservations are required for lunch (request when booking your ticket).

To save a few francs, it's fine to bring your own **picnic**. Seats in panoramic cars even come with handy tables—perfect for a grocery-store feast.

THE JOURNEY BEGINS

I'll describe the route starting at Chur and heading towards Zermatt. (For details on the trip from St. Moritz to Chur, see Bernina Express, page 234.)

As you leave Chur, you'll be following the **Ruinaulta Gorge**, carved by the Rhine River (though way down here in Switzerland, it's a little tyke, and not navigable). After about nine miles, the train diverges from the Rhine and enters a pastoral region called Surselva, centered on the town Ilanz. This is Romansh country, where the fourth official language of Switzerland is kept alive—barely—in communities like this one. Romansh, like French and Italian, is a Romance language—but it's more directly descended from Latin than most.

As you approach **Disentis**, the tracks begin to twist along the edge of canyon—making the scenery more dramatic (a taste of what's to come). You'll pull into Disentis, with its big Benedictine Monastery looming in your window. Your car will jiggle as the cog-wheel locomotive is attached. Without this system, the train could never make it up the next, very steep stretch.

You'll work your way up the mountain and enter a long series of snow sheds—designed to protect the tracks (and trains) in case an avalanche strikes. You'll emerge from the sheds at **Oberalp Pass**, the literal high point of this journey (6,670 feet). Waaay up top,

notice the extensive network of avalanche fences—a reminder of the many generations of Swiss farmers who have learned to live on the land. The reddish streaks you might see on the snow? Believe it or not, that's sand from the Sahara Desert—caught up in high-altitude winds and carried all the way to the Swiss Alps.

As you descend from the pass, you'll travel over, then through, the modern town of **Andermatt**—which feels like a return to civilization. In this desolate terrain, notice the huge boulders embedded in the ground, deposited there by glaciers. Soon after, you'll go through the 9.5-mile-long Furka Basis Tunnel. While it might seem like a view-killer, realize that this tunnel—finished in 1982—made it possible for the Glacier Express to continue running through the winter.

You'll emerge into the region of **Goms**, with more pretty villages. The village of Kühboden has a cable car up to Eggishorn, boasting views of all the Alps All-Stars: Matterhorn, Mont Blanc, Eiger, Mönch, and Jungfrau. Soon after, the train meets up with another one of Europe's great rivers, the Rhône.

Finally, you'll arrive at **Brig**, an ugly industrial town with good connections to other train lines (transfer here if you're not continuing on to Zermatt). From Brig, it's on to Zermatt and the Matterhorn, following the craggy Nikolaital Valley. Think about how much the terrain has changed since you started the trip: from fertile farmlands, to tundra above the tree line, to this rough and rocky terrain. Keep an eye out for vineyards—we're out of milk country, and into wine country.

As you continue along the valley, lined with quarries, you'll begin to get your first glimpses of the unmistakable shape of the **Matterhorn**—a fitting exclamation point at the end of this long journey. **Zermatt** lies just around the bend.

TRANSPORTATION CONNECTIONS

From Chur by train to: Zürich (hrly, 1.5 hrs), **Luzern** (hrly, 2.25 hrs, transfer in Thalwil).

From Zermatt: Zermatt is connected to the outside world via the 90-minute train ride to Brig. Brig is also a handy place to bail out of the Glacier Express route, if you're coming from Chur and not going all the way to Zermatt.

From Brig by train to: Bern (hrly, 1.75 hrs), **Lausanne** (hrly, 1.75 hrs), **Interlaken** (hrly, 1.5 hrs with transfer in Spiez), **Luzern** (nearly hrly, 3.5 hrs, transfer in Olten), **Zürich** (hrly, 3 hrs, sometimes with transfer in Bern).

Chur

The routes of the Glacier Express and the Bernina Express intersect in Chur—supposedly Switzerland's oldest and warmest town. It's a handy transportation hub for these two scenic train lines, and has a charming enough old town. Overall, Chur (koor) is just a typical Swiss burg—fine for passing through, but not worth a detour. If you've got time to kill, you can wander up through the old town to two big churches (the Romanesque Cathedral and the Gothic Church of St. Martin), some remains of the medieval city wall, and the town museum (Rättisches Museum).

ORIENTATION

Chur fans out over the foothills from the Rhine River. The newly renovated train station is at the bottom (north end) of the town center.

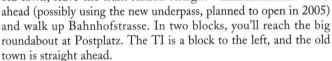

Tourist Information: Chur's TI offers a town map (marked with sights, hotels, restaurants, and a convenient walking-tour route) and a brochure with hotel listings (both free). They're one block from Postplatz, at Grabenstrasse 5 (Mon 13:30–18:00, Tue–Fri 8:30–12:00 & 13:30–18:00, Sat 8:00–12:00, closed Sun, tel. 081-252-1818, www.churtourismus.ch). The TI will probably move into its new digs at the renovated train station by the end of 2005.

Arrival in Chur: To get to the TI and old town, leave the train station straight ahead (possibly using the new underpass, planned to open in 2005) and walk up Bahnhofstrasse. In two blocks, you'll reach the big roundabout at Postplatz. The TI is a block to the left, and the old town is straight ahead.

Internet Access: The library (Kantonsbibliothek Graubünden) offers 15 minutes online for free (thereafter 2 SF/15 min, Tue and Thu 9:00–17:45, Wed and Fri 9:00–18:45, Sat 9:00–15:45, closed Sun-Mon, Karlihofplatz, tel. 081-257-2828).

SLEEPING

Sleep here only if you must, in order to connect to one of the scenic rail lines. These moderately priced places are in the old town, an easy 10- to 15-min walk from the train station.

Hotel Freieck has 37 clean, tasteful rooms with wood floors and fun, old-fashioned furniture, over a low-key café (Sb-90–110 SF, Db-150–180 SF, Tb-180–230 SF, prices depend on season—highest May–mid-Oct, Reichsgasse 44-50, tel. 081-252-1792, fax 081-253-3419, www.freieck.ch, hotel@freieck.ch, Stockmann family).

Hotel Zunfthaus Räblüta, in a 500-year-old building, overlooks a quiet little square a block off Kornplatz. The eight rooms are rustic but comfortable, and the hotel is warmly run by the Stöhr family (Ss-50 SF, Sb-80 SF, Db-140 SF, Pfisterplatz 1, tel. 081-257-1357, www.rebleuten.ch, info@rebleuten.ch).

TRANSPORTATION CONNECTIONS

Chur is a convenient spot to catch either the Glacier Express or the Bernina Express. It also offers speedy, frequent connections to Zürich, making it an ideal junction for spicing up your trip with a scenic train.

From Chur by train to: Zürich (hrly, 1.5 hrs), **Luzern** (hrly, 2.25 hrs, transfer in Thalwil). To reach destinations in northern or western Switzerland—such as Bern, Interlaken, or Lake Geneva—you'll transfer in Zürich (see Zürich's "Transportation Connections," page 54).

APPENDIX

Winter Sports in Switzerland

I admit it: This is a summertime book. I've included plenty of tips on hiking, while ignoring the winter-sports scene entirely. But winter activities are an important part of the Swiss culture (and tourist industry). Here are the basics.

Skiing had its roots in Scandinavia 4,000 years ago as a method of wintertime transportation. Just a century ago, clever entrepreneurs in the Swiss Alps realized that the sport could be a profitable extension of their resorts' spring and summer seasons. Telemark (cross-country skiing) came first, then alpine (downhill) skiing, and today snowboarding rules. Generations of Swiss skiers have honed their skills on these slopes. Today's biggest names include Erica Hess, Vreni Schneider, and Maria Walliser.

You don't have to be a skier or snowboarder to enjoy Switzerland in the winter. Ski resorts offer plenty of other activities, including snowshoeing, sledding, ice skating...and shopping. Or just ride up a lift, rent a chair in the sun, and warm up with a glass of *Pflümli* (plum liqueur).

The winter-sports season begins in December and runs through Easter. During this period, hotel prices in resort towns surpass summer highs. For those who can afford them, the best winter activities are in the Berner Oberland (Mürren, Wengen, Grindelwald, and Gstaad); the southern canton of Valais (Zermatt, Saas-Fee, Crans-Montana, and Verbier); and the eastern canton of Graubünden (St. Moritz, Davos, Klosters, and Arosa).

The **Berner Oberland** offers the ultimate variety in terrain and character (see Gimmelwald and the Berner Oberland chapter). Three resort areas cluster around the Lauterbrunnen Valley. The cliff-hanging town of Mürren is a good home base, with the 10,000-foot

Schilthorn peak as the backbone of its ski area (great steep sections up top, especially the Kanoneruhr; lower down, it caters to all levels, but can suffer from icy conditions or lack of snow). Across the valley, Wengen offers challenging skiing, fine accommodations, and shopping, with a complex lift system connecting it to Kleine Scheidegg, Männlichen, and Grindelwald. Each January, the World Cup ski races take place on Wengen's tough Lauberhorn run. Grindelwald, a little closer to Interlaken, is another fine base—with multiple funicular railways, cable cars, lifts, and over 100 miles of downhill runs (www.grindelwald.com).

Further to the west, Gstaad has more of a French accent. With a perfect location at the intersection of several valleys, it enjoys great sun exposure and a decent elevation (www.gstaad.ch). This famous, glamorous resort—mingling German coziness and French modernism—is *the* place to see and be seen. Skiing is secondary (see "Golden Pass," page 225 of Scenic Rail Journeys chapter).

The canton of **Valais** ("Valley") is known for its excellent winemaking along the banks of the Rhône, but it's also a popular skiing destination. Connected by several high-mountain passes to Italy, Valais is home to Switzerland's best-known sight: the Matterhorn. The area around the Matterhorn, including the villages of Zermatt and Saas-Fee, enjoy a high elevation and good skiing. Whereas Zermatt sits surrounded by groves of fir trees, with tacky tourist souvenir shops lining its main street (see Zermatt chapter), Saas-Fee lies in a deep valley that seems to pour out from the huge Fee ("Fairy") glacier (www.saas-fee.ch). Its town center—also very touristy—is circled by mountains, among them Switzerland's highest peak, the Dom (14,908 feet).

The resorts of Crans-Montana lack the village charm of other Swiss resorts, but offer great skiing with expansive views over the Rhône valley and the Valais Alps (www.crans-montana.ch). The resort town of Verbier is also very modern (www.verbier.ch). It features a high-tech, state-of-the-art sports complex that links four valleys with Switzerland's most famous transit network, Téléverbier: 12 gondolas, five cable cars, 32 chairlifts, and 46 ski lifts, providing access to more than 250 miles of runs (www.televerbier.ch). Other activities here include rock and ice climbing, snowshoeing, and cross-country ski excursions.

The **Graubündener Alps** contain 14 different passes. St Moritz, situated in the Upper Engadine valley, is so well-known that it's a registered trademark (see Pontresina, Samedan, and St. Moritz chapter). This resort town offers designer boutiques, luxury accommodations, a natural mineral spring spa...oh, and ski slopes, too. In addition to skiing, winter visitors to St. Moritz play polo and cricket on snow, go bobsledding on natural ice, or try *Skijöring*—skiing pulled by riderless horses.

St. Moritz is also home to the famed Cresta Run, a difficult toboggan run that was started by a group of eccentric 19th-century invalids who were sent to Swiss hospitals to recuperate. Instead, they fled their beds, invented the toboggan, and created a treacherous route down the mountain. Screaming perilously down the slopes, members of this exclusive club were known as the fastest men on earth. The tradition continues today (www.cresta-run.com).

Other Graubünden resorts include Davos (more urban, good for hockey and Nordic skiing, www.davos.ch) and Klosters (a favorite of the British royal family, www.klosters.ch). A less-discovered, Back Door-style option is Arosa, a village whose natural beauty, isolated location, and quiet atmosphere set it apart (www.arosa.ch). Visitors to Arosa can take the train one hour from Chur or drive along a 19-mile road so twisty that it's said there's a curve for every day of the year. In this village horse-drawn sleighs outnumber cars. The ski slopes are just five minutes from the town center, and there's also an ice arena, curling center, and racetrack, where a hot-air balloon lifts off regularly in winter.

One of my favorite Swiss memories happened one winter night on the snowy slopes of the Berner Oberland. My friend Walter (who runs Hotel Mittaghorn, see page 132) and I, warmed by hot chocolate laced with schnapps, decided to go sledding between mountain-high villages. We strapped flashlights to our heads, miner-style, and zoomed through the crisp, moonlit night.

Let's Talk Telephones

For specifics on Switzerland, see "Telephones" in this book's Introduction.

Making Calls Within a European Country: About half of all European countries use area codes (like we do); the other half uses a direct-dial system without area codes.

To make calls within a country that uses a direct-dial system (Belgium, the Czech Republic, Denmark, France, Italy, Portugal, Norway, Spain, and Switzerland), you dial the same number whether you're calling across the country or across the street.

In countries that use area codes (such as Austria, Britain, Finland, Germany, Ireland, the Netherlands, and Sweden), you dial the local number when calling within a city, and you add the area code if calling long-distance within the country.

Making International Calls: You always start with the international access code (011 if you're calling from the United States or Canada, or 00 from anywhere in Europe), then dial the country code of the country you're calling (see chart below).

What you dial next depends on the phone system of the country you're calling. If the country uses area codes, drop the initial 0 of the area code, then dial the rest of the number.

European Calling Chart

Just smile and dial, using this key:
AC = Area Code, LN = Local Number.

European Country	Calling long distance within ...	Calling from the U.S.A./ Canada to ...	Calling from a European country to ...
Austria	AC + LN	011 + 43 + AC (without the initial zero) + LN	00 + 43 + AC (without the initial zero) + LN
Belgium	LN	011 + 32 + LN (without initial zero)	00 + 32 + LN (without initial zero)
Britain	AC + LN	011 + 44 + AC (without initial zero) + LN	00 + 44 + AC (without initial zero) + LN
Czech Republic	LN	011 + 420 + LN	00 + 420 + LN
Denmark	LN	011 + 45 + LN	00 + 45 + LN
Estonia	LN	011 + 372 + LN	00 + 372 + LN
Finland	AC + LN	011 + 358 + AC (without initial zero) + LN	00 + 358 + AC (without initial zero) + LN
France	LN	011 + 33 + LN (without initial zero)	00 + 33 + LN (without initial zero)
Germany	AC + LN	011 + 49 + AC (without initial zero) + LN	00 + 49 + AC (without initial zero) + LN
Gibraltar	LN	011 + 350 + LN	00 + 350 + LN From Spain: 9567 + LN
Greece	LN	011 + 30 + LN	00 + 30 + LN

European Country	Calling long distance within...	Calling from the U.S.A./ Canada to...	Calling from a European country to...
Ireland	AC + LN	011 + 353 + AC (without initial zero) + LN	00 + 353 + AC (without initial zero) + LN
Italy	LN	011 + 39 + LN	00 + 39 + LN
Morocco	LN	011 + 212 + LN (without initial zero)	00 + 212 + LN (without initial zero)
Netherlands	AC + LN	011 + 31 + AC (without initial zero) + LN	00 + 31 + AC (without initial zero) + LN
Norway	LN	011 + 47 + LN	00 + 47 + LN
Portugal	LN	011 + 351 + LN	00 + 351 + LN
Spain	LN	011 + 34 + LN	00 + 34 + LN
Sweden	AC + LN	011 + 46 + AC (without initial zero) + LN	00 + 46 + AC (without initial zero) + LN
Switzerland	LN	011 + 41 + LN (without initial zero)	00 + 41 + LN (without initial zero)
Turkey	AC (if no initial zero is included, add one) + LN	011 + 90 + AC (without initial zero) + LN	00 + 90 + AC (without initial zero) + LN

- The instructions above apply whether you're calling a fixed phone or cell phone.

- The international access codes (the first numbers you dial when making an international call) are 011 if you're calling from the U.S.A./Canada, or 00 if you're calling from anywhere in Europe.

- To call the U.S.A. or Canada from Europe, dial 00, then 1 (the country code for the U.S.A. and Canada), then the area code and number. In short, 00 + 1 + AC + LN = Hi, Mom!

Countries that use direct-dial systems (no area codes) vary in how they're accessed internationally by phone. For instance, if you're making an international call to the Czech Republic, Denmark, Italy, Norway, Portugal, or Spain, simply dial the international access code, country code, and phone number. But if you're calling Belgium, France, or Switzerland, drop the initial 0 in the phone number.

Country Codes

After you've dialed the international access code (00 if you're calling from Europe, 011 from the United States or Canada), dial the code of the country you're calling.

Austria—43	Ireland—353
Belgium—32	Italy—39
Britain—44	Morocco—212
Canada—1	Netherlands—31
Croatia—385	Norway—47
Czech Rep.—420	Poland—48
Denmark—45	Portugal—351
Estonia—372	Slovenia—386
Finland—358	Spain—34
France—33	Sweden—46
Germany—49	Switzerland—41
Gibraltar—350	Turkey—90
Greece—30	U.S.A.—1

Directory Assistance

National—111
International—191
Train info—0900/300-300

U.S. Embassy

In Bern: Jubilaeumsstrasse 93, tel. 031-357-7234, www.us-embassy.ch

Festivals and Public Holidays

For specifics, contact the Swiss national tourist office (U.S. tel. 877/794-8037, www.myswitzerland.com, info.usa@switzerland.com) and check www.whatsonwhen.com.

Jan 1	New Year's Day
Jan 2	Harder Potschete (parade), Interlaken
Jan 6	Epiphany (closings)
Feb	Karneval, especially celebrated in Luzern, Zürich, and Bern
March 3–20	International Easter Music Festival (www.lucernefestival.ch), Luzern

2005

JANUARY
S	M	T	W	T	F	S
						1
2	3	4	5	6	7	8
9	10	11	12	13	14	15
16	17	18	19	20	21	22
23/30	24/31	25	26	27	28	29

FEBRUARY
S	M	T	W	T	F	S
		1	2	3	4	5
6	7	8	9	10	11	12
13	14	15	16	17	18	19
20	21	22	23	24	25	26
27	28					

MARCH
S	M	T	W	T	F	S
		1	2	3	4	5
6	7	8	9	10	11	12
13	14	15	16	17	18	19
20	21	22	23	24	25	26
27	28	29	30	31		

APRIL
S	M	T	W	T	F	S
					1	2
3	4	5	6	7	8	9
10	11	12	13	14	15	16
17	18	19	20	21	22	23
24	25	26	27	28	29	30

MAY
S	M	T	W	T	F	S
1	2	3	4	5	6	7
8	9	10	11	12	13	14
15	16	17	18	19	20	21
22	23	24	25	26	27	28
29	30	31				

JUNE
S	M	T	W	T	F	S
			1	2	3	4
5	6	7	8	9	10	11
12	13	14	15	16	17	18
19	20	21	22	23	24	25
26	27	28	29	30		

JULY
S	M	T	W	T	F	S
					1	2
3	4	5	6	7	8	9
10	11	12	13	14	15	16
17	18	19	20	21	22	23
24/31	25	26	27	28	29	30

AUGUST
S	M	T	W	T	F	S
	1	2	3	4	5	6
7	8	9	10	11	12	13
14	15	16	17	18	19	20
21	22	23	24	25	26	27
28	29	30	31			

SEPTEMBER
S	M	T	W	T	F	S
				1	2	3
4	5	6	7	8	9	10
11	12	13	14	15	16	17
18	19	20	21	22	23	24
25	26	27	28	29	30	

OCTOBER
S	M	T	W	T	F	S
						1
2	3	4	5	6	7	8
9	10	11	12	13	14	15
16	17	18	19	20	21	22
23/30	24/31	25	26	27	28	29

NOVEMBER
S	M	T	W	T	F	S
		1	2	3	4	5
6	7	8	9	10	11	12
13	14	15	16	17	18	19
20	21	22	23	24	25	26
27	28	29	30			

DECEMBER
S	M	T	W	T	F	S
				1	2	3
4	5	6	7	8	9	10
11	12	13	14	15	16	17
18	19	20	21	22	23	24
25	26	27	28	29	30	31

March 25–27	Easter Weekend
March–May	International Jazz Festival (www.jazzfestivalbern.ch), Bern
April 24	Open-Air Parliament (public selection of delegates), Appenzell
April	Sechseläuten (Spring Festival, www.sechselaeuten.ch), Zürich
May 5	Ascension Day (religious festival, closures)
May 16	Whit Monday (religious festival, closures)
June 1–11	Berner Tanztage (dance festival, www.tanztage.ch), Bern
June–July	Zürich Festival (www.zuercher-festspiele.ch)
Late June–early Sept	William Tell Performance (open-air theater, www.tellspiele.ch), Interlaken

July	Montreux International Jazz Festival (www.montreuxjazz.com)
	City Festival (www.festivalcite.ch), Lausanne
	Estival Jazz (free open-air festival, www.estivaljazz.ch), Lugano
	Gurten Open-Air Rock Festival (www.gurtenfestival.ch), Bern
	Blue Balls Jazz Festival (www.blueballs.ch), Luzern
Aug 1	Swiss National Day (parades and fireworks)
Mid-Aug–mid-Sept	Luzern Festival (classical, www.lucernefestival.ch), Luzern
Oct	Festa d'Autunno (food and wine festival), Lugano
Nov 1	All Saints' Day
Nov	Traditional Onion Market Fair, Bern
	Luzern Music Festival (piano, www.lucernefestival.ch)
Dec 6	St. Nicholas Day
Dec	Christmas Fairs

Numbers and Stumblers

- Europeans write a few of their numbers differently than we do. 1 = 1, 4 = 4, 7 = 7. Learn the difference or miss your train.
- In Europe, dates appear as day/month/year, so Christmas is 25/12/05.
- Commas are decimal points and decimals, commas. A dollar and a half is $1,50, and there are 5.280 feet in a mile.
- When counting with your fingers, start with your thumb. If you hold up your first finger to request one item, you'll probably get two.
- What Americans call the second floor of a building is the first floor in Europe.
- Europeans keep the left "lane" open for passing on escalators and moving sidewalks. Keep to the right.

Metric Conversion (approximate)

1 inch = 25 millimeters	32 degrees F = 0 degrees C
1 foot = 0.3 meter	82 degrees F = about 28 degrees C
1 yard = 0.9 meter	1 ounce = 28 grams
1 mile = 1.6 kilometers	1 kilogram = 2.2 pounds
1 centimeter = 0.4 inch	1 quart = 0.95 liter
1 meter = 39.4 inches	1 square yard = 0.8 square meter
1 kilometer = .62 mile	1 acre = 0.4 hectare

Climate

First line, average daily low; second line, average daily high; third line, days of no rain.

J	F	M	A	M	J	J	A	S	O	N	D

Bern

29°	30°	36°	42°	49°	55°	58°	58°	53°	44°	37°	31°
38°	42°	51°	59°	66°	73°	77°	76°	69°	58°	47°	40°
20	19	22	21	20	19	22	20	20	21	19	21

Temperature Conversion: Fahrenheit and Celsius

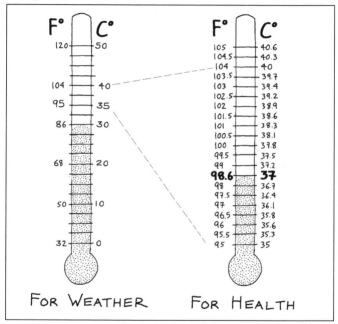

Making Your Hotel Reservation

Most hotel managers know basic "hotel English." Faxing or e-mailing are the preferred methods for reserving a room. They're more accurate than telephoning and much faster than writing a letter. Use this handy form for your fax or find it online at www.ricksteves.com/reservation. Photocopy and fax away.

One-Page Fax

To: _____ @ _____
             hotel   **fax**

From: _____ @ _____
             name   **fax**

Today's date: _____ / _____ / _____
                day   month   year

Dear Hotel _____ ,
Please make this reservation for me:

Name: _____

Total # of people: _____ # of rooms: _____ # of nights: _____

Arriving: _____ / _____ / _____   My time of arrival (24-hr clock): _____
            day   month   year   (I will telephone if I will be late)

Departing: ____ / ____ / ____
             day month year

Room(s): Single _____ Double ____ Twin _____ Triple ____ Quad _____

With: Toilet _____ Shower _____ Bath _____ Sink only _____

Special needs: View ____ Quiet ____ Cheapest ____ Ground Floor ____

Please fax, mail, or e-mail confirmation of my reservation, along with the type of room reserved and the price. Please also inform me of your cancellation policy. After I hear from you, I will quickly send my credit-card information as a deposit to hold the room. Thank you.

_____
Signature

_____
Name

_____
Address

_____
City   **State**   **Zip Code   Country**

_____
E-mail Address

German Survival Phrases

When using the phonetics, pronounce ī as the long I sound in "light."

English	German	Phonetics
Good day.	Guten Tag.	**goo**-tehn tahg
Do you speak English?	Sprechen Sie Englisch?	shprehkh-ehn zee **ehng**-lish
Yes. / No.	Ja. / Nein.	yah / nīn
I (don't) understand.	Ich verstehe (nicht).	ikh fehr-**shtay**-heh (nikht)
Please.	Bitte.	**bit**-teh
Thank you.	Danke.	**dahng**-keh
I'm sorry.	Es tut mir leid.	ehs toot meer līt
Excuse me.	Entschuldigung.	ehnt-**shool**-dig-oong
(No) problem.	(Kein) Problem.	(kīn) proh-**blaym**
(Very) good.	(Sehr) gut.	(zehr) goot
Goodbye.	Auf Wiedersehen.	owf **vee**-der-zayn
one / two	eins / zwei	īns / tsvī
three / four	drei / vier	drī / feer
five / six	fünf / sechs	fewnf / zehkhs
seven / eight	sieben / acht	**zee**-behn / ahkht
nine / ten	neun / zehn	noyn / tsayn
How much is it?	Wieviel kostet das?	**vee**-feel **kohs**-teht dahs
Write it?	Schreiben?	shrī-behn
Is it free?	Ist es umsonst?	ist ehs oom-**zohnst**
Included?	Inklusive?	in-kloo-**zee**-veh
Where can I buy / find...?	Wo kann ich kaufen / finden...?	voh kahn ikh **kow**-fehn / **fin**-dehn
I'd like / We'd like...	Ich hätte gern / Wir hätten gern...	ikh **heh**-teh gehrn / veer **heh**-tehn gehrn
...a room.	...ein Zimmer.	īn **tsim**-mer
...a ticket to ___.	...eine Fahrkarte nach ___.	ī-neh **far**-kar-teh nahkh
Is it possible?	Ist es möglich?	ist ehs **mur**-glikh
Where is...?	Wo ist...?	voh ist
...the train station	...der Bahnhof	dehr **bahn**-hohf
...the bus station	...der Busbahnhof	dehr **boos**-bahn-hohf
...tourist information	...das Touristen- informationsbüro	dahs too-**ris**-tehn- in-for-maht-see-**ohns-bew**-roh
...toilet	...die Toilette	dee toh-**leh**-teh
men	Herren	**hehr**-rehn
women	Damen	**dah**-mehn
left / right	links / rechts	links / rehkhts
straight	geradeaus	geh-**rah**-deh-**ows**
When is this open / closed?	Um wieviel Uhr ist hier geöffnet / geschlossen?	oom **vee**-feel oor ist heer geh-**urf**-neht / geh-**shloh**-sehn
At what time?	Um wieviel Uhr?	oom **vee**-feel oor
Just a moment.	Moment.	moh-**mehnt**
now / soon / later	jetzt / bald / später	yehtst / bahld / **shpay**-ter
today / tomorrow	heute / morgen	**hoy**-teh / **mor**-gehn

In the Restaurant

English	German	Pronunciation
I'd like / We'd like...	Ich hätte gern / Wir hätten gern...	ikh **heh**-teh gehrn / veer **heh**-tehn gehrn
...a reservation for...	...eine Reservierung für...	ī-neh reh-zer-**feer**-oong fewr
...a table for one / two.	...einen Tisch für ein / zwei.	ī-nehn tish fewr īn / tsvī
Non-smoking.	Nichtraucher.	**nikht**-rowkh-er
Is this seat free?	Ist hier frei?	ist heer frī
Menu (in English), please.	Speisekarte (in Englisch), bitte.	**shpī**-zeh-kar-teh (in **ehng**-lish) **bit**-teh
service (not) included	Trinkgeld (nicht) inklusive	**trink**-gehlt (nikht) in-kloo-**zee**-veh
cover charge	Eintritt	**īn**-trit
to go	zum Mitnehmen	tsoom **mit**-nay-mehn
with / without	mit / ohne	mit / **oh**-neh
and / or	und / oder	oont / **oh**-der
menu (of the day)	(Tages-) Karte	(**tah**-gehs-) **kar**-teh
set meal for tourists	Touristenmenü	too-**ris**-tehn-meh-**new**
specialty of the house	Spezialität des Hauses	shpayt-see-ah-lee-**tayt** dehs **how**-zehs
appetizers	Vorspeise	**for**-shpī-zeh
bread	Brot	broht
cheese	Käse	**kay**-zeh
sandwich	Sandwich	**zahnd**-vich
soup	Suppe	**zup**-peh
salad	Salat	zah-**laht**
meat	Fleisch	flīsh
poultry	Geflügel	geh-**flew**-gehl
fish	Fisch	fish
seafood	Meeresfrüchte	meh-rehs-**frewkh**-teh
fruit	Obst	ohpst
vegetables	Gemüse	geh-**mew**-zeh
dessert	Nachspeise	**nahkh**-shpī-zeh
mineral water	Mineralwasser	min-eh-**rahl**-vah-ser
tap water	Leitungswasser	**lī**-toongs-vah-ser
milk	Milch	milkh
(orange) juice	(Orangen-) Saft	(oh-**rahn**-zhehn-) zahft
coffee	Kaffee	kah-**fay**
tea	Tee	tay
wine	Wein	vīn
red / white	rot / weiß	roht / vīs
glass / bottle	Glas / Flasche	glahs / **flah**-sheh
beer	Bier	beer
Cheers!	Prost!	prohst
More. / Another.	Mehr. / Noch ein.	mehr / nohkh īn
The same.	Das gleiche.	dahs **glīkh**-eh
Bill, please.	Rechnung, bitte.	**rehkh**-noong **bit**-teh
tip	Trinkgeld	**trink**-gehlt
Delicious!	Lecker!	**lehk**-er

For more user-friendly German phrases, check out *Rick Steves' German Phrase Book and Dictionary* or *Rick Steves' French, Italian & German Phrase Book*.

French Survival Phrases

When using the phonetics, try to nasalize the n̲ sound.

Good day.	**Bonjour.**	bohn̲-zhoor
Mrs. / Mr.	**Madame / Monsieur**	mah-dahm / muhs-yur
Do you speak English?	**Parlez-vous anglais?**	par-lay-voo ahn̲-glay
Yes. / No.	**Oui. / Non.**	wee / nohn̲
I understand.	**Je comprends.**	zhuh kohn̲-prahn̲
I don't understand.	**Je ne comprends pas.**	zhuh nuh kohn̲-prahn̲ pah
Please.	**S'il vous plaît.**	see voo play
Thank you.	**Merci.**	mehr-see
I'm sorry.	**Désolé.**	day-zoh-lay
Excuse me.	**Pardon.**	par-dohn̲
(No) problem.	**(Pas de) problème.**	(pah duh) proh-blehm
It's good.	**C'est bon.**	say bohn̲
Goodbye.	**Au revoir.**	oh vwahr
one / two	**un / deux**	uhn̲ / duh
three / four	**trois / quatre**	twah / kah-truh
five / six	**cinq / six**	san̲k / sees
seven / eight	**sept / huit**	seht / weet
nine / ten	**neuf / dix**	nuhf / dees
How much is it?	**Combien?**	kohn̲-bee-an̲
Write it?	**Ecrivez?**	ay-kree-vay
Is it free?	**C'est gratuit?**	say grah-twee
Included?	**Inclus?**	an̲-klew
Where can I buy / find...?	**Où puis-je acheter / trouver...?**	oo pwee-zhuh ah-shuh-tay / troo-vay
I'd like / We'd like...	**Je voudrais / Nous voudrions...**	zhuh voo-dray / noo voo-dree-ohn̲
...a room.	**...une chambre.**	ewn shahn̲-bruh
...a ticket to ___.	**...un billet pour ___.**	uhn̲ bee-yay poor
Is it possible?	**C'est possible?**	say poh-see-bluh
Where is...?	**Où est...?**	oo ay
...the train station	**...la gare**	lah gar
...the bus station	**...la gare routière**	lah gar root-yehr
...tourist information	**...l'office du tourisme**	loh-fees dew too-reez-muh
Where are the toilets?	**Où sont les toilettes?**	oo sohn̲ lay twah-leht
men	**hommes**	ohm
women	**dames**	dahm
left / right	**à gauche / à droite**	ah gohsh / ah dwaht
straight	**tout droit**	too dwah
When does this open / close?	**Ça ouvre / ferme à quelle heure?**	sah oo-vruh / fehrm ah kehl ur
At what time?	**À quelle heure?**	ah kehl ur
Just a moment.	**Un moment.**	uhn̲ moh-mahn̲
now / soon / later	**maintenant / bientôt / plus tard**	man̲-tuh-nahn̲ / bee-an̲-toh / plew tar
today / tomorrow	**aujourd'hui / demain**	oh-zhoor-dwee / duh-man̲

In the Restaurant

I'd like / We'd like...	**Je voudrais / Nous voudrions...**	zhuh voo-dray / noo voo-dree-oh<u>n</u>
...to reserve...	**...réserver...**	ray-zehr-vay
...a table for one / two.	**...une table pour un / deux.**	ewn tah-bluh poor uh<u>n</u> / duh
Non-smoking.	**Non fumeur.**	noh<u>n</u> few-mur
Is this seat free?	**C'est libre?**	say lee-bruh
The menu (in English), please.	**La carte (en anglais), s'il vous plaît.**	lah kart (ah<u>n</u> ah<u>n</u>-glay) see voo play
service (not) included	**service (non) compris**	sehr-vees (noh<u>n</u>) koh<u>n</u>-pree
to go	**à emporter**	ah ah<u>n</u>-por-tay
with / without	**avec / sans**	ah-vehk / sah<u>n</u>
and / or	**et / ou**	ay / oo
special of the day	**plat du jour**	plah dew zhoor
specialty of the house	**spécialité de la maison**	spay-see-ah-lee-tay duh lah may-zoh<u>n</u>
appetizers	**hors-d'oeuvre**	or-duh-vruh
first course (soup, salad)	**entrée**	ah<u>n</u>-tray
main course (meat, fish)	**plat principal**	plah pra<u>n</u>-see-pahl
bread	**pain**	pa<u>n</u>
cheese	**fromage**	froh-mahzh
sandwich	**sandwich**	sah<u>n</u>d-weech
soup	**soupe**	soop
salad	**salade**	sah-lahd
meat	**viande**	vee-ah<u>n</u>d
chicken	**poulet**	poo-lay
fish	**poisson**	pwah-soh<u>n</u>
seafood	**fruits de mer**	frwee duh mehr
fruit	**fruit**	frwee
vegetables	**légumes**	lay-gewm
dessert	**dessert**	duh-sehr
mineral water	**eau minérale**	oh mee-nay-rahl
tap water	**l'eau du robinet**	loh dew roh-bee-nay
milk	**lait**	lay
(orange) juice	**jus (d'orange)**	zhew (doh-rah<u>n</u>zh)
coffee	**café**	kah-fay
tea	**thé**	tay
wine	**vin**	va<u>n</u>
red / white	**rouge / blanc**	roozh / blah<u>n</u>
glass / bottle	**verre / bouteille**	vehr / boo-teh-ee
beer	**bière**	bee-ehr
Cheers!	**Santé!**	sah<u>n</u>-tay
More. / Another.	**Plus. / Un autre.**	plew / uh<u>n</u> oh-truh
The same.	**La même chose.**	lah mehm shohz
The bill, please.	**L'addition, s'il vous plaît.**	lah-dee-see-oh<u>n</u> see voo play
tip	**pourboire**	poor-bwar
Delicious!	**Délicieux!**	day-lee-see-uh

For more user-friendly French phrases, check out *Rick Steves' French Phrase Boo* *and Dictionary* or *Rick Steves' French, Italian & German Phrase Book.*

Italian Survival Phrases

Good day.	**Buon giorno.**	bwohn JOR-noh
Do you speak English?	**Parla inglese?**	PAR-lah een-GLAY-zay
Yes. / No.	**Si. / No.**	see / noh
I (don't) understand.	**(Non) capisco.**	(nohn) kah-PEES-koh
Please.	**Per favore.**	pehr fah-VOH-ray
Thank you.	**Grazie.**	GRAHT-seeay
I'm sorry.	**Mi dispiace.**	mee dee-speeAH-chay
Excuse me.	**Mi scusi.**	mee SKOO-zee
(No) problem.	**(Non) c'è un problema.**	(nohn) cheh oon proh-BLAY-mah
Good.	**Va bene.**	vah BEHN-ay
Goodbye.	**Arrivederci.**	ah-ree-vay-DEHR-chee
one / two	**uno / due**	OO-noh / DOO-ay
three / four	**tre / quattro**	tray / KWAH-troh
five / six	**cinque / sei**	CHEENG-kway / SEHee
seven / eight	**sette / otto**	SEHT-tay / OT-toh
nine / ten	**nove / dieci**	NOV-ay / deeAY-chee
How much is it?	**Quanto costa?**	KWAHN-toh KOS-tah
Write it?	**Me lo scrive?**	may loh SKREE-vay
Is it free?	**È gratis?**	eh GRAH-tees
Is it included?	**È incluso?**	eh een-KLOO-zoh
Where can I buy / find...?	**Dove posso comprare / trovare...?**	DOH-vay POS-soh kohm-PRAH-ray / troh-VAH-ray
I'd like / We'd like...	**Vorrei / Vorremmo...**	vor-REHee / vor-RAY-moh
...a room.	**...una camera.**	OO-nah KAH-meh-rah
...a ticket to ___.	**...un biglietto per ___.**	oon beel-YEHT-toh pehr
Is it possible?	**È possibile?**	eh poh-SEE-bee-lay
Where is...?	**Dov'è...?**	DOH-veh
...the train station	**...la stazione**	lah staht-seeOH-nay
...the bus station	**...la stazione degli autobus**	lah staht-seeOH-nay DAYL-yee OW-toh-boos
...tourist information	**...informazioni per turisti**	een-for-maht-seeOH-nee pehr too-REE-stee
...the toilet	**...la toilette**	lah twah-LEHT-tay
men	**uomini, signori**	WOH-mee-nee, seen-YOH-ree
women	**donne, signore**	DON-nay, seen-YOH-ray
left / right	**sinistra / destra**	see-NEE-strah / DEHS-trah
straight	**sempre diritto**	SEHM-pray dee-REE-toh
When do you open / close?	**A che ora aprite / chiudete?**	ah kay OH-rah ah-PREE-tay / keeoo-DAY-tay
At what time?	**A che ora?**	ah kay OH-rah
Just a moment.	**Un momento.**	oon moh-MAYN-toh
now / soon / later	**adesso / presto / tardi**	ah-DEHS-soh / PREHS-toh / TAR-dee
today / tomorrow	**oggi / domani**	OH-jee / doh-MAH-nee

In the Restaurant

I'd like...	**Vorrei...**	vor-REHee
We'd like...	**Vorremmo...**	vor-RAY-moh
...to reserve...	**...prenotare...**	pray-noh-TAH-ray
...a table for one / two.	**...un tavolo per uno / due.**	oon TAH-voh-loh pehr OO-noh / DOO-ay
Non-smoking.	**Non fumare.**	nohn foo-MAH-ray
Is this seat free?	**È libero questo posto?**	eh LEE-bay-roh KWEHS-toh POH-stoh
The menu (in English), please.	**Il menù (in inglese), per favore.**	eel may-NOO (een een-GLAY-zay) pehr fah-VOH-ray
service (not) included	**servizio (non) incluso**	sehr-VEET-seeoh (nohn) een-KLOO-zoh
cover charge	**pane e coperto**	PAH-nay ay koh-PEHR-toh
to go	**da portar via**	dah POR-tar VEE-ah
with / without	**con / senza**	kohn / SEHN-sah
and / or	**e / o**	ay / oh
menu (of the day)	**menù (del giorno)**	may-NOO (dayl JOR-noh)
specialty of the house	**specialità della casa**	spay-chah-lee-TAH DEHL-lah KAH-zah
first course (pasta, soup)	**primo piatto**	PREE-moh peeAH-toh
main course (meat, fish)	**secondo piatto**	say-KOHN-doh peeAH-toh
side dishes	**contorni**	kohn-TOR-nee
bread	**pane**	PAH-nay
cheese	**formaggio**	for-MAH-joh
sandwich	**panino**	pah-NEE-noh
soup	**minestra, zuppa**	mee-NEHS-trah, TSOO-pah
salad	**insalata**	een-sah-LAH-tah
meat	**carne**	KAR-nay
chicken	**pollo**	POH-loh
fish	**pesce**	PEH-shay
seafood	**frutti di mare**	FROO-tee dee MAH-ray
fruit / vegetables	**frutta / legumi**	FROO-tah / lay-GOO-mee
dessert	**dolci**	DOHL-chee
tap water	**acqua del rubinetto**	AH-kwah dayl roo-bee-NAY-toh
mineral water	**acqua minerale**	AH-kwah mee-nay-RAH-lay
milk	**latte**	LAH-tay
(orange) juice	**succo (d'arancia)**	SOO-koh (dah-RAHN-chah)
coffee / tea	**caffè / tè**	kah-FEH / teh
wine	**vino**	VEE-noh
red / white	**rosso / bianco**	ROH-soh / beeAHN-koh
glass / bottle	**bicchiere / bottiglia**	bee-keeAY-ray / boh-TEEL-yah
beer	**birra**	BEE-rah
Cheers!	**Cin cin!**	cheen cheen
More. / Another.	**Ancora un po.' / Un altro.**	ahn-KOH-rah oon poh / oon AHL-troh
The same.	**Lo stesso.**	loh STEHS-soh
The bill, please.	**Il conto, per favore.**	eel KOHN-toh pehr fah-VOH-ray
tip	**mancia**	MAHN-chah
Delicious!	**Delizioso!**	day-leet-seeOH-zoh

For hundreds more pages of survival phrases for your trip to Italy, check out *Rick Steves' Italian Phrase Book & Dictionary* or *Rick Steves' French, Italian, and German Phrase Book.*

INDEX

RESEARCHERS

To write this book, Rick relied on the help of these fantastic researchers:

CAMERON HEWITT

Cameron Hewitt edits, researches, and writes guidebooks for Rick Steves. He recently took a break from *Rick Steves' Best of Eastern Europe* (which he co-authors) to return to Switzerland, his favorite Western European country, and write new chapters on Luzern, Zermatt, and the Glacier Express.

SUSANA MINICH

Susana Minich was born in Czechoslovakia, grew up in Switzerland, and now divides her time between Spain and Seattle. She's multi-lingual, and holds a degree in art history with a minor in architecture. She has been leading Rick Steves' tours since 1999.

Start your trip at
www.ricksteves.com

Rick Steves' website is packed with over 3,000 pages of timely travel information. It's also your gateway to getting FREE monthly travel news from Rick — and more!

Free Monthly European Travel News

Fresh articles on Europe's most interesting destinations and happenings. Rick will even send you an e-mail every month (often direct from Europe) with his latest discoveries!

Timely Travel Tips

Rick Steves' best money-and-stress-saving tips on trip planning, packing, transportation, hotels, health, safety, finances, hurdling the language barrier...and more.

Travelers' Graffiti Wall

Candid advice and opinions from thousands of travelers on everything listed above, plus whatever topics are hot at the moment (discount flights, packing tips, scams...you name it).

Rick's Annual Guide to European Railpasses

The clearest, most comprehensive guide to the confusing array of railpass options out there, and how to choo-choose the railpass that best fits your itinerary and budget. Then you can order your railpass (and get a bunch of great freebies) online from us!

Great Gear at the Rick Steves Travel Store

Enjoy bargains on Rick's guidebooks, planning maps and TV series DVDs—and on his custom-designed carry-on bags, wheeled bags, day bags and light-packing accessories.

Rick Steves Tours

Every year more than 5,000 lucky travelers explore Europe on a Rick Steves tour. Learn more about our 26 different one-to-three-week itineraries, read uncensored feedback from our tour alums, and sign up for your dream trip online!

Rick on TV

Read the scripts and see video clips from the popular Rick Steves' Europe TV series, and get an inside look at Rick's 13 newest shows.

Respect for Your Privacy

Ordering online from us is secure. When you buy something from us, join a tour, or subscribe to Rick's free monthly travel news e-mails, we promise to never share your name, information, or e-mail address with anyone else. You won't be spammed!

Have fun raising your Travel I.Q. at
www.ricksteves.com

Travel smart…carry on!

The latest generation of Rick Steves' carry-on travel bags is easily the best—benefiting from two decades of on-the-road attention to what really matters: maximum quality and strength; practical, flexible features; and no unnecessary frills. You won't find a better value anywhere!

Convertible, expandable, and carry-on-size:

Rick Steves' Back Door Bag $99

This is the same bag that Rick Steves lives out of for three months every summer. It's made of rugged water-resistant 1000 denier Cordura nylon, and best of all, it converts easily from a smart-looking suitcase to a handy backpack with comfortably-curved shoulder straps and a padded waistbelt.

This roomy, versatile 9" x 21" x 14" bag has a large 2600 cubic-inch main compartment, plus three outside pockets (small, medium and huge) that are perfect for often-used items. And the cinch-tight compression straps will keep your load compact and close to your back—not sagging like a sack of potatoes.

Wishing you had even more room to bring home souvenirs? Pull open the full-perimeter expando-zipper and its capacity jumps from 2600 to 3000 cubic inches. When you want to use it as a suitcase or check it as luggage (required when "expanded"), the straps and belt hide away in a zippered compartment in the back.

Attention travelers under 5'4" tall: This bag also comes in an inch-shorter version, for a compact-friendlier fit between the waistbelt and shoulder straps.

Convenient, durable, and carry-on-size:

Rick Steves' Wheeled Bag $119

At 9" x 21" x 14" our sturdy Rick Steves' Wheeled Bag is rucksack-soft in front, but the rest is lined with a hard ABS-lexan shell to give maximum protection to your belongings. We've spared no expense on moving parts, splurging on an extra-long button-release handle and big, tough inline skate wheels for easy rolling on rough surfaces.

This bag is not convertible! Our research tells us that travelers who've bought convertible wheeled bags never put them on their backs anyway, so we've eliminated the extra weight and expense.

Rick Steves' Wheeled Bag has exactly the same three-outside-pocket configuration as our Back Door Bag, plus a handy "add-a-bag" strap and full lining.

Our Back Door Bags and Wheeled Bags come in black, navy, blue spruce, evergreen and merlot.

For great deals on a wide selection of travel goodies, begin your next trip at the Rick Steves Travel Store!

Visit the Rick Steves Travel Store at
www.ricksteves.com

Rick Steves

COUNTRY GUIDES 2005

France
Germany & Austria
Great Britain
Greece
Ireland
Italy
Portugal
Scandinavia
Spain
Switzerland

CITY GUIDES 2005

Amsterdam, Bruges & Brussels
Florence & Tuscany
London
Paris
Prague & The Czech Republic
Provence & The French Riviera
Rome
Venice

BEST OF GUIDES

Best European City Walks & Museums
Best of Eastern Europe
Best of Europe

More *Savvy*. More *Surprising*. More *Fun*.

PHRASE BOOKS & DICTIONARIES

French
French, Italian & German
German
Italian
Portuguese
Spanish

MORE EUROPE FROM RICK STEVES

Easy Access Europe
Europe 101
Europe Through the Back Door
Postcards from Europe

DVD
RICK STEVES' EUROPE

Rick Steves' Europe All Thirty
   Shows 2000–2003
Britain & Ireland
Exotic Europe
Germany, The Swiss Alps
   & Travel Skills
Italy

For a list of Rick Steves' guidebooks, see page 9.

Avalon Travel Publishing
1400 65th Street, Suite 250
Emeryville, CA 94608
AVALON Avalon Travel Publishing is an Imprint of Avalon Publishing Group, Inc.
publishing group incorporated

Printed in the United States of America by Worzalla
First printing October 2004
Distributed by Publishers Group West

ISBN 1-56691-882-0
ISSN 1552-1818

For the latest on Rick's lectures, guidebooks, tours, and public television series, contact
Europe Through the Back Door, Box 2009, Edmonds, WA 98020, 425/771-8303, fax
425/771-0833, www.ricksteves.com, rick@ricksteves.com.

Thanks to my hardworking team at Europe Through the Back Door, and most of all to my
wife, Anne, for her support.

Europe Through the Back Door Managing Editor: Risa Laib
Europe Through the Back Door Editors: Cameron Hewitt, Christine Grabowski,
  Jennifer Hauseman
Avalon Travel Publishing Series Manager: Roxanna Font
Avalon Travel Publishing Editor: Patrick Collins
Copy Editor: Mia Lipman
Indexer: Stephen Callahan
Research Assistance: Susana Minich, Cameron Hewitt, Julie Coen (winter sports),
  Gene Openshaw (art and history)
Production & Typesetting: Patrick David Barber
Cover Design: Kari Gim, Laura Mazer
Interior Design: Jane Musser, Amber Pirker, Laura Mazer
Maps & Graphics: David C. Hoerlein, Zoey Platt, Lauren Mills, Mike Morgenfeld
Photography: Cameron Hewitt, David C. Hoerlein, Rick Steves, Susana Minich
Front cover photos: Front image, Sidewalk Café on Lakeside Promenade, Lucerne,
  Switzerland © John & Dallas Heaton/Corbis; Back image, Alpine town of Steinen,
  Switzerland © Royalty-Free/Corbis
Front matter color photos: p. i, View from the Schilthorn © Cameron Hewitt; p. iii,
  Zürich's Grossmünster © Cameron Hewitt; p. iv, Lauterbrunnen Valley © David C.
  Hoerlein
Avalon Travel Publishing Graphics Coordinator: Deborah Dutcher